SEASON
of WITCH
the

Also by Gail B. Griffin

CALLING:
Essays on Teaching in the Mother Tongue

SEASON
of *the* WITCH

BORDER LINES, MARGINAL NOTES

Gail B. Griffin

TRILOGY BOOKS
Pasadena, California

Cover Illustration, "The Wicked Witch of the West," from the Pennyroyal Press edition of *The Wonderful Wizard of Oz*, by Frank L. Baum, used by permission of artist, Barry Moser.

Cover design: J. Stevens Art & Design

Permissions appear on page 272.

Publisher's Cataloging in Publication

Griffin, Gail B.
    Season of the witch: Border lines, marginal notes / Gail B. Griffin.
    p. cm.
    Includes bibliographical references.
    ISBN 0-9623879-5-9

    1. Women college teachers--United States--Biography. 2. Feminism. 3. Teaching--Philosophy. 4. Essays. I. Title. II. Title: Border lines, marginal notes.

LB2332.3.G75 1995   378.12'092
                                     QBI95-20499

Library of Congress Catalog Card Number: 95-61711

for the ones who burn

When I look out my window,
Many sights to see,
And when I look in my window,
So many different people to be

That it's strange,
So strange,
You've got to pick up every stitch
You've got to pick up every stitch. . .

Oh, no—
Must be the season of the witch. . .

—Donovan

Table of Contents

Part Three:
The Giant Waking
On Memory, Myth, and Transformation

Acknowledgements

First of all, I'm grateful to Kalamazoo College, primarily for the sabbatical leave in which this book was written, but also for that community's support of my work, and (as always) for the contradictions, painful or delightful, that prompt so much of what I write. A grant, via the college, from the MacArthur Foundation (not a Genius Grant; more like a Moderately Intelligent Grant) supported my work during this year.

And second, I owe a great deal to the Five College Women's Studies Research Center at Mt. Holyoke, where I completed this volume as a Research Associate. To the remarkable staff, to the audience who took my work very seriously and responded helpfully when I presented it, and especially to the Girls of Dickinson House, I am indebted for a sanctified year of feminist scholarly community.

A few of these essays were drafted at the Virginia Center for the Creative Arts during my second residency there, a wonderful place for thinking and writing. I'm grateful to the administration there and to my fellow colonists, especially the ones who were so eager to talk about "The Wizard of Oz."

My scholarship is often generated and always deeply informed by my students. Their continual challenges to me and their consistent support of me are the best part of my professional life. To all of them, past and present, especially those who responded so movingly to my first book and were eager and curious about this one, I am tremendously grateful. They are all woven in here, between the lines, among the metaphors.

Somewhere in this book I refer to my mother, Barbara Hanna Hamel, as my first teacher, the one "who gave me words." I hope she's proud of what I've done with them. I thank her for gracefully enduring the tribulation of having an autobiographical child, and for allowing me to make sometimes painful memories public. I also thank my niece, Katherine Hanna Griffin, whose letter generated one of these pieces.

Finally, my deepest thanks and my love to Diane, my girlfriend, my "best mind"; and to Bob, who kept the fire stoked downstairs while this got written upstairs by the shores of Lake Wyola. They are both in the margins of every page, and their belief in me is necessary as paper and ink.

. . . you may go no further this way,' said they,

for this is the edge of things, here,

and beyond is another country.

We are defined by the lines we choose to cross

or to be confined by.

—A. S. Byatt, *Possession*

Introduction
Marginalia: In the Borderland of Dreams

margin: *the blank space bordering the text on a page, usually left blank,*
but sometimes partly occupied with notes, variant readings or
references.

A particular embarrassment: finding old textbooks from high
school or college, margins full of my loopy handwriting in whatever color
ink I was affecting at the time. Sometimes I spy what are clearly the
teacher's words: "epiphany!" "phallic." Sometimes, page references or
other textual notations. But more often than not, my marginal notes seem
to have been responsive and emotional: exclamation points (sometimes
following expletives) to indicate my anger at a character's obtuseness; dis-
agreements with the author; effusions at beauty, passion, and truth. I was
talking with the book, or talking back to it — both in the sense of
responding in conversation with the text, and in the sense of contradict-
ing, being uppity, talking out of turn — the talking back that got swiftly
punished in my family and that serves bell hooks as a wonderful book
title. In my marginal notes, I was writing a sporadic kind of counter-text.

My old copies of *Wuthering Heights*, outlined in purple, black,
and blue to indicate different emphases at different points in my life or
different courses taken, margins crowded with notations. When I think of
my first really overwhelming experience of reading adult literature, I think
of the weeks after I first finished *Wuthering Heights* in, I think, eleventh
grade. I literally could not get it out of my head; I walked around in a
kind of trance, slipping sporadically through the sheer membrane
between Ann Arbor, Michigan, and darkest Yorkshire.

The novel begins with the arrival at the eponymous house of a
fussy, pretentious, self-deluded urbanite named Lockwood, who is renting
Thrushcross Grange from a Mr. Heathcliff. After a couple of dazzling
chapters in which he mistakes everything and everyone and makes a
thorough fool of himself, Lockwood is trapped at the Heights by a snow-
storm which turns the landscape into a blank page he cannot read. He is
rudely shunted into an upstairs bedroom which, he will discover,

belonged to the mythical dead Cathy. To read himself to sleep, he picks up a grim Evangelical tract belonging to the surly servant Joseph. He finds its margins completely filled with tiny girlish handwriting. It is there, in the margins of a patriarchal sermon, that Lockwood (and we) read the beginnings of Cathy's story of her unhallowed devotion to the despised, dark-skinned, surly, uncouth Heathcliff. It gets even better: the part of Cathy's story Lockwood quotes for us bemoans the rigors of Sundays, protests the oppressiveness of Joseph and her brother Hindley, and recounts escaping outdoors with Heathcliff (the singular need that defines Cathy to the end of her life). It's all we hear from Cathy in her own voice, but in the small marginal space she finds to write in, she manages to indict patriarchal religion, male authority, and entrapment "indoors" — the world of culture versus nature. A truly "marginal" story, in more ways than one.

Girls writing in the margins, inscribing the counter-text. What else has women's studies been about?

———

margin: an edge and the area immediately adjacent to it.
           a border, edge, brink, verge, rim.

border: a boundary; also a frontier.

It is difficult even to think about, to grasp: a line, and also a space. An end, and also a beginning. A limit, and also the edge of what is beyond limits. The margin defies dualism; it is both/and, and it is wholly other. Perhaps its slippery ambivalence accounts for its imaginative allure and its current popularity as image and metaphor.

Sharon Olds describes the doorsill of a baby's room as representing, for a young mother, a boundary between competing realities:

. . . When she nurses
it feels like being drunk, the swallows
pulling at her breast, delicious, but when she leaves the small
room, closes the door,
she is sure the baby's not breathing. . . .

In her primal anxiety, the baby becomes a version of herself, the doorsill a boundary between selves:

Crossing the sill again, she inhales that
peace like ether. Leaving again she
enters the dream of murder, mutilation, her
old self bleeding in pieces on the butcher paper.

The line of the doorsill, the mystical border, suddenly opens into a marginal space of metamorphosis:

There is no language
between these worlds.
On the sill all is dark, the transformation
rushes through her like a train in a tunnel.

Take it in slow motion, you see the young mother
swimming over the threshold through silted air,
the soot falling like black rice. . . .

The poem ends in a densely multivalent transformation of imagery:

. . . she is
struggling down the corridor, her own mother
hanging on to her ankles and bearing down.[1]

The woman who, earlier, was a tunnel is now inside one; is it the corridor outside the baby's room, or her own mother's birth canal? Does the final "her" refer to the baby's mother, or the mother's? In other words, is "her own mother" hanging on to her own ankles, "bearing down" in the process of giving birth, or is she hanging on to her daughter's ankles, bearing down on her oppressively or protectively, pulling her back as she tries to move away, into her own dangerous life?

Right down to that ambiguous pronoun, this poem deals with boundaries and margins in a specifically female context. The blurriness of mother-daughter boundaries is one dimension: in the course of the poem, it is not only described (in the breast feeding and the mother's inability to leave her child alone) but enacted, as the young mother becomes both her child and her own mother. That mysterious Twilight Zone of a doorsill becomes boundary-as-vagina: what patriarchy imagines as a "hole" is actually a passage between two worlds, collapsing upon itself or expanding, alternately containing space and containing none.

No wonder that issues of female development and identity so often have to do with lines and boundaries. If human development has been constructed in the European male terms of individuation — that is, of boundary clarification and linear margins — then the female project has been to revise identity in terms of connection, the crossing or softening of lines, or the reconceiving of boundaries as sites of proximity, intimacy, as much as separation. I think of my female students, who want clarity and self-definition, but worry about connection and responsibility. They yearn to be the line drawings in which they first represented themselves, but they remember watercolors, too, the exquisite moment when the blue and pink bled to lavender. They stand in the doorsill, vacillating, unable to remain immured in the nursery of enmeshment or to walk away, down the corridor into separation.

"There is no language / between these worlds." Yet this is the world we struggle always, ceaselessly, to voice, as women: the world between, the darkness on the sill, where transformation rushes through us.

margin: *a limit beyond which change cannot take place without the cessation of certain activities or phenomena; the limit of a state or process, e.g., "the margin of reality."*
a measure, quantity, or degree of difference.

marginal: *at a margin.*
pertaining to the fringe of consciousness.
barely within a lower standard or limit of quality.

The variant definitions capture our cultural anxiety about the marginal: it is at the edge, on the frontier, but also barely within a lower standard, as in "marginal intelligence." That contradiction is the kernel of much of the struggle taking place in the academic world today: marginal people are staking claims, "taking over," speaking as authorities.

And they are doing so from the margins; that is, they are claiming marginality as a desirable location. Bell hooks makes "a definite distinction between that marginality which is imposed by oppressive structures and that marginality one chooses as site of resistance — as location of radical openness and possibility."[2] It is, for her and others, like that door-sill: a tense, mysterious dimension between worlds, a seemingly restrictive or definitive line that opens outward into space, onto new worlds. "For me," writes hooks, "this space of radical openness is a margin — a profound edge. Locating oneself there is difficult yet necessary. It is not a 'safe' place. One is always at risk."[3] A sweeping paradigm shift: from thinking of the margin as an assigned location, an imposed position, to regarding it as a choice, a destination, a consciousness to be cultivated. This, I think, is what Isabel Allende means when she says that a writer's breadth of vision "depends on [her or his] own capacity to become a 'marginal'; a writer has to be a marginal."[4] In Meena Alexander's words, "It's a dangerous thing to be a writer, like being at the outposts of your consciousness."[5] Can this be something of what Emily Dickinson meant when she wrote, "My business is Circumference" — that she saw her marginality, with splendid Dickinsonian irony, as affording a wide, encompassing view of the world?

The margin is usually conceived as relative to the center, defined by the center: women have been represented as marginal, framing and decorating a male center. But geometrically it is the margin, after all, that locates and defines the center; logically, then, it can also disrupt that center. A margin might be seen as looking outward, as well as in, its energy expansive, "pushing the envelope." Above all, the margin might be thought of not as a static position, but as a ring of motion, energy, movement around the periphery.

Toni Morrison, annoyed by being asked yet again when she's going to write about white people, translates the question: "'You write well enough. You could come on into the center if you wanted to. You don't have to stay out here on the margins.' And I'm saying, Yeah, well I'm gonna stay out here on the margins, and let the center look for me."[6] When the center looks for the margins, the center has moved.

People of color and women are rich cultural resources precisely because they are usually adroit negotiators of the margin. The circumstances of their lives demand expertise in translation and transition. Polyglots, they become adept at moving between worlds, acculturating and reculturating. This is why they are leading the way, moving the center after them.

And this is why they are producing most of the healthy, vibrant art in an age of postmodern cynicism. "Revolutionary art dwells, by its nature, on edges," explains Adrienne Rich. "That is its power: the tension between subject and means, between the is and the what can be. Edges

between ruin and celebration. Naming and mourning damage, keeping
pain vocal so it cannot become normalized and acceptable. Yet, through
that burning gauze in a poem which flickers over words and images,
through the energy of desire, summoning a different reality."[7] Who better
to summon that reality — to call it from the dark — than those far
enough out to glimpse it, dimly, beyond the edge where they stand, rec-
ollecting ancient tongues, timeless powers flushed from the memory of
the Center?

marginal: *pertaining to conscious states not the focus of*
                attention, but felt dimly and indistinctly.

borderland: *land on the frontiers of two adjoining countries;*
                often used figuratively, as in "the borderland of
                dreams."

To occupy the margins is to hang out in a "bad" neighborhood —
what the Center calls irrationality, madness, gibberish, voodoo, witchcraft.
Like the frontier itself, the margin is at once primal and progressive,
ancient and avant garde. To cultivate it begins with trusting the perceptions at the edge of our vision, which must find their way to us through
and around the admissible evidence of the Center. Terry Tempest
Williams writes of "peripheral perceptions [that] are short, sharp flashes of
insight we tend to discount like seeing the movement of an animal from
the corner of our eye."[8] When we turn and follow the animal into the
dark, the world is changed.

Seeing marginally, then, means seeing indirectly, circuitously, and
dynamically. Instead of stasis, marginal vision sees movement, shape-
shifting, blurriness, transformation. Instead of certainties and stable truths,
it tends to ambivalence; it is not ashamed to be tentative. And instead of
either homogeneity or crippling dualisms, it values and seeks multiplicity.
"It is this perspective," writes Patricia Williams, "the ambivalent, multivalent way of seeing, that is at the core of what is called critical theory, feminist theory, and much of the minority critique [of culture]. It has to do
with a fluid positioning that sees back and forth across boundary. . . ."[9] It
resists the subsuming of difference. It is always skirting the law. And at
the first sign of closure, it takes off, lighting out for the borderland of
dreams.

Paul Tillich wrote: "I thought that the concept of the boundary might be the fitting symbol for the whole of my personal and intellectual development. At almost every point, I have had to stand between alternate possibilities of existence, to be completely at home in neither and to take no definitive stand. Since thinking presupposes receptiveness to new possibility, this position is fruitful for thought; but it is difficult and dangerous in life . . . ."[10] In fact, it is part of a marginal vision to acknowledge and describe that difficulty, that danger, rather than using the metaphor of the margin to bring a false but poetic closure to the open questions and chaotic experience of living.

Living, even identity itself, can be understood as a series of positions; most of us shift between various centers and margins. As someone born to the privileges of the center in many ways, marginal in others, I have often felt the strain of being in two places at once, or of commuting back and forth from one position to the other. In my relationships to institutions I often experience the same sense of dividedness, part of me welcome, central, even comfortable, part of me exiled or demonized or just ill at ease. In another sense of the metaphor, I have frequently felt myself wavering on edges, walking a border, dwelling in margins between two worlds, unable to commit to either. To accept my commuting as necessary, even possibly advantageous, didn't occur to me until very recently. Likewise, it has taken me a long time to see my wavering ambivalence as other than a character flaw — to begin to see the margin as tenable, a valid position in many cases, even a place of vision. Many feminist writers and writers of color have provided structure and confirmation in this process, which culminated in this book.

The essays themselves write across boundaries in various ways — boundaries of genre, temporal and chronological boundaries, the crumbling boundaries between "personal" and "intellectual," "academic" and "political." In writing them, I have been drawn to the notion of margins as places where worlds collide, or elide — places where one thing touches, confronts, or becomes another, and the ineffable, immeasurable doorsill between them. My life as a scholar, writer, and teacher has been energized by the friction at the margins of gender, racial, and cultural identities. And from childhood I've been fascinated by the permeable boundaries of memory — eruptions of the past into the present; the way what is gone shapes and shadows what is with us.

Each of the three sections uses the metaphor of margins in different ways. The first set of essays, on girlhood, comes from my sense of the personal and historical margins in my life, the times of personal change and fundamental cultural shift between the chronological middle of the century, when I was born — its center, if you will — and its outside margin, the coming millennium (which in the sixties, of course, I couldn't imagine living to see). In another sense of the metaphor, these pieces often trace the intersection of my life with the larger social and cultural life around me in the late fifties and sixties. The essays often deal with alternate worlds, beyond the border of the mundane — summer camp, Oz, Canada, the London of adolescent imagination. They also explore girlhood as a space between conditions and desire. I'm especially interested in female adolescence as a deeply marginal time, a period of sometimes agonizing and debilitating acculturation, a movement from the outer edge between culture and wilderness into the tight heart of cultural constructs of femininity. Finally, these essays often take place in that startling intimacy between past and present that occurs in middle age: where the past suddenly penetrates the present like one of Scrooge's ghosts, or the present veers around to the past; where the woman looks into the mirror and sees the girl looking back.

The second section, on teaching, deals with the classroom as a borderland — between home and "the world," adolescence and adulthood — where marginal thinking can be safely cultivated. Some of these essays explore the marginality of women — defined positively and negatively — to institutions of higher education and to the production of knowledge. Some walk the tense borders of race, looking for places where a clear view might be had, where real contact might be made. They try to capture the tension between margin and center in an academic world in the midst of revolution, as barricades between the knowable and the unknowable are falling everywhere.

The final section deals with cultural, racial, and national memory. These essays come from my sense of western culture in the painful throes of profound change, and of the United States specifically as a nation troubled by the bad dreams that come of repression and willed forgetting. The boundaries here are often between what has been and what might be, or between innocence and knowledge — my own included.

In this book, I worked to keep myself at my own margins, "words coming together to reveal what was unknown to me until I wrote them," as Adrienne Rich has so wonderfully put it.[11] "I can't write a poem that transcends my own limits," she continues, "though poetry has often pushed me beyond old horizons, and writing a poem has shown me how far out a part of me was walking beyond the rest."[12] In this border walking I have heard in myself the voice of the figure who begins and ends the final section, who appears sporadically elsewhere, and who gives the book its title: the witch, a marginal person in her society, haunting the edges, familiar with their madness and their magic, a powerful, powerless person. Midwife, shaper, healer, spell-caster, she dances in the borderland of our dreams, just over the line where the law ends.

Patricia Williams reminds us that although we fear destruction when we cross that line, "[t]he transgression is dizzyingly intense, a reminder of what it is to be alive. It is a sinful pleasure, this willing trans- gression of a line, which takes one into new awareness, a secret, lonely, and tabooed world — to survive the transgression is terrifying and addic- tive. To know that everything has changed and yet that nothing has changed; and in leaping the chasm of this impossible division of the self, a discovery of the self surviving, still well, still strong, and, as a curious consequence, renewed."[13] It is this transgression — this small death, with its very real terrors and losses — that begins to make, from the line crossed, a space, a margin.

> We come to this space through suffering and pain, through struggle. . . . We are transformed, individually, collectively as we make radical cre- ative space which affirms and sustains our sub- jectivity, which gives us a new location from which to articulate our sense of the world.[14]

We begin to feel sane and strong. And in the place between worlds where there was no language, we begin to form words.

Part One

Snapshots from an Uncolored Girlhood
On Growing Up Female

. . . the past breaks through and changes
and enlightens the present, and vice-versa.
The reason that we remember a past moment at all
is that our present-day life is still a working-out
of a similar situation. . . . And the ever-evolving present
changes the significance of the past.

—Maxine Hong Kingston

In this misty land the borderline between myth,
legend, and fact is not decisive, my father says,
as a stone arc might be between this world and another,
but more like a series of moving veils or woven webs
between one room and another. . . .
In my childhood, . . . I would curl up in a small ball,
like a hedgehog or sleeping caterpillar,
and lie as still as death,or the time before birth,
or between autumn and spring (the hedgehog)
or the crawling state and the flying (the grub).

—A. S. Byatt

. . . what else is meaning but the need to mark
the irretrievable loss of beginnings and endings?

—Patricia Willliams

1

Points of Departure

1. *Boundary Waters*

Residents of the first or second coasts of the United States speak of the Midwest as landlocked. This is why they regard our lives claustrophobically: they think of us as immured in land (corn-covered, usually), horizontally impoverished, without escape. From these assumptions, of course, they derive a notion of our mental landscape as well.

To grow up in Michigan is to feel the proximity of water. Not lakes, but Lakes, *the* Lakes, the Inland Sea. Huge bodies of water on three sides. Small freshwater oceans, with their great beauty, their vast lore and mythology, their complicated political history, their spirit power. Places of *manitou*. To come to their shores is to sense, as you do at the ocean, immense presence, and also to feel you have come to an end — land's end, literally, but also the margins of customary modes of thought, feeling, being.

The places where the Big Lakes come together — the straits — are charged with mystery and power. The four such junctures involving Michigan have always been especially mystical for me because of my sense of what lies on the other side. Lakes Michigan and Huron meet in the Straits of Mackinac, spanned by Big Mac itself, full of arching, aerodynamic energy, like a great bird or leaping fish. When it opened in 1957, a marked day for Michiganders, everyone called it a miracle of engineering, the longest suspension bridge on the planet; but the real wonder was that now you could drive to the U.P. The Upper Peninsula, wild, dark-green, obscure Otherworld, the anomalous Outland bought for a strip of northern Ohio. The Yoo Pee, where even the heart of summer couldn't warm the nights, where winter settled in early and stayed late and wolves still ran the forests and anything might happen.

But the other three Michigan straits bring us into intimate relation with that truly alien, mythic domain called Canada. Far north, there is Sault Ste. Marie, the Soo, the place where the St. Mary's River used to "jump" (*sault*) the rapids from Lake Superior — the Wolf's Head, the cold, grim Gitche Gumee of Longfellow and Lightfoot — down to Lake Huron. The Locks brought the lakes into carefully managed proximity. From childhood my fantasies had accumulated there, visions of the huge ore freighters slowly, miraculously raised up or let down. One night, aged thirty, I found myself there at last, in a threadbare, mildewey motel room right on the Locks. When I saw a vast banks of lights passing slowly in the dark just outside the window, I thought at first that the room was moving.

Far south is much the most mundane, unromantic of the three, where the French named a fort for the straits themselves: Detroit. It has always been a site of confluence and conflict, cultural, national, racial. Today white people drive into or out of Detroit from Canada or from its suburbs and lock their doors. Detroit has come to occupy a special place in a really frightening kind of racial mythology: many suburban whites regard it as the absolute outer limit of the urban nightmare, abandoned entirely to Them. When local whites talk about the city, even in the total absence of overtly racial language, you can hear black people in the sub-text of whatever they say, unnamed, unnameable. In the white mind, Detroit is the urban Heart of Darkness, the mythical Dangerous Place, where white fears are barely contained, waiting to ambush us when we pass through.

Today it is difficult to glimpse any magic as one follows the "Bridge to Canada" signs through the hollow-eyed, desperate city, up and over the Ambassador Bridge, and down onto a strip of motels, fast food, and "exotic dancing" in the unremarkable Windsor. But growing up out-side Detroit you felt the pulse of Motor City, barely an hour away. You heard the deep hum of the city. Big, ugly cars rolled endlessly off the line at Ford and GM; we put America on wheels. Down at Briggs Stadium, Kaline was at bat and the crowd roared in the sun. One hot day in August you drove downtown with your mother to Hudson's, to get school clothes for fall. For this momentous pilgrimage you dressed up and you ate lunch in a restaurant. You listened to CKLW, which reminded you that just moments further on, beyond a brief flash of water, lay another country.

Summer began when you drove up, north of the city, to Port Huron. There, where Lake Huron rolls down into Lake St. Clair and on toward the Detroit River, you sped onto the Blue Water Bridge. As you rose above the silver, sunstruck water stretching away on both sides, you felt that lurch in the stomach. Nearing the apex of the bridge, you held yourself suspended for that moment when you could think to yourself, "Half of us is in America and half in Canada." There was even a split sec-ond, you would think you caught it, when you yourself, your very body, was in two countries. Then down the other side toward that awful, breathless moment at Customs, while your father and mother in the front seat answered questions politely, seriously, and you feared that your big brother would follow through on his threat, uttered moments earlier, to say he was born in Hawaii, which was not yet a state. The relief when you were waved through the magic gate by the humorless guardians of Canada. That you had come down in extremely unromantic Sarnia was no impediment; you were in Another Country. Soon you would be out of lower Ontario and into the woods. Canada (which in the gendered economy of young minds I always thought of as female), stretching away to the north, limitless, incomprehensible, dangerous, wonderful.

There is something about the proximity of great waters that shapes the Michigan consciousness. There was something about the nearness of Otherlands that fed my imagination as a girl. I became conscious of the unspoken, the hidden, the subversive. Edges drew me. I came to love secret spaces, imaginary dimensions. I grew attentive to the points, in time or space, where things open out into something else, or where they come together in terrible, thrilling intimacy and confrontation, or in goodbye. I learned to fear and to treasure crossings.

2. Margaret

The first sailing vessel on the upper Great Lakes, which carried LaSalle and his party through the straits called Missilimakinac into Lake Dauphin (Michigan) in 1679, was called the Griffin. I grew up knowing that my dead father's grandfather was Captain William Griffin the Ore-Boat Captain. There is a photo of him, bushy-bearded, wide-eyed, somehow baby-faced. I liked to think of him standing on the bridge, eyeing the horizon as his vessel rolled up Lake Michigan, down Lake Huron. (I had in mind something like the Edmund Fitzgerald until one day I realized that his son, my paternal grandfather, died in the early years of this century.) My mother told me that Captain Will married a girl from Potsdam, New York, so I assumed he was from upstate as well.

Then one day in my adulthood, she mentioned a rumor in my father's family, some vague hint or suggestion that as a baby my father himself had been smuggled over the border. From Canada. Of course, I realized with a romantic surge: Captain Will was a Canadian freighter captain. He himself crossed the mystical border to marry Jane Sabrina Ellis of Potsdam, she of the sweet, sad face in the album. The miniature Welsh-English testament came down to me from double emigrants: from Wales to North America, and then from Canada to the States.

Crossings. To leave a home after many years is an emigration as well. You take stock, render accounts, demarcate past from future consciously and materially. When my mother and stepfather moved out of the house in which they had lived for twenty-five years, into a leaner condominium, she did a lot of sloughing off. Furniture, books, pictures, china, odd knicknacks were brought out and offered to the first comer amongst the children. I got the Griffin family albums. One I had perused before; the other I had never seen. Like the first it is huge and heavy, wooden-sided, padded and upholstered, but while the first is red velvet, this one is coarse, dun-colored cloth. Inside it was a canvas mailing envelope, stamped "3 cents paid," and addressed to "Griffin Dry Goods Store, 1553 Devon Ave., Chicago, Ill." I barely had time to record the fact that my family at some point sold dry goods before my attention was seized by two sheets of yellowed paper folded inside.

They were covered in pencilled names and dates, in my paternal grandmother's hand, recognizable from notations in other albums. Quickly I realized it was a history of her husband's family, the first detailed Griffin family record I had seen.

Under the heading "Marriage of Paternal Grandparents": Edward Griffin, born in Montreal in 1808, married Margaret Kelley, of St. John's, Newfoundland, born in 1809. She I recognized as the great-great grandmother whose face, somewhat startled, with its rim of dark hair pulled severely up and back, looks out from a deep, gilded wooden frame on my bedroom wall, on the back of which, in something like chalk, is written "Capt. Griffin's Mother." Then, under the heading "Births," an astonishing list:

Capt. William Griffin, Montreal, 1833.

So he was the eldest..

James Griffin, Montreal, 1835.

The name that found its way to his great-grand-nephew, my brother.

Mary A. Griffin, Sacket's Harbor, 1837.

Mary Ann? Mary Alice? Mary Agnes? I check my atlas: Sacket's Harbor is in New York. . . .

John Griffin, Kingston, 1839.

The family moved twice in three years, across the border and back again. Then two named for the parents:

Margaret Griffin, Kingston, 1841.
Edward Griffin, Kingston, 1843.

And finally, the baby, afforded a somewhat more extravagant name:

Celia Griffin, Port Dalhousie, 1845.

    I sat for some minutes, relishing these new relations, saying their names over, wishing I had their faces before me. Then, reviewing the dates again, I suddenly saw the unmistakable 19th-century pattern: a baby every two years, like clockwork, like Queen Victoria herself. Seven babies in thirteen years, taking Margaret from twenty-three to thirty-six. The "natural" rhythm of a female body at the mercy of its own reproductive system.

    Then, amid jumbled questions (How much joy can find room in such prolonged exhaustion? What occasioned the moves around Canadian seaports?), I moved to page two. Another list, briefer, only five lines long:

Edward Griffin 1st , died Nov. 8, 1845, age 37 yrs + 3 days.
Mary A. Griffin, died Sept. 24, 1837, age 1 day.
John Griffin, died Jan. 15, 1840, age 1 year + 7 mos.
Margaret Griffin, died Sept. 18, 1845, age five years.
Celia Griffin, died Nov. 30th, 1845, age 3 mos.

I can swallow the human reality of this list only in pieces: Four children dead in childhood. Three before their second birthday, two before their first. All three of the girls, lost? All three? Then I see that the two youngest girls, Margaret and Celia, died barely two months apart. It takes several readings before I understand that their father, the elder Edward, died between them. In one dreadful autumn, a century-and-a-half ago, having already watched a son and a daughter die, Margaret Kelley Griffin lost her two babies and her husband.

    What happened here? Brontë-like congenital illness? Some epidemic in eastern Canada? Did these children conceived and born by the sea stumble into it and drown? Was their father, like his eldest son, a seaman, and did the sea take him too, in one of those deadly November gales? But I have only names and numbers. The rest, as Hamlet says, is silence.

    In the last century, I remind myself, neither of these lists would have seemed extraordinary; families were big, and infant mortality high. Even now, I remind myself further, in much of the world, people have many children in order to raise the odds that a substantial number will survive childhood. But did the commonness of her family's fate render it any less painful for Margaret Kelley Griffin, I wonder? I try to picture her, widowed at thirty-six, with three boys remaining, all under thirteen. I reach for her across the borders of time. My own single, childless, professional life is so far from hers that I can make no contact. I see her seated quietly in a rocker, by a window in Port Dalhousie, looking out at the water, wondering what she will do next.

One of the things she did, in fact, was to marry again, seven years later, to one John Jones, in April of 1852. After that, the record is blank, except for the picture on my wall. I would give much to know how those children died, what that husband did with his life. But most of all I yearn to know Margaret's heart. Whether she loved her husbands. Whether Edward was a good man, and John. Whether she had family, friends, enough money. Whether she welcomed all those children. What she most feared. Above all, I want to know how she understood this unimaginable litany of deaths. Whether she believed, whether she lost faith. How she survived, internally. If the death of one child does what I have seen it do to parents, how she remained sane in the loss of four. How she integrated such monumental loss into her life, her self, her view of the world. What country her grief took her to, what world she found across that dark water from the one she had lost.

But the hearts of women are not the stuff of history. Their silence, despite all that we have managed to unearth in the past twenty years, still looms over their great-great-granddaughters, I think, folding the yellowed sheets, putting them back in the canvas envelope.

And then I realize that my grandmother recorded all these details of her husband's family. "Marriage of Paternal Grandparents" means *his* paternal grandparents. Of her own family, not one name or date, not one word.

3. Hanna Women

Summer, 1987: I am in the living room of my Aunt Joyce's condo in Flint, Michigan, where she is a travel agent and her husband, my small dynamo of a Uruguayan uncle, Eduardo, was a musician. I am here for his funeral. In the living room with me are two of my cousins, David, son of Eduardo and Joyce; and my only girl-cousin, Rhys, daughter of my Aunt Dot and Uncle Dike. In the adjoining dining room my mother and her two sisters — Joyce, the youngest, and Dot, the middle — are conferring. Joyce's voice is high and soft, a little nasal, and, after all the years functioning in Uruguayan Spanish, ever-so-slightly accented. Dot's is a dark alto. My mother's, Barbara's, is insistent, matter-of-fact, muscular, dynamic.

Rhys and David and I have been silent for some time. Suddenly David looks up at us, smiles, cocks his head toward the dining room, and says, "Hanna Women." We hold each other's eyes for a moment, smiling, nodding, listening to the three-part fugue in the dining room and feeling, beneath the overlay of our disparate adult lives, our deep common matrix.

———•——《○⊗○》◦——•———

My mother used to speak of her great-great-grandmother as "the First White Woman in Livingston County," Michigan. I used to picture her, striding along alone, upright and forthright, past a sign saying "Livingston County," into deep woods toward a group of startled Indians. Her granddaughter was Mary Katherine Haven, my mother's adored maternal grandmother. Mary Katherine's husband, Chester Van Wormer, fought in the Civil War, spent time in Andersonville, and brought home to Howell, Michigan, a chest nubbled with shot. My grandmother and her sisters remembered clearly fingering the bumps as girls, reading their father's war stories in the Braille of his chest. The Van Wormers had a boy who died young and four girls, three of whom lived long enough for me to know them: Aunt Anna, Aunt Grace (always called by my mother's childhood name for her, 'Bis'), and my grandmother, Antoinette, who would later go by her husband's truncation of her last name, "Van." After Chester's death, Mary Katherine supported herself and her girls with her baking — demonstrating the talent with pastry transmitted genetically through the female line in her family. Bound and determined that her girls would be able to make their way in the world, she managed to send the two youngest to nursing school in Detroit in the early years of the century, when nursing was one of precious few viable options for girls.

Aunt Bis served in England during the First World War and came back with a completely charming Englishman in tow, my Uncle Steve, who would dazzle me late in his life, during my love affair with theater, by telling me he had seen Henry Irving and Ellen Terry on the London stage. Antoinette married a young surgeon, E. Howard Hanna, one of ten children of a dour Protestant Irish immigrant, originally O'Hanney, a farmer in Birmingham, north of Detroit. And like her mother, Antoinette had multiple girls: Barbara Jeanne, Dorothy Grace, and Joyce Antoinette, born over eleven years, beginning in 1915.

Growing up, I relished seeing them together. They struck me as much different — in looks, style, personality — and much alike: stubborn, vocal, funny, opinionated, deeply gracious, devoted to each other. My mother was the classic older sister/functional son, always running the show, arguing, critiquing, praising. Aunt Joyce was the perfect baby of the family: soft spoken, sweet, apologetic, gentle, catching her flies with honey tinged with just the slightest trace of ironic vinegar. Aunt Dot was the classic middle child, accommodating, surviving, enduring, delightful in her bursts of humor, wackiness, girlishness.

They were, for their time and class, well educated: my mother had two years at the University of Michigan School of Music, Dot studied design, Joyce pursued music at Westminster Choir College, where she met the mad Uruguayan who threw the family into an uproar by spiriting Dr. Hanna's baby away to the wilds of Montevideo before she was twenty. In some ways the other two also made inappropriate marriages. Just as the war began, Dot married a small businessman whose heart was in acting, and she raised her three kids in his family home, a vast, dark, dusty, crannied old wedding-cake house in Birmingham, while they spent every single weekend building, with their own hands, what we called for years "the new house," a ranch in Bloomfield. My own father was fifteen years my mother's senior, nearly forty when she married him at twenty-four; nearly fifty when I was born. My grandmother warned her that she would be a young widow, and that she was. Whatever joys they held, these marriages can not have been easy; lovable, funny, and talented, all three of these men could also be querulous, self-centered, demanding, domineering, though in three very different keys. Growing up, though I loved them all in certain ways, I viewed my father and my two maternal uncles as overgrown children, ridiculous or pitiful or endearing or infuriating in turn. Their wives I saw as transcendent, powerhouses of competence, grace, and emotional breadth.

Like many women of their generation, I think they were all at least skeptical of, maybe hostile to, contemporary feminism. I suspect that in demanding for women choices they never had, the movement implied to them that their limitations had been unnecessary or their aspirations too small or their sacrifices and achievements worthless. They were women who swallowed disappointment and grew on it, who lay down with yearning and got up with disillusion. They made their choices and took their consequences, choked their anger and kept on singing. We who "wanted it all" must have seemed spoiled and naive.

Like many of my generation of women, I turned my back on what I saw as their version of female destiny and kept on walking, across the great divide of the sixties. Yet when I conjure the matrix from which my own feminism bubbled up, I hear the sound of the three of them (the trinity in which all mythic women appear, fates, fairies, witches) in a kitchen, laughing, arguing, getting a dinner on the table, resonating throughout my childhood. And I see them in trouble's eye, converging like natural forces that, to my girl's imagination, made the world go on turning. Hanna Women.

4. 1959

My father was born four months after the death of Queen Victoria. My mother's earliest memory is of her grave, decorous father turning handstands in the yard at the news of the Armistice in 1917. I have to remind myself that when I was born, Truman was president. George VI reigned over a British Empire, Stalin presided in the Soviet Union. "The War" bled into my vague childhood consciousness as a recent event to which all subsequent developments were constantly referred for context: "Before the war . . . ." "Since the war . . . ." "During the war, we . . . . " My mother tells me that Ike waved to me from the back of a train in 1952. One of my earliest treasures was a leftover campaign button that mesmerized me by turning, with a flick of the wrist, from "I LIKE IKE" to a photo of his grinning face.

That bald white head: the benign wizard presiding over the Oz of my childhood. I grew up in the deepest heart of the American dream, imbibing all its nutrients, all its carcinogens. When I picture myself, running across my vast suburban lawn, I realize I was wrapped in a safety unknown to even most suburban upper-middle-class white kids today. And then when I remember how easily I incorporated duck-and-cover nuclear attack drills into my notion of kindergarten, I see that safety's grim underside and realize I lived with a sense of danger likewise unknown to kids today. Their dangers are different, maybe worse. There are worse things, perhaps, than the end of the world.

In December of 1959, my father died — a week before the decade closed. The following summer I turned ten. Four months later we had a president-elect who seemed worlds away from Ike. An enormous cultural shift began — I think of it almost in terms of tectonic plates realligning — just as I hit puberty, the great divide between girlhood and womanhood. I came of age on the crest of a youth culture with unprecedented power to influence politics. economics, the larger American culture. "Postwar America" transformed itself into the contemporary U. S. Within so short a span of years, before even the end of the astonishing decade to come, the American vista would explode in a vision of psychedelic beauty and horror, confusion and hope.

Just as I held my breath for the moment at the top of the bridge, I watched and waited for the moment when winter turned to spring, or summer to autumn. I sniffed the air, studied the light. Though I sought out these boundary moments, changes and departures agonized me, then as now. I wanted to hold myself suspended in the in-between, where before and after melted. I wanted nothing to leave me for good and I wanted to leave nothing behind. I watched the river run at the foot of the yard.

The eastern margin of our property, between our yard and the Webbs', was a line of trees and foliage. I knew a thicket there between some bushes. When I needed to escape or dream or sulk, I crawled into it and the bushes closed behind me. The air was so cool it was almost chilly. A lush blanket of lilies-of-the-valley cushioned the ground. I sat, admiring the light dribbling in through the branches, breathing the dark, holding myself still.

2

Snapshots from an Uncolored Girlhood

*I grew up in the vast encircling presumption
of whiteness — that primary quality of being
which knows itself, its possessions, only against
an otherness that has to be dehumanized.
I grew up in white silence that was utterly obsessional.
Race was the theme whatever the topic.*

—Adrienne Rich[1]

1. Gloria

In the mid-fifties, I had a black baby doll. I forgot about her for a long time, but then I remembered her very clearly, the hard plastic of her body, the golden-shaded brown skin, the hair molded in hard plastic waves on her head. I named her Gloria. That was my favorite girl's name. In my mind it connoted the color gold, as well as luxurious beauty. Adults laughed at the doll's name in a way that conveyed to me that it had something ludicrous and extreme about it, something excessive. White girls, in the northern Detroit suburbs in the fifties, were named Susan and Linda and Cathy. Exotic was Kerry, or Julia, or Dana. Nobody was named Gloria. But Mary's granddaughter was, and that's where I got the name. Mary cleaned our house. I had never met her granddaughter, but she was the only little colored girl I even knew of, and I loved her name, so I named my doll for her.

It seems almost incredible to me that I had this doll. I can't imagine that black baby dolls were common then. My mother says she bought Gloria after a considerable search of downtown Detroit. Why would she have bought this doll for me except to encourage infantile racial liberalism? Twenty years later the television landscape would be full of white families raising black children. There is confusion about Gloria's fate. What is clear is that I gave her away, to her namesake, Mary's little granddaughter, littler than I. My mother says it probably occurred in the process of sorting out adolescence from childhood when were packing up to move. But by that point I was eleven, and I'm convinced I relinquished Gloria earlier, while still a little girl. What I remember is doing so at Mother's behest: I remember her asking me if it didn't seem right to me that Gloria should go to a little colored girl who didn't have a baby doll, when I had others. The justice of this appeal seemed obvious to me. So I gave Gloria up.

These memories are tangled and troubling, as if there is some factor missing. Why would my mother give me the doll and then urge me to give it up? I remember its being a sacrifice, painful and reluctant. I wonder if this was the first time I "knew" I was white. I wonder if this was the first time I thought, in, five- or six-year-olds' terms, about what white owed to black, about whether and how white could love black, about what blackness was available to whiteness. I wonder if the sadness was not simply the loss of a doll I loved, but the vague, partial understanding of difference, distance, deprivation, and estrangement. I wonder whether Gloria's relinquishment constituted, or symbolized, a bigger loss, one I still feel, one that perhaps cannot be healed at this time, in this country, on this earth.

2. Background shots

I was born in Detroit. My nine-years-older brother went to school with black kids from the projects, one of whom was his good buddy. That is a world I never knew. On January 2, 1954 — the day I turned three-and-a-half — my father moved us out to the suburb of Franklin, fourteen miles north, where I lived to adolescence. Franklin, named for Benjamin, called itself "The Town that Time Forgot." Now a chi-chi suburb, it was then truly a village, with a tiny library, a vine-covered elementary school, a hilltop cemetary full of time-softened Civil War-era gravestones looking down over the town, and a village green in front of a generic white-steepled community church.

But the town's forgottenness was limited. I grew up with television, among other revolutions, and as we watched the Civil Rights Movement unfold, appalled at the specter of segregation, it would never have occurred to me to call the world in which I grew up "segregated." Yet the suburbs were about segregation: a white margin (ironically) around a dangerous black center called Downtown.

"We can agree, I think," writes Toni Morrison, "that invisible things are not necessarily 'not-there'; that a void may be empty, but is not a vacuum." There were no black people in my neighborhood, or my school, or the stores where we shopped in nearby Birmingham. But they were there, always, like dark spots on the periphery of our vision. "[C]ertain absences," Morrison continues, ". . . arrest us with intentionality and purpose, like neighborhoods that are defined by the population held away from them."[2] As sociologist Ruth Frankenburg discovered when talking to white women who came out of childhoods like mine, "segregation bespoke the presence rather than the absence of people of color."[3] To segregate is to acknowledge, to foreground, that which you wish to keep out. In defining your place exclusively, you make the absent present. Thus it is that in white settings, and psyches, black people are never forgotten, never "absent," always haunting the conversation.

One way in which black people were present to me was in the literature of childhood. I loved reading, being read to, the sound of rhythm and rhyme, the sound of strange words I didn't understand that filled my mouth. "Little Black Sambo" enchanted me, largely because of tiger butter. Black Mumbo, Black Jumbo, and Black Sambo: the first family of color I ever knew.

Then there was Uncle Remus: African folk tales winding their way down to me through various permutations and purloinings. What I remember most powerfully from those tremendous stories is the fascination of that cryptic figure, the Tar Baby. The sticky blackness that wouldn't respond and wouldn't let go, becoming a kind of opaque mirror of the anxiety of its interrogator.

But the highlight was my mother's chilling, mesmerizing recitation of James Whitcomb Riley's poem "Little Orphant Annie." As I listened to Annie's gallery of spiteful, disrespectful children meeting with terrible supernatural ends, my flesh would ripple when my mother came to the part about the little girl who, after mocking and shocking her elders, suddenly sees "two great big b-b-b-black things a-standin' by her side."

Was that it, our deepest fear?

3. Calling names

Eenie, meanie, miney, MO!
Catch a tiger by the TOE!
If he hollers, let him GO!
Eenie, meanie, miney, MO!

But tigers don't holler. Something wasn't being said here, or it was being said only by the bad boys on the playground, to provoke horror and wonder. I thought about a colored boy being held up by one toe, a startling, frightening picture. Why would anybody "catch" a Negro, anyway?

————— ·•═──•◄○8○►═──•·─ —————

The polite white word was "colored." The more clinical, analytical, newspaper word was "Negro." It was permissible, but sounded a little harsh somehow. From Stephen Foster, I learned "darky," which sounded to my kid's ears archaic and foreign, and which I was told was considered (illegitimately) offensive.

The other word, the "N" word, was never spoken. I was told in no uncertain terms never, ever to use it. Ignorant southerners used that word, I was told. But as in the counting rhyme, it seemed always to threaten to be spoken, to thrust itself up through the surface of our smooth white language.

In the early sixties, Afro-American, which I then thought neological, resurfaced, sounding to me very dignified. In the mid-sixties, the shock of "black," the awkwardness of saying it: It seemed harsh, abrasive, even insulting. What a watershed in my relationship with words when I began to think about why "black" felt ugly to me. And then about what it meant that I assumed that black people needed a euphemism to bear their own skin.

Meanwhile, there was only one word for us. We were white. But only in racially oppositional contexts. By ourselves, we weren't racial at all. We were just people. Uncolored.

As with race, so with gender: linguistic distinctions unexplained but fraught with power. Ladies were people like our mothers. Women were something else. We didn't know what, but it was rude to call a lady a woman. Therefore, if we wished to be polite about colored people of the female gender (and we did), we said "colored lady." It was deliberately generous. It ennobled us to say it.

One night at dinner, I asked, "Is Mary our maid?"

The table rippled with attention. "Why do you ask that?" my mother inquired. I replied that somebody at school had asked if she was. In my mind, "maid" suggested vast wealth, mansions, the British aristocracy, a servant in a black uniform and white cap — not us, not Mary. So I wondered.

"No," my father said tersely. "She's not."

"She's our cleaning lady, right?" Another fine, if irrational, linguistic distinction.

My father was visibly discomforted. "Just say she's a friend. A friend of our family."

I remember feeling unease, smelling adult obfuscation. So did my mother. "For heaven's sake, Griff," she said, and then, to me:

"Yes, Mary is our cleaning lady. You can tell your friends that, if they ask."

So even then, we couldn't talk about it very well, even amongst ourselves. And we couldn't find the word that would tell us who she was, the black woman in the other room, or allow us to speak clearly of her — not to mention to her.

4. Aside: True Colors

A family story, repressed and muffled: a female relative walks into a room full of people in a stunning new dress. Her husband greets her arrival by saying, "Well, here's my wife, the one in nigger blue." The woman in question has told this to me with her face so tight and pained that it might have happened yesterday. For her, it was mostly a case of deliberate, nasty public humiliation, not a matter of race.

Though I don't remember seeing it and never asked, I know exactly what color that dress was. It was a blue that was beyond — well, beyond the "pale" (or the navy). It was a blue that was excessive, too hot, too deep, to bright, too brilliant for the wives of suburban manufacturer's representatives. It was a blue too expressive and too strong for a wife who should know her place, and too sexual a blue for a white Lady.

The word that polite white folks didn't use in public, the word their children were instructed never to use, could sudden explode into the room like that, rushing up from the realm of the repressed, loaded with raw, unexamined racial assumptions.

My world was positively cross-hatched with color lines.

5. Mary

Mary Jones Jepson[4] was born in 1917, the same year as my mother. Her mother cleaned our houses for many years when my older brother was small. On her first day, my mother tells me, she introduced herself as follows: "They call me Mrs. Jones." Thus did this tiny person — I remember her as white-haired and diminutive — insist on naming herself, overturning the titular decorum of cleaning ladies and employers. Mrs. Jones still substituted for Mary in staying with my brother and me sometimes.

Mary lived with her mother and children, and then grandchildren, in the projects of Detroit. She commuted to Franklin to clean our house and later some of our neighbors' houses too. She rode up on the bus to Northland, the first shopping mall in the country, where my mother picked her up. Mary stayed overnight one day a week, usually, but when my parents went on vacation to Sea Island, Georgia, in the late winter, she stayed for a week.

Mary was pretty, plump (always dieting), gentle, very feminine, somehow girlish. She giggled rather than laughed, at least at our house, and I think she was quite shy.

Mary was no disciplinarian, but I don't think I ever tried to get around her in any serious way; I had too much deference to rules, and I would never have wanted to abuse or exploit Mary. I did, however, like to tease her, to surprise her with my daring or cheek, and I liked to cajole her into things that weren't expressly forbidden by my parents. I especially loved watching TV with her — "Wagon Train" being our favorite — sitting together on the sofabed in the den, at the far end of the house watching white men "tame" the west.

I loved Mary very much. When I said my prayers, she came right at the end of the family names. The days she came to our house were highlighted in my week; I would brighten up and hurry, coming home from school, when I remembered she'd be there. I think she loved me, too. And neither of these facts negates a third: that I didn't regard her as an adult. I thought of her as — and loved her, in part, because of it — an overgrown child. I was eternally amazed to remember that she and my mother, the apex of authority in my world, were of an age. I certainly interacted with her as I would never have dared to interact with a white adult — on a basis of familiarity, intimacy, and condescension. What white adult, excepting family, would I have called by her first name?

There is no telling where I learned to think of her this way, because there was no source of authority in my world that would have taught me otherwise. In our house she was treated with kindness and consideration. But there was nothing that would have taught me to respect her as, say, I respected my best friend's mother, or my aunt, or the dental hygienist, or the librarian. When Mary stayed overnight, she slept in the other bed in my room — a sign of her status as an intimate and a child.

Certain questions could not form until much later: How did Mary's children fare when she was taking care of me, cooking my meals, washing my clothes, playing with me, cleaning my house, scooping up my goldfish from the jaws of death on the kitchen floor? How did they feel about me? How did she deal with her own family's needs when she got home tired, with few hours left in the day, after cleaning our sprawling three-bedroom ranch house?

It was the fifties, a suburb of a northern city. The Civil Rights movement rumbled in the background, soon to burst through into the foreground of my consciousness. And yet still, for the daughter of a progressive white home, racial awareness came mediated through the mammy system. The same false, costly intimacy, painfully lost in adulthood, sentimentalized in memory, glazing a troubled, complicated truth whose roots stretch far away underground, into the past.

Ruth Frankenburg writes of her interviews of white women:

> . . . one startling feature of several descriptions
> of apparently all-white childhoods was the sud-
> den appearance in the narratives of people of
> color as employees, mainly Black, mainly female,
> and mainly domestic workers. What is striking
> here is not the presence of domestic workers as
> such but the way in which they were talked
> about. For, oddly, these Black women were not
> summoned into white women's accounts of their
> lives by means of questions like "Were there any
> people of color in your neighborhood?" or "Who
> lived in your household when you were growing
> up?" Rather, they arrived previously unheralded,
> in the context of some other topic.[5]

But how could these women appear in response to those questions?
Neither question describes their situation: They were not "in our neighborhood"; our neighborhood was, de jure or de facto, completely segregated. And they didn't *live* in our households, even if they stayed
overnight, even if they spent weeks at a time. Just as it was hard for my
family to find the word to say what Mary was to us, it is hard to find the
indirect question that would summon them in an interview, these black
women who were among us on intimate terms but not "in our neighborhoods" or "living in our houses." They inhabited a marginal space, almost
another level of reality that we struggle to name, at once intimate and
endlessly distant.

6. Michael

Once my mother and I drove Mary home, to the projects. I don't
know what occasioned this departure from tradition; I suspect I might
have been taken along so that I could see that the world was bigger than
the rolling green suburban bliss I lived in. In less than an hour, I was
miles, years from my home, in another country. I remember long, low,
dark buildings, many doors. I have few clear memories of Mary's house,
but I think I got out of the car with my mother and went up to the door. I
remember faces gathered at Mary's door. One of them belonged to her
grandson, Michael. He was her joy. We heard about him a lot. He was
close to my age. I have a very indistinct memory of a small face at the

door, watching me with large, dark, unblinking eyes, imprinting himself on my memory as Michael.

Have I made this up? If I have, what does it mean, that I see this face looking back at me, across this enormous gulf? I see this scene, as if I'm looking at a photograph in a frame: the two of us, feet or yards apart, taking each other in. My blue eyes, his brown ones, full of each other.

7. Big Pictures, in Black and White

The other day, an African American colleague told me that her husband was a childhood playmate of Emmett Till. Today, forty years later, he can't talk about Till's death. The summer his young, outraged body was dredged from the river, I turned five. It happened in what I grew up thinking of as the dark, hot, guilty South, simmering with loathings and terrors, incomprehensible to me.

When I think of my individual life projected against a historical background, a screen on which the motion and shadows of the greater world appear, I see people marching. The Civil Rights Movement was the great struggle of the times of my early life, the definitive showdown of good and evil as I came to understand them — unmistakable, unambiguous. That struggle came to me as directly and powerfully as it did because of television. Mine was the first generation surrounded by that steady stream of visual and aural images of our world.

My sense of Blackness was deeply informed by vivid images of struggle: people driven backward into walls by fire hoses, young men dodging snarling dogs, women of my mother's and grandmother's ages walking tired, endless circles with signs. And especially images of kids, so tidily dressed, quiet and contained, looking neither left nor right, walking quickly alongside tall impassive troopers toward school doors.

What I have not thought about until now is the images of whiteness impressed into my own skin by those years. What I remember first are the monstrous versions: grownups screaming, spitting, throwing rocks at children; bulky, crew-cut police chiefs; the oily-haired governor, his face twisted with meanness, blocking the schoolhouse door. What does a child do with such images? I had that convenient repository for them: the South, as we understood it. Southerners were hicks, crackers, rednecks; ignorant people. At a very young age I internalized the notion that racism was largely a matter of ignorance. Perhaps because my parents' educations were terminated prematurely by family needs, my family believed absolutely in education as the fundamental liberator. As in Black families, any effort toward education, toward bettering oneself, was laudable, worthy of expenditure and sacrifice. This value system, of course, ennobled and intensified the struggle for school integration in our eyes. What we saw in TV was "ignorant Southerners" trying to keep well-brought-up colored kids from an education. If Eisenhower's and Kennedy's troops could get and keep the school doors open, justice and equality were simple matters of time.

By the early sixties, I had access to other white images in this now monumental struggle. I was dimly aware that there were white people, mostly young, who were dropping their lives to venture down into that lethal southern miasma. And no one in the Detroit Metropolitan Area could have been unaware of Viola Liuzzo, always described by the media as "Detroit housewife" or "Detroit wife and mother," dead in a car on the road from Montgomery to Selma. On the other hand, the Black people whose lives were routinely snuffed out were part of my awareness only in the nameless aggregate.

My white students today have not only a very vague notion of the breadth and complexity of the Movement, but a simplistic, sanitized picture of segregation itself. They suffer from a double deprivation, these mostly privileged children wrestling awkwardly with racial consciousness. They lack the memory of a clear struggle with a clear evil; but closer to home, they lack images of people like themselves — privileged, white — who struggled, who helped, who behaved bravely, took risks, contributed, were hurt, sometimes killed.

White heroism was perhaps easier to imagine in those days, when the song said "black and white together." It all seemed very clear to me at ten or twelve. If adolescence means learning how complicated the world is, part of that lesson for me was that black and white together was no simple matter of piano keys.

The backdrop for the Civil Rights struggle was the Civil War centenary, and I became a ten-year-old Civil War buff. I learned that after the War, things happened very rapidly, including many of the things that were now happening again. Why was history repeating itself? If colored people could vote in 1870, why couldn't they vote now? What had happened? Why was it such a big deal for colored candidates to be elected, if during Reconstruction they had gone to state capitols and to Washington in numbers?

I remember the answer I got — my first memory of the social construction of historical narrative: Reconstruction had "failed." It had been too much too soon; colored people, having so recently been slaves, weren't "ready" for freedom (as the emerging African nations hadn't been "ready" for independence from their colonial parents until just recently). The education ethos entered in here: freedom was a dangerous commodity one had to be educated to handle. Implicit in this view was the notion of African Americans as childlike that colored my relations with Mary.

It frightens me to think how malleable a child's mind is, how eagerly it absorbs and shapes itself to the notions it is given from sources it has no reason to doubt, no choice but to trust. This notion of postbellum America stayed with me far into adulthood, unexamined and unrevised. One day I was reading a contemporary view of Reconstruction where the retreat from full black citizenship was attributed to the backlash of violence and conservativism, the lynching and other Klan activity that I certainly knew about but that hadn't disrupted the version I had carried with me from childhood.

At home, on the piano, I played the songs of Stephen Foster, full of sentiment for the Old South that never jarred against my abolitionist and civil rights allegiances. Neither did my passionate consumption of *Gone With the Wind* in one week during my tenth summer. So the sinister, mean, jungle-like South I had in mind when I watched or read the news co-existed happily with a mythical, glamorous South, tragically gone with the wind.

What a strange, confused America I inherited. Monstrous, in the nineteenth-century sense of the word: unnaturally and chaotically hybrid. What a weird stew of truths, semi-truths, lies, gaping silences, and yawning omissions was represented by the flag to which I pledged my allegiance five mornings a week. And yet I took a clear lesson away, one which shaped all my political thinking subsequently. I grew up alongside a movement toward justice that taught me to question authority, law, and social structures and to affirm and even normalize political struggle. A useful inheritance.

8. Can't Forget the Motor City

For a baby-boomer, part of the kick of seeing "The Big Chill" was what happened in a theater full of white folks during the dinner sequence, on the first two or three notes of "Ain't Too Proud to Beg." A palpable jolt ran across the aisles. People seized up in their seats, emitting low moans of joy, grabbing their companions' arms. A film about a reunion of white sixties survivors (whose gauge of how far they've fallen is their memories of wanting to "teach ghetto kids"), and the soundtrack is predominantly black. And that's the way it was: the soundtrack to our white suburban lives was mostly black. There is still no faster way to raise the energy level in a room full of white people in their forties than to put on a Temptations song. It's "our" music.

When did it become "ours"? At the moment it stopped being "race music" and went "mainstream" — that is, onto white radio stations and into white record stores. Asked when R&B turned into rock & roll,

Ruth Brown said, "When the white kids started to dance to it."[6] This earlier moment made possible the flowering of Motown in the early sixties. It
was of such marginal moments — when forces converged in the throes of
becoming — that what we now call "the sixties" was born.

It is impossible to speak of that time without talking about music
— and not as detail or background. Sometimes it seems that the music is
simultaneously the readiest point of access, a kind of summation of it all,
and the secret heart of the time. Yet the early sixties — the pre-sixties, if
you will, since the sixties started in 1964 — were an odd moment in
American popular music. The white music scene was heterodox and
amorphous. Elvis and the Everlys were still around, though getting a bit
long in the tooth. The mass-produced Teen Idols — Frankie Avalon, Paul
Anka, Bobby Rydell — were hopeless. Frankie Valli, of the glass-shatter-
ing nasal falsetto, seemed to be everywhere, with his gallery of goddess-
es: Dawn, Marlena, Candy, Rag Doll, Big Girls who Do Cry. From the
west blew the lush harmonies of the Wilson extended family and a ready-
made fantasy of sun, sand, surf, and blonde, tanned bodies — as white a
myth of privileged indolent youth as pop music ever knew. As for black
male artists to whom white kids had access, they were iconoclastic figures
who likewise seemed to be holdovers from our older siblings' record col-
lections: Little Richard, James Brown, Jackie Wilson, Little Anthony, the
Platters.

The girls, were an equally motley crew. The female counterparts
to Bobby and Frankie were probably Brenda Lee and Connie Francis —
likewise beginning to seem very dated. The queen of the white girl
singers, for my age-mates, was certainly Leslie Gore, in her immobilized
bouffant and shirtwaist dresses. She provided an acutely particular soundtrack for suburban gender socalization, in which parties became epic confrontations. She collaborated with the general airwave indoctrination with
songs like "Maybe I Know," where the girl defiantly asserts her helplessness in the face of any form of humiliation from the man she loves; but
she countered with the subversive and equally defiant "You Don't Own
Me." Perfect for girls like me, caught between submission and rebellion.
And perfect for that rumbling, changeful time.

It was from across the race line that the great girl-music came, via
the Girl Groups, with their frothy names, Chiffons and Shirelles, and their
nasal harmonies riding Phil Spector's wall of sound. It's interesting how
many of their truly wonderful songs were written by Carol King or Ellie
Greenwich, white female sensibilities that produced solid gold — "One
Fine Day," "Will You Still Love Me Tomorrow?" — along with horrors like
"He Hit Me (But It Felt Like a Kiss)."

What we inhabited on the edge of our teens, via the AM radio
and American Bandstand on Saturday afternoon, was an edgily integrated

musical landscape that was formless, if not entirely void. Black-leather rebelliousness boogied with the most conventional messages. We white kids who were five or eight years younger than Elvis' fans waited for some music we could claim, something that would claim us, tell us who we were. To answer Martha Reeves' question, we were ready for a brand-new beat.

I think it must have been Smokey Robinson I heard first, that high, cool voice singing "Shop Around." But suddenly there was a flood, rushing up from Grand River downtown. A whole generation of white girls started pantomiming "Stop! In The Name of Love" at slumber parties. Just as I was beginning to ponder the Name of Love, I had these soulful philosophers to feed my visions. The fifteen-year-old me conceived of true love as consisting of the basic dramatic intensity of the Four Tops' "Reach Out," layered with the Temps' sweet sincerity on "My Girl," cut with with the coy sexiness of Mary Wells on "My Guy." Suddenly I saw women singing in the foreground, with male back-ups: Gladys and her Pips, Martha and her Vandellas. Teamwork like Marvin Gaye and Tammie Terrell. And the boy I thought of myself as growing up with, as his piping voice got lower and edgier: Steveland Morris, Little Stevie, born in the same year in the same city, a whole universe away from me.

When the Beatles arrived in Detroit in September of 1964, everybody wanted to meet them. But they wanted to meet Barry Gordy. They knew, if we didn't, the debt they owed to the black music industry: Not just their covers of black songs — "Twist and Shout," "Money," "Kansas City," "Please Mr. Postman," "You Really Got A Hold On Me," "Baby, It's You" — but the rhythms, melodies, chord progressions, background vocals of much of *Meet the Beatles* and the albums that followed fast upon it. John Lennon would later say that "the Beatles were always supposing that they were Smokey Robinson."[7] The movement in music that carried us forward into what we call the Sixties seemed to come from two directions, but what was coming from England was only coming home to where it started.

It is and isn't ours, this music we bought, big-time, and loved. We white kids line-dancing in the basement and lip-synching in the bedroom, we needed it, no question. We have overlaid it with our memories, our coming-of-age; we have dubbed it into the movie of our lives. But it is not ours. And our love for it had, and has, no necessary relation to racial respect or justice. Bernice Reagon has recently explained why music often crosses the color line in this country without eroding it, and why black folks are not necessarily overjoyed by white "adoption" of their music:

"The African-American sound has always been very accessible, out there for other people to try on. The problem with that comes because of racism. We experience diminished access to our own sound. We see our music going into places we're not welcome. It angers us to see people so readily embracing that which belongs to us, but still shutting us out."[8] In 1962 or 3, in music as in the auto factories, black labor in Detroit produced beauty for white leisure in the suburbs. The fruit of black culture was "hired" for white entertainment. And the only black folks traveling north from Detroit were the mothers and sisters, aunts and grandmothers of Stevie and Diana and Smokey, coming out on buses to clean our houses.

We cannot claim this music. But there is no denying our history with it, or our need for it. Again I come up against the absence, the hunger, the big chill in white middle- to upper-class culture that drives it to the black fire to warm itself. It was undeniably cold in those suburbs, and too quiet, and too neat. The martinis flowed and bridge got played; the pool got filtered and the lawn was mowed religiously. Angers and betrayals were swallowed with the meat loaf. Daughters and sons prowled their spacious upstairs rooms. The music that came out to us from Downtown: even now when I strain my ears back into the past, trying to hear it as I heard it then, I can't tune it in. The signal is scrambled: what we danced and finger-popped to, was it a clear, vivid apprehension of something that black people knew about freedom, about movement, about the soul stretching in song? Or was it just jungle fever, white adolescent slumming, a musical safari?

"Come into the / black / and live," offered African American poet Lucille Clifton in a particularly generous moment, after the prospect of white fathers murdering their own children at Kent State had driven her to outright pity for the poverty of the white spirit.[9] How often have we done so — forced our way in, crept in, danced in, listened in toward the black so we could live. From Miss Ann drawing from Mammy the sustenance — spiritual as well as physical — that the Big House wasn't giving her, on down through generations of white folks asking, or demanding, that black women, men, and children provide or represent something lacking in their own white spaces.

Behind this phenomenon stretch centuries of complicated racial politics. White people demonized blackness as "savage" and essentialized it as "primitive." Blackness," as a sign, has been seized from black people and made to mean whatever whites need it to mean: "savage" can mean "noble," representing a symbolic dignity that we deny to real, flesh-and-blood black people; or "savage" can mean "subhuman, inferior," legitimizing all manner of injustice. "Primitive" can mean "not worthy of study," or it can mean "pure, unsullied, basic." Both mean, always, sexual. And we

who are in charge of the signifiers can use them as extensions of ourselves: we can buy back from black people (cheap) the "primitive" that
we ourselves have assigned to their music. We can use it to relieve our
own cultural, social, and sexual anxieties. We can say (to ourselves, in a
whisper) it helps us get in touch with our "primitive," "savage" selves —
by which we might mean any number of things. Toni Morrison calls this
"Playing in the Dark."[10]

To be white and to have come up in those times is to recognize
that I and my love for this music are implicated in this tangled history. It's
not my music. Yet it is in me, undeniably. As much as purloined treasure,
the spoils of cultural raiding, it was also a gift and a blessing. An invita-
tion, across the nation. A chance for folks to meet. And at that time, in
that season, it really seemed possible that there might be dancing in the
streets.

9 . Fast Forward

June, 1963: I'm about to become an official teenager. A Civil
Rights worker named Medgar Evers has been assassinated in his front
yard, his wife and children inside. I'm not sure who he is, but I'm confused. I don't understand how white people can keep shooting and
lynching colored people without getting caught and going to jail. This
conundrum opens a crack in the plaster of a privileged child's confidence
in justice..

August, 1963: A sea of faces, mostly dark, around the Lincoln
Memorial. The man has a dream today.

September, 1963: I have just started eighth grade. Four colored
girls are blown apart by a bomb in the basement of a church in
Birmingham, Alabama, during Sunday morning services. They are
younger than I am.

November, 1963: The Thursday before Thanksgiving, my sixth-
period American History class is interrupted twice by the faltering voice of
the principal over the P.A. First, the president has been shot. Then, the
president is dead. We are to go quickly and quietly to our lockers and
then out to the buses that are waiting to take us home from Bloomfield
Hills Junior High, where there are precisely two "colored" students, a
brother and sister, painfully shy.

July, 1964: I am living to see the Beatles in concert in September.
White kids and colored kids just a little older than I am are going south in
droves. This is what comes to be called Freedom Summer.

February, 1965: Malcolm X has been shot, by his own people

we're told, the Black Muslims from whom he's separated himself. Malcolm is the bad one, of course; Dr. King is the good one. This is, at fifteen, my understanding of racial politics, but I am hardly unique. Dr. King looks Christlike, dignified, sad. Malcolm X looked angry, scary. Black anger is the most frightening thing the white mind can imagine.

July, 1967: I get up early for a lousy job at Scotty's, a fast-food place, all the more contemptible because I know I won't ever have to do it for a living. It's already steaming hot when I get down to breakfast. My mother has the radio on, her face is troubled. In this Summer of Love, Detroit has exploded. The city is a war zone. When we used to go "downtown" to shop at J. L. Hudson's, we dressed up; it was an occasion. We don't go there anymore, now that we live in Ann Arbor, now that the city is "dangerous." The city, where Michael lived, where Mary lived. Where both Glorias, hers and mine, lived. The city where I was born. The city is full of anger, black anger. The city is in flames. That very night, Martha and the Vandellas are singing "Dancing in the Streets" downtown.[11] Their anthem will become Mick Jagger's demonic parody: fighting, not dancing, in the streets.

I go to Ann Arbor Pioneer High, a vast complex of nearly four thousand students of every color and class. There are many black students. I count as a friend exactly one of them, who sings in the choir with me. They are a world apart within the school. Next spring, what are always called "racial tensions" will be such that the police will patrol our hallways, armed, in the weeks before graduation. At that point in the history of American education, this is a big deal.

I am slightly more knowledgeable now. In AP American History I have read *The Strange Career of Jim Crow*. It has filled in important blanks, so that what has gone on in my lifetime has context. I have done a big research paper on slavery in Brazil and have begun to draw connections.

But the book that has transfixed me is John Howard Griffin's *Black Like Me*. Is it because Griffin's epidermal self-transformation opens a path for a white imagination to enter into blackness? Or is it because a white man "turning" black and voluntarily entering the madness, reporting back, is somehow more heroic, more reliable, than a black man would be, speaking simply from his everyday, livelong life?

Do I even know that black women write books at all?

10. The View from Arlington

April 4, 1968. After some days in New York, our senior class trip has brought us to Washington. Tonight we are to leave, directly from Arlington National Cemetery, our last stop, where we will visit the eternal flame at President Kennedy's grave. Then we will head out to National Airport to fly home to Detroit, recovering very slowly from the riots nine months before. In six more weeks we will graduate.

As we're packing, someone comes in to tell us that Martin Luther King has been shot dead in Memphis. I am amazed, and then frightened. As we gather to board the bus, I speak to one of the black students whom I know. I tell her I'm sorry (thinking how stupid I sound) and ask how she's doing.

"Well," she answers, her voice composed formal, "we're pretty upset."

"Yeah," I mumble, "of course." I don't know what to say. I hear, I feel the "we," to which I don't belong. In her response I catch a brief glimpse of these black students, my peers, as a community unto themselves, submerged in my huge high school. A community transcending particular friendships, alliances, family backgrounds, personalities. They are a We. My feelings are tangled. I want to be part of their mourning, but I know I can't. The rage beneath it frightens me. The distance between us gapes, insurmountable.

On the bus to Arlington, I'm thinking about King's grave, intelligent face. I'm frightened. I wonder what will happen, and I want to stop it before it does. I feel the lid is going to blow off. As it turns out, of course, I'm right. I feel a loss of control, over an idea of America that will slowly, inexorably crumble over the next few years, as I leave my Republican home, and the war in Asia drags on, and kids like me are killed at Kent State and kids like those black kids sitting together on the bus, conferring quietly, are shot down at Jackson State.

By the time we reach the cemetery, the sun has set, leaving only a violet-peach smear in the western Virginia sky. Darkness seeps down over Washington, spread out below us. I'm standing at Kennedy's grave with a bunch of other white kids. In little more than two months, another grave will appear here. Before we've graduated, my mother will wake me early, tears streaming down her face, to tell me that Bobby Kennedy's been shot in Los Angeles. To the right, about five hundred feet away, the black students stand in a closed circle, talking in low voices.

And suddenly we hear a siren, then another, wailing across the city. "Look, look!" people are saying, pointing down at the city. Sporadic smoke is rising. Fires have broken out. It's begun.

I climb on the bus with the others to begin the trip home.

3

Into the Woods

Land of the silver birch, home of the beaver,
I will return to thee, hills of the north;
Blue lake and rocky shore,
I will return once more . ... .

—a camp song

July, 1989

I am Up North. Ask a Michigander where Up North begins as you
drive north on 131 or 75, and you will get an array of answers, but we are
no less sure of where it *is* or of when we are there.

The capital of Up North is T. C., Traverse City, which sits at the
bottom of Grand Traverse Bay, just where Mission Peninsula reaches up
to divide the Bay into east and west. The particular corner of Up North
where I find myself is southeast of Traverse City on the Boardman River,
a cold, clear, fast stream that runs through dense forest. I'm sharing with
my buddy Marigene a spacious A-frame cabin owned by a mutual friend.
Marigene climbs trees and saws off dead limbs; I sit in the sun and read.
She plays with her dog, Rigby (as in Eleanor); I sit in the shade and read.
Iridescent turquoise dragonflies circle and land, veer away, coupling in
air. The afternoons buzz. The sun drips down through the trees.

One day, bored with tree surgery, Marigene suddenly pipes up,
"Wanna go look for your camp?" I have told her that I navigated the
Boardman on a raft during my years at Camp Arbutus, a camp for girls on
one of a chain of five small, pristine lakes southeast of T.C.

I went to Camp Arbutus every summer from 1960, when I turned
ten, through 1965, when I got too old. For the first two years I attended
month-long sessions; thereafter, nothing but the whole eight weeks. I
remember those months very simply. Endless depths of mottled green
sunlight, clear blue water, the smell of dry pine needles and tar in the
heat, and the sounds of girls' voices. With effort I can dredge up tears,

anger, fear, jealousy, illness, rain. But, I recognize with a slight shock, those summers were the most entirely happy time in my life.

Yet they weren't a time. They were a series of times, six times, brief timeless times between the ordered real-time of the school year. Camp lay at the margins of my real life, where my real friends didn't go, where my parents played no part after they dropped me off. Perhaps this explains why my recollections of camp seem somewhat dreamlike. Camp had its distinct culture, its rituals, heroes, values, standards, lore. Camp was down the rabbit hole, through the looking glass, over the rainbow. And one day late in each June, I crossed over.

Literally, physically, Camp was something of a secret, hidden place. As Marigene and I drive off in search of it, I remember only the feeling of turning in off the main road (what road? what road was it?), parking in a small lot to the left, and walking down a long, dusty entry road, overarched with dense trees, until the woods closed behind me and the sounds of the outside world died away. Then, suddenly, Camp opened up before me as I walked into its heart: an open place where several major paths came together, with the Lodge on a rise to the right, the road down to the directors' cabins straight ahead, the trail to Happy Hollow, for the littlest campers, to the left. Throughout the rolling woods behind the lodge were the cabins, idiosyncratically named. And further ahead, beyond it all, the hill sloped suddenly, steeply down to the shore of small, tranquil Lake Arbutus, ringed with jagged, black-green evergreens.

I have been down this road so often in my dreams; it was only after I realized in my thirties how often I dreamed of Camp that I began to look back more attentively. It was my primal place somehow, my enchanted place. And when I wake from dreams in which I've gone back, I always yearn for a while, like one in exile who has dreamed of home.

I have told Marigene that I have no idea how to get there. Her road map gives us only the location of the lake. "That's all we need," she says confidently. "We'll find it." Marigene is an anthropologist. We drive around the general area between Mayfield and the lake for a while. Somehow it all looks far too civilized; I remember a darker, more mysterious, Twin Peaks sort of landscape. We've been at this for only about fifteen minutes when suddenly, coming around a curve of blacktop, there it is: a sign, the one I used to crane my neck in the back seat of my mother's car to see, announcing in letters made of rope, "CAMP ARBUTUS."

I yelp. Marigene laughs and turns into the entry drive. As we park in the lot on the left, I announce I'm a little scared.

"Why?" Marigene asks, loving this.

"I have no idea."

Because it's the Twilight Zone, that's why. Because I don't know

what lies down that road.
Or who.

———— ••◄○8○►•••• • ————

By the third or fourth summer, coming back here was as close as my suburban white post-fifties life got to mystical. The place waited for me, always the same, and that continuity was at least half its value, as my life between ten and fifteen erupted with disorienting, profound changes. My Happy Hollow month was July of 1960, when I turned ten; the preceding December my father had died. After my third summer, in 1962, my mother remarried. For me this meant a new house in a different suburb, a new school just as I entered junior high, a new stepbrother and stepsister and extended family, new people everywhere in my life. Between my fourth and fifth summers, 1963 and 64, my only brother married and moved to Oregon, and my stepfather died suddenly. And in May of 1965, a month before my last Arbutus summer commenced, my mother married again, and so we moved again — another new stepbrother and stepsister, new city, new house, new school, this time just as I entered high school.

When I map it out like this, my own life seems so dramatic I hardly recognize it. And on top of it all — or rather, beneath it — came puberty. My first summer at camp, I was a tall-for-my-age ten-year-old with a pixie haircut whose chief joys in life were playing the piano and watching "Bonanza." By the time I left Arbutus for the last time, weeping profusely, I had turned fifteen, had breasts and periods and long bleached hair and had discovered, via Paul McCartney, rock and roll and the meaning of passion. Those years, from ten to fifteen, form an arduous, perilous passage in any girl's life. For girls like I was, they are the Danger Zone defined by Carol Gilligan and others, the time of loss of voice, both literally and metaphorically. The tough, limber, little girl falls silent, weakens, looks away, forgets how to say "I want," "I know," "I see." Her self-expressions become corrupt, convoluted, self-destructive. In my life, family events had made these years positively tumultuous. But as a kid, in the midst of such experience, you normalize it. It's the only life you know, so it can't be extraordinary to you. I see myself at twelve or fourteen, raised to be cooperative, obedient, a trouper, a good sport, and I find myself hanging on to the saddlehorn of a runaway, bucking life. But when I walked down this entry road again each summer, a promise was reconfirmed: something remained unchanged, something waited — the dark pines reflected in the lake exactly as they had been last summer, the same faces calling, the same songs and rituals. This was a place where my belonging deepened with every turn of the seasons, unlike the rest of my life, where family was repeatedly reconfigured, where home did not exist either as a temporal or as a spatial concept, and everyone and everything was new, awkward, without past. Here I was met at the end of the road not only by old friends but by an old familiar self. I stepped up to her and we ran off into the woods.

That was half the mystery and wonder of Camp — that it endured. But the other half was that it didn't. It was transitory, ephemeral. Though I never saw it disappear, I knew it did. I tried to imagine it in winter, snowbound and silent, the lake frozen grey, doors and gates locked, horses transported south, boats in drydock. It scared me and I stopped. It was easier to imagine that Camp simply vanished into a wrinkle in time, reappearing with the summer. My own private Brigadoon.

By the time Marigene and I reach the point where I know Camp is about to appear around the next bend in the dirt road, I am breathless with eagerness and anxiety. Maybe I don't even want to see it again. Thomas Wolfe, etc. This tempts fate.

But there it is.

The first thing I notice is a long wooden table at the bottom of the rise to the Lodge where a bunch of pubescent girls and younger boys seems to be lounging around, in chairs or on top of the table. Don't they have a schedule to follow? And —

Wait a minute:

BOYS?

There are *boys* at Camp Arbutus?

Marigene is smiling into the sun, looking around, taking it all in. One of the girls, about twelve, long honey-colored hair in a thick pony-tail, saunters over and says in a distinct English accent, "Can I help you?" Who ARE these children? I stammer that I used to go to camp here, that I just want to walk around if it's all right. "Sure it is," she shrugs. "But Mac's here, if you want to see her. She'd probably remember you.

Mac is here? Twenty-five years after I left my last sneaker print in the pine-needled dust, Grace MacDonald still exists, here? Well, of course. This is Never Never Land.

Mac was the Assistant Director. The directors, a somewhat regal older couple, were the Elizabeth-and-Philip figureheads; Mac was the prime minister, beloved and a little feared. She did gruff-with-a-heart-of-gold to perfection. And she ran the motorized barge that took us on sud-denly announced trips to First Lake Store to get candy. At the periphery of any camp activity, there she'd be, standing silent, cross-armed, smiling a small ironic smile.

Not only is Mac still here, but she looks exactly the same. Well, a little gray in the dark, wavy, modified D.A. And she remembers me. "Griffin," she repeats several times, narrowing her eyes to see me at eleven or twelve. And then to my amazement she reels off the names of counselors and fellow campers of my era. "What about Sam?" I ask. "Have you heard anything about her?"

She nods deeply, then shakes her head. "Born again."

"No! Sam?" Wild, profane, tomboy Sam?

"Yep, born-again Christian."

As long as we're into heresies, I ask about the boys. The answer is depressing: Insurance has become so formidable that they've had to expand. "But we only take the younger ones," she assures me. "Pre-teenage." Small comfort.

Mac owns the camp now, I'm gratified to hear — bought it when Elizabeth and Philip abdicated south. But she fears she can't hold it long. Costs are staggering. She shakes her head. I think of the very worldly, obviously wealthy girl who met us. At the table with her were a couple brown Indian faces. Of course: the camp has been internationalized by the influx of business and professional families from overseas who send their kids to private schools and private camps. I picture the faces gathered in the Lodge in 1962: not one non-white face among them. Nearly all of us were from Michigan and northern Ohio, suburbs like Bloomfield Hills or Upper Arlington. The depth of my innocence then, coming back here for six summers and never knowing that this was an absolute luxury.

With Mac's blessing, Marigene and I head off on a walking tour. It occurs to me that I might be in one of my dreams. I put my feet down softly, quietly, afraid it will all crumble. We range up over "the Hill" beyond the Lodge, dotted with the cabins of middle-aged campers, twelve to fourteen; and down into "the Hollow," a cluster of cabins for younger girls. I am ransacking my memory for the names of the cabins I was in; I know they're wedged somewhere in a fold of my brain. They float back: Cedar, West Wind . . . . As we move to higher ground, scraps of the blue lake appear and vanish through the trees just as they used to.

The ache in my shoulders is like a low hum in the background. I have learned to stroke through it, on and on, turning my wrists forward at the end to put a tail on the J. If I hold it just a fleet second, the bow will swing to the left. But I don't, and the canoe surges gently across the water. One day I am standing up in the stern of a huge war canoe, feet apart, calling out "Stroke! Stroke!" to the eight girls sitting in front of me, feeling like something out of "Ben Hur." What does coxing a war canoe have in common with the nineteen-sixties, Swinging London, the dead Kennedys, we shall overcome? What does it have to do with Capezios, white eyeliner, strawberry vanilla lipstick,? Nothing. Not a blessed thing. I stand there timeless, ridiculous, mythic, in command of my boat.

We stand still and breathe. The warm smell of dry pine needles mingles with the other woodscents. Small rushes of wind bend the tops of the pines. It is quiet, deserted, but I hear muffled sounds — shots from the riflery range, arrows thwopping into straw-stuffed targets. "I was really good at archery," I tell Marigene.

"Yeah?" she says.

"I still have the certificates and medals someplace."

I get so that I can find almost by feel the particular spot in the air where my arrow tip belongs: just to the right of the bullseye and up slightly. The feathers hiss over my fingers and the metal tip buries itself in the red vinyl, the shaft quivering in the air. My right bicep throbs quietly, it's a heavy bow. Last summer I couldn't draw the string back far enough, to the place alongside my right cheek, so tight that sometimes when I straighten my three fingers the string burns my skin as it shoots forward.

Beyond the archery range I begin to lose my bearings. Paths converge and separate, heading off into the woods. I know that at some point my feet will know, my body will know which one to take, the one that led toward the horses. You had riding three days a week, MWF or TTS. Those were the best days. It was an uphill trek, maybe a quarter mile, and then the green pine smell would give way to warm brown horse smell.

It's a peculiar, difficult gesture, holding him back and urging him forward at once, so that he breaks from a walk straight into a canter without slipping into a trot. It's especially hard bareback. But so is sitting a trot. He's a big bay, sixteen hands, black mane and tail, with those huge, lucid, intelligent brown eyes that only horses have, and only some of them. His name is Toy, for his bigness. You rotate to a different horse every class, with some allowances made for size and temperament — of horse and of rider, that is. But the days I know I have Toy waiting for me are days of swallowed anticipation. To swing my right leg over and settle onto his solidity, to feel his muscles shift, the forward lurch of him, the steady gait. The moment he breaks into a canter, the fear followed by something like ecstasy. Pelvis moving to his rhythm, hands quiet and close to his withers, trying to keep still from the waist up, the slight lean into a turn, hugging his round sides with my thighs, trying to remember to sit tall, not to lean down toward his beautiful neck. The sun rushing by through the blurry trees. Don't stop. Don't ever stop. Stop time here, right here.

For a fleet moment I wonder if Toy is still here, and then I realize it's been twenty-three years. And I have not been on a horse since the last summer I was here. I am thirty-nine years old. When I was here, I could not imagine thirty-nine. Mac was probably not yet thirty-nine then. For me, the depth of sophistication, wisdom, and general coolness was seventeen, the age of most of the CIT's, Counselors-in-Training. They laughed at things we didn't understand, went to TC on Saturday nights and wouldn't tell us about it on Sunday, had great haircuts and breasts, boyfriends at home and stories to tell. They sang suggestive songs, winked at us, implied always that although they had to enforce the rules, things would be different if they ran the place.

I am running from the softball diamond, up the hill toward my cabin. I am crying, desperately, passionately. I have hurt Sam somehow, thrown or swung wild and watched the ball connect with her shoulder or back. Am I running away from her? After her? Away from my shame, from proffered solace, from and into my conviction that I am a Jonah, an awkward, graceless loser? Sam the invincible, the freckled, grinning everybody's-favorite, the born winner: wounded, bruised by my stupidity. Sam was a camper at age eight, so she is now the elect of the elect, the one who knows all the lore, the secrets, the precedents, the songs and stories, the drill, the program, the style. She was the camp's child; I couldn't imagine her having a regular home, and parents. The mischief shining in her eyes was barely held in check by her CIT responsibilities and loyalty to Arbutus, and no authority figure could stay angry at her. She was the androgyne, solidly built, muscular, with short, slick black hair. Completely unselfconscious, always in motion. To see her throw her head back and laugh would stop my heart. I would have died to please her, to get her attention, to impress her, to make her laugh. I would have died to be born again as Sam.

There is no feeling like the crush of a pubescent girl on an older one, none on this earth.

What did it mean to be a girl here? It seems, in memory, that all the lines were redrawn, all the Outside World rules, categories, labels, requirements were irrelevant. Neither femininity nor ladylikeness raised her tiresome head all summer. Prissy, fastidious, or vain girls were ridiculed: they had come to the wrong place. We ran and sweated and yelled and laughed, we made alliances and fought, we wore no make-up and outfits that didn't match, we let our hair dry in the sun after swimming and washed it once a week if we remembered; we were always on our way into or out of the lake,.so it was wet most of the time anyway. We giggled at the two males in our world, the dour, decrepit busdriver and the teenaged handy- man, and were completely satisfied with ourselves and each other.

1963: Betty Friedan published *The Feminine Mystique*. Sylvia Plath gassed herself in England.

———•·══◄◙⊗◙►══·•———

Heading back toward the Lodge, I can't resist running down to Slide-Inn, the cabin in which I spent my third summer. The origin of its name is obvious from its situation, perched halfway down the bluff to the lake. Coming down the path from the Lodge on a rainy day, you often did literally slide in.

I am running down from the Lodge on a hot afternoon, sneakers slapping the path. If my toe catches on a root, I'm gone. The momentum carries me up the steps and through the cabin door, which slams behind me.

Inside, it seems unbearably close, hot. It couldn't have been this small, but it must have been, because the walls are covered, completely covered, in names and dates: in ink, pencil, marker, calcified toothpaste. And one of them is mine. Marigene spots it first, on a rafter above a top bunk. In the middle of the wood floor, I stand, sweating, looking up at it. GAIL GRIFFIN '62 in pale green — probably Crest, then a new brand.

I always try to grab the top bunk. You can hide there, if you need to. And at night you can lie on your side at the inside edge of the metal frame, your face close to the screen, watching the darkness settle down. Taps blow, sometimes sweetly, at 9 p.m., when dark is just gathering at the western edge of the Eastern Time Zone on daylight savings in July and August. When dark comes it is absolute. The cabins have no electricity, so if someone goes out to the bathroom, a flashlight's bright circle bounces along a path. I feel the edge of the air turn chill, I hear a zillion crickets. I hear the footsteps of two counselors along a path, their soft laughter. And one night, with a cold jolt to the stomach, I hear a wild, utterly clear, utterly insane laugh from across the still lake.

We are teenaged girls, or nearly, and we know about dangers in the dark. We tell stories about The Hook, The Babysitter. "The call's coming from inside the house!" "And hanging on the door handle was a HOOK!" The maniacal laugh came from inside the woods, our woods. It came from the deep heart of the woods, that even we don't know, don't visit. It's like the animal skull we found on South Manitou Island — the vacant eyes, the memento mori at the center of paradise.

The next day our counselor tells me about loons.

Something wants to stay forever, something wants to go. Our last stop is the Lodge itself, and this is a small shock: again, of course, smaller than the vast, woody shrine I remember, but also clearly in disrepair, dusty, almost seedy. The wonderful smell is the same: decades of woodsmoke coating the walls, ceiling, windows. Down the lake side of the central living room, with the big stone fireplace, runs the long porch lined with tables where we gathered three times a day, sang a grace ("Oh, the Lord is good to me, / And so I thank the Lord / For giving me the things I need, /The sun and the rain and the appleseed . . . .") ate, sang again, something funny this time, and went on to the next phase of a day organized by the clanging Lodge bell.

At the opposite end of the central room from the fireplace, the birchbark canoe still hangs. Not *a* but *the* birchbark canoe. Supposedly the genuine article, Indian-made. And at the end of every summer, in the holiest, most secret-shrouded ritual of all, the CIT's carefully took it from the log where it hung, bore it down to the lake, and held it by the gunwales as, out of the woods, emerged the one camper chosen worthiest to paddle it out across the glassy waters of Lake Arbutus at sunset.

It was always an older girl, a long-time camper, resident of Donut or Nejee. In 1965 — August, my last days at Camp although I didn't know it then — I prayed it would be me. Back in the World, I would never get the honors that counted among girls. This is my world, I prayed, let it be me.

It wasn't me. It was Annie, a sunny, warm, wonderful girl whom everybody, including me, adored. I was given the first-runner-up honor: that of writing the long narrative poem that would be read at the final ceremonies. I was, if you will, that summer's Camp Arbutus Homer. So that I would have time to compose this epic, I was told far in advance, sworn to secrecy. Unable to share my sorrow, I went away to my top bunk and sobbed. A counselor found me there asked why I wasn't wherever I was supposed to be. I lied and said I didn't feel well, had cramps. She insisted on taking me to Pill Hill, the infirmary, where I lay on a cot all afternoon feeling miserable and ashamed.

Ingrate that I was, little shit. Second place in the whole camp wasn't good enough? Didn't I know how appropriate this honor was for me? Well, yes, I did. That was why I didn't want it. I didn't want to be me, articulate and literary. I wanted to be the other thing, the one everybody loved, chosen to kneel in that canoe and pull the water past its swelling white flanks with a perfect J-stroke, no waves, no wake. I wanted to strike out toward sunset, across the cool lake, a silhouette against the peachy sky, with the entire camp population on shore, silently watching me.

Instead, I wrote the poem, which everybody said was the best one anybody had ever written. And for the rest of my life I have written the poem and yearned to paddle the birchbark canoe.

———— · ····◄◦⊗◦►···· · ————

On the way out, I notice a huge wooden sign hanging outside the Lodge. CAMP ARBUTUS 25th BIRTHDAY 1962. Below are a dozen or so squares of shellacked wood, attached to each other like quilt pieces, each made by one cabin in the summer of 1962. Quickly my eyes find "Slide Inn," burned sloppily into the pine. And a list of our names — me, Annie, Lisa, Mary Ann . . . . "There you are again!" Marigene hoots, delighted. "Do you remember doing this?"

I do.

There we are, twenty-seven years later, for these new-age campers to peruse and wonder about and probably sneer at. These girls who probably like Madonna and do drugs and lose their virginities at eleven — and these BOYS. What do they know? We were mighty. "Campers, campers, hats off to you," went one of our songs. It had been a time, hadn't it, a vintage time. And we had left our marks, hadn't we? Burned in wood. Looped in toothpaste.

"Arbutus moon," went a song sung at the end of campfires just before we crept back to our cabins to sleep. "I'd like to be as lovely as you are, Arbutus moon."

———— · ····◄◦⊗◦►···· · ————

It is not until we are back at our outpost on the Boardman that I know what I have understood in returning, the subliminal discovery that has been whispering in me all day.

Camp was a holy place for me always, for many reasons. If you are vulnerable to the particular blue-and-green, pine-smelling, deep-souled beauty of Up North, it is haunting. It was also a place of belonging in years when I felt transient. It was a place where, in the very years when girls weaken toward womanhood, I became strong, had certificates and ribbons and biceps and hard thighs to show for it. In the time when the power born in us seeps out of us into things and people around us, and we begin our lifelong search to find it again, I found it here, in wind and water and the muscular back of a bay horse.

But above all, it was a female place, a girl place. In the very years when we begin that long, complicated slide into the world of men, this was a world of women, little and big. A place out of time, stretching from little-girlhood across the great divide into womanhood. It was a place where girls could be strong and weak, stupid and smart, silly and serious, plain and pretty, could learn and take chances and fail and triumph, all of it apart from the gender police, the sexual strait-jacketing of Real World adolescence. It was the only place where a girl like me could approach something that felt like freedom.

Was it the first time in my life I felt free?

It was certainly the last.

June, 1992

I have one week squashed between Commencement and the first day of summer-quarter classes. In desperate need of some Up North, but unusually short of friends' and family's cottages, I rent myself one of the three at Paul's Paradise Resort on Little Traverse Lake, halfway between Glen Arbor and Leelenau.

Then I am on my way south again, back to my life.

From TC I turn south on what I think is the road that will take me to US 131, which stretches all the way down to the Indiana line. After ten minutes I begin to wonder. After twenty minutes the road comes up over a steep rise. From the top I look out over a sudden, broad vista of dense, unbroken forest. Stunning, beautiful, and somehow eerie, forbidding. I know I'm on the wrong road. I am heading into something I don't understand.

Ten more minutes and the road narrows and I accept that I, who am never lost, am lost. If I just keep going, I think, I'll come out the other side. But I don't. Houses appear along the roadside, then a store and a post office and a sign.

"Mayfield."

I pull off the road, stop and think. I turn around a drive back to a fork and take a right. A sign reads, "Arbutus Motel, Efficiencies, Fishing." I am making turns as if I know what I'm doing, as if I had radar. The woods are thick, bright green, silent. The road leads straight up to a little store on a bluff, at the bottom of which, I know without having to see it, is a lake. Can this be First Lake Store? I drive past it, up along the bluff, never glimpsing the water. This feels like the Twilight Zone episodes where somebody finds himself in a town in the past. *What if I keep going. Will I find it? Will it be there, around some corner? What if I keep going. What if I just keep driving, and never show up back there. How long would it take them to notice my absence? Where would they start looking?*

At some undefinable point, surrounded by strangeness and familiarity, I stop again. I listen to the hot summer afternoon for a while. Then

I turn the car around and drive back to the main road. And I drive through Mayfield, out the other side, on toward Kingsley and 131, south, toward my life.

September, 1993

I move temporarily to an A-frame on a little lake in western Massachusetts. The moment I arrive and step out of the car, the smell is there — pines, dry needles, earth. Within a few days I can send myself back to camp at will. Watching the water can do it, or feeling morning sun on my shoulder.

The first few nights I am full of dreams, as always when I arrive in a new place. Around the third or fourth night, I have a two-part dream, a diptych. The beginning is cloudy, but at the end of part one I am leaving camp again, walking down the long dirt road, out to the blacktop.

In part two I am surrounded by several men I work with. They are explaining to me why my behavior is unacceptable, why the way I operate is not professional. Finally one of them, smiles and says, "What we've got to do with you, Gail, is domesticate you."

I wake laughing, watching myself run back into the woods.

4

A Good Little Girl Like You
Revisiting *"The Wizard of Oz"*

- for Diane -

I had to leave that space called home
to move beyond boundaries,
yet I needed also to return there.

—bell hooks[1]

1. The Small and Meek

This Christmas past, I was given L. Frank Baum's *The Wonderful Wizard of Oz*, a reproduction of the 1900 original, complete with W. W. Denslow's marvelous illustrations. I have read it eagerly, trying to imagine myself back into the "virginity" of this text, before it was forever compromised by comparison with the film. That's hard to do. With a film version that has so permeated the popular consciousness, the text almost inescapably becomes the secondary term of comparison: I read along, thinking how it differs from the film, rather than the reverse.

The differences are legion. Baum's original is much more straightforward: there is no knock on the head, so Dorothy couldn't have dreamed it all. There are no "real-life," black-and-white Kansan originals for the people of Oz, so there is no Freudian layer to the book, no sense that Oz is in Dorothy's mind or that the journey is an inner one. There is no Miss Gulch plot to precipitate Dorothy's "flight" from home. The book has much less humor and much more violence: a remarkable number of amputations and decapitations. There are sub-plots entirely eliminated from the film. But the first difference you notice, perhaps the most significant one, is visual. It's Dorothy.

It came about by accident of Hollywood politics. 20th Century Fox wouldn't release the ten-year-old Shirley Temple to play Dorothy, so MGM reluctantly went with the original choice: sixteen-year-old Judy Garland. That substitution worked a profound transformation on Baum's myth. His Dorothy, a very small girl who looks about six in the illustrations, shot up, Alice-like, into adolescence. She's nearly as tall as Aunt Em, Uncle Henry, and the farmhands; she's as tall as the witch. In Denslow's original illustrations, the Munchkins are interesting precisely because they are Dorothy's size. But in the film, Dorothy towers over them, Gulliver in Lilliput. They accentuate her dislocation, her outsizeness. She seems gawky, too old for the pinafore and the braids. The actual binding of Garland's breasts for the role, which apparently caused tissue damage, makes her chest seem to be straining, painfully confined by that gingham. The anklets look ridiculous. Everything about her seems awkward, clumsy, too big for its assigned place, *bound*. Including her vision, her outrage, her desire.

And that's how it is, to be an adolescent girl. That's how it was for me when I first saw the film. I was a lot like Judy's Dorothy, in spirit and circumstances. While the Detroit suburbs aren't exactly Kansas, I was white and midwestern, and like her I was awkward, spirited, dreamy, smart, a sucker for underdogs, much given (then as now) to towering righteous indignation and urgencies which I expected everyone around me to share. Like her, I was prone to violent homesickness for a "home" hallowed by imagination. Like her, my rebelliousness wrestled constantly with politeness, deference, fear of exile and hunger for approval. Above all, I hated not being listened to and not being believed. These experiences can still jolt me back into my raging child-self. I think they are especially common and infuriating experiences for women. Our emergencies are ignored or diminished; our dreams meet with condescension. And these are the experiences that frame Dorothy's journey, quite literally: as the film opens, her outrage over Miss Gulch's injustice is dismissed and deflected by Aunt Em and Uncle Henry; as it closes, her "family" is chuckling patronizingly and exchanging knowing glances over her account of her vision quest. Both scenes still annoy me.

Salman Rushdie, remembering the power the film had for him as a boy in Bombay, says its "driving force is the inadequacy of adults, even of good adults." For him, the mythos of the film is about seizure of power and autonomy: "the weakness of grownups forces children to take control of their own destinies, and so, ironically, grow up themselves." Dorothy undergoes a classic "rite of passage . . . into a world where people are her own size and she is never, ever treated as a child but as a heroine."[2] Literally speaking, he is wrong about the Munchkins' size relative to Dorothy; they are smaller, and their weird *impersonations* of childhood and (even weirder) of childhood impersonating age serve in a sense to destabilize her age and to call chronological age into question altogether. He is certainly accurate about Dorothy's rite of passage, but the male developmental trajectory toward control and autonomy (no wonder he can't understand her desire to return home) distorts her actual journey down the yellow brick road — which begins as a spiral. Dorothy's is a classically female passage from girlhood toward womanhood, and her engagement with the forces in and around her takes specifically female forms. Alongside the other figures of potent girlhood — Joan of Arc, Jane Eyre, Alice, Juliet, Mary, even Stephen King's Carrie — belongs Dorothy Gale, whose first name means "gift of god" and whose last name is the big wind that seems to be born of her own girlish fury, her towering indignation over the injustice of the world. It circles upon itself until it drives her persecutors underground, lifts her out of her hopeless environment, and spins her into the alternate world she has dreamed up, somewhere over the rainbow.

2. Cyclone

Terry McMillan, recalling the film as she watched it, a young black girl in Port Huron, Michigan, remembers its thrust toward escape. In her world, "Violence was plentiful, and I wanted to go wherever Dorothy was going where she would not find trouble. To put it bluntly, I wanted to escape because I needed an escape."[3] When Dorothy is revealed to have dreamed Oz, it occurred to McMillan "that this very well might be the only way to escape. To dream up another world. Create your own."[4]

Dorothy's "voyage out" is generated by the repressions and confinements of her surroundings, by the flattening, leeching effect of Kansas. Her technicolor imagination is forced into bloom by a black-and-white landscape. The film is pervaded by a tension between liberation and confinement, centrifugal and centripetal forces, like the convergence of high and low fronts that generates a cyclone. This is the ambivalence of adolescence, the confusion and contradiction. After all, as Rushdie has pointed out, the film is driven by Dorothy's relentless desire to return to a place presented as completely unpleasant. Such is home, he continues: the origin and terminus of all quests, the place we are always either dying to leave or trying to find.[5] In Oz, Dorothy herself is an ambivalent figure: in the first scene alone, she is hailed as a savior-hero, indicted as a murderer, and threatened as a potential victim. She has killed the tyrannical Witch of the East, but not through any action of her own. She is helpless lost girl and stalwart questing hero. Even those cumbersome ruby slippers are ambiguous: Glinda herself doesn't know what they're about, "but they must be very powerful, or [the Witch of the West] wouldn't want them so badly." That is, Dorothy, again without her own agency, has inherited a tool of great power and value which she cannot comprehend and is powerless to use.

This doubleness belongs to the world of adolescence, ·especially the female version. In history, literature, and mythology, not to mention reality, female adolescence is the ground for a definitive clash of power and powerlessness. The inherent psychic, emotional, intellectual, physical, and spiritual power of the girl-woman locks in battle with the cultural and social forces restraining and diminishing her. Like Lewis Carroll's Alice, she is alternately and simultaneously oversized and undersized: huge in her possibilities, tiny in her social power. Bodily, she is swelling; cultural-ly, she must be contained. The dissonance is so much sharper for girls, for whom the size of the body and its parts is a particularly crucial issue: for them, the imperative of "normal" adulthood is to get small, not big like their brothers. In other words, you must somehow complete the growth process by defeating it. To grow up, you must, as Annis Pratt has noted, "grow down."[6] When I was Dorothy's age, to become a woman meant, more than anything, to bind yourself physically: not just bras but girdles and heels, gloves and slips and nylons. Adolescence, for girls, is the wilderness of appetites that demand indulgence but must be denied and punished: a prescription for bulimarexia and sexual craziness.

A suggestive image for Dorothy's predicament appears in what has always struck me as one of the weirder scenes in the film (absent from the book): Dorothy trying to walk the fence of the pigpen, losing her balance, and tumbling into the mud amid the snorting, restive, hungry swine. Just prior, she has been told to get lost, to go play, to stop inter-rupting the chicken-counting with her outrage over Toto. Once, when she was smaller, she could probably traverse that fence easily. But now she's too tall, too heavy, too clumsy; she is out of balance. Hers is a sort of slapstick version of the archetypal Fall, into knowledge, sexuality, com-plexity, experience, womanhood. Surely those pigs are connected to her own physicality, appetite, and aggression — everything that gets her into the "trouble" Aunt Em warns her away from.

But of course Dorothy has another, more primary animal-self: her familiar, her *totem*. Toto plays a much larger role in the film than in Baum's story, not only as the source of the opening conflict, but as the ongoing "hero," in the sense of the one who saves the day. In Baum, his interventions in the story are much more accidental, whereas Dorothy is the more intentional agent of much that happens. The cinematic Dorothy, though so much bigger than Baum's original, is more polite, more fearful, more self-diminishing. The film, in fact, feminizes Dorothy by displacing much of her agency and assertion to her animal self. [7]

Above all, Toto is an escape artist. He has escaped from Miss Gulch as the film opens and is about to do so again, popping out of the basket on the back of her bike. His escape from the Witch's castle will save Dorothy's life. And his final escape — from Dorothy's arms, in pur-suit of an Ozian cat — saves her from the bogus Wizard's helplessness in balloonery, almost saves her from returning to Kansas, and precipitates her final recognition of her own power. If Dorothy's quest has something to do with escaping her various confinements, Toto's role is to enact and re-enact that escape. No wonder she cherishes him and fights for his survival. He is a wiry bundle of primary energy. He is that small, insouciant, determined, resourceful thing in adolescent girls that will not be denied, confined, tamed, or destroyed. He is exactly what's at stake.

3. Which Ol' Witch?

"A striking aspect of 'The Wizard of Oz,'" Rushdie observes, "is its lack of a male hero."[8] Well, that's one way of putting it. What is really striking is the presence of a female hero. Half the power of the film for us girls was that, unlike the rest of the cultural fare on which we starved, it had a protagonist who was one of us, without a human male presence to relegate her to "heroine-ism."

In its male images, what the film offers is mock-heroes, beginning with her trio of companions. If, in Rushdie's view, "it is impossible to see the Scarecrow, the Tin Man, and the Cowardly Lion as classic Hollywood leading men,"[9] it is entirely possible to see them as wonderful parodies of leading men, not to mention as some of our worst dates. They're the men who are missing something: the goofy, clumsy aspiring Intellectual, the heartless would-be Romantic, and the spineless Animal Macho Man — caricatured tellingly by Bert Lahr as a limp-wristed, effeminate gay stereotype who is "just a dandy-lion."[10]

But from another angle, this trio represents dimensions of the female hero that she is discovering and exploring through her journey: her quick intelligence, her empathic heart, and her animal courage. That Dorothy's quest is not so much about achievement or even probation as about self-discovery is underscored by the film's thematic emphasis: that what you set out to acquire, you discover within. It's a major theme in women's lives, too: struggling through a culture that defines us as fundamentally lacking (a penis, mathematical ability, the Right Stuff, the right body, whatever), we learn that we have and always have had exactly what we need. This is what Dorothy's journey is about, I think: the critical experience that brings that understanding. And in the indelible image of her and her comrades linking arms and skipping down the Yellow Brick Road, we see Dorothy literally joining her forces, integrating herself incrementally, and moving on.

The "absence of a male hero" from this myth allows us not only to see Dorothy clearly as its protagonist, but to focus attention on the film's remarkable triptych of powerful female images. But first, remember that Dorothy is motherless, like almost every memorable girl/woman in literature and folklore. Motherlessness, in female mythology, signifies detachment from female tradition, sources, power, and protection, as well as, sometimes, resistance to the culturally inscribed feminine, rejection of gender expectations. Dorothy's encounters with three alternate mothers are engagements with female possibility. And this, rather than autonomy or control, is the crux of the film.

Aunt Emily Gale is left out of the triangular "power center"[11] Rushdie defines at the center of the movie: Dorothy, Glinda, the Witch of the West. The discrepancy between his account of Aunt Em and McMillan's is telling: while Rushdie discusses her entirely in the context of poverty, passivity, and Good Christian Womanhood that won't speak its mind to Miss Gulch, McMillan remembers quite a different woman: "Auntie Em sounded just like my mother — bossy and domineering. They both ran the show . . . . Auntie Em's husband was a wimp, and for once the tables were turned: he took orders from her."[12] She associates Aunt Em with the example of her own mother, which showed her that "being a woman didn't mean you had to be helpless."[13] Where Rushdie sees victimization, McMillan sees power, albeit distorted and unpleasant. I think Aunt Em is both, and more. She haunts Dorothy throughout her journey precisely because she is so multivalent. If she is simply victim or shrew, why is Dorothy so desperate to return to her — specifically to her, not Uncle Henry? If she's the classic inadequate or bad mother-figure, how is it that Professor Marvel can propel Dorothy into a guilty about-face merely by hinting that he sees in his crystal ball a woman named Emily, crying? In Oz, Dorothy's immediate, visceral, uncritical homesickness is inseparable from Aunt Em.

Once Dorothy is in Oz, however, the two controlling forces in her journey seem to be the classically opposed feminine archetypes, wonderfully exaggerated, who also represent sides of Dorothy: the loving, helpful Good Girl and the subversive, raging troublemaker. One of the greatest differences between Baum and Hollywood is the foregrounding of Glinda, the Good Witch of the North, and the interestingly nameless Wicked Witch of the West. In Baum's text, Glinda is the Witch of the South and doesn't appear until very late in the story; Dorothy is greeted in Munchkinland by a Witch of the North who is an old woman, Munchkin-sized. And the Witch of the West isn't even heard of until Oz sends Dorothy & Co. on the broomstick errand. In the film, they are the poles defining Dorothy's entire journey.

Glinda, the "positive" pole, benevolent, nurturing, protective, magical, pink-and-blonde princess/bride/fairygodmother, is what we can hope to become if we are good and kind — and pretty (for, as she explains to Dorothy, "Only bad witches are ugly.") But Glinda is not without complication herself. Chiefly, we have to wonder why she seems alternately knowledgeable and ignorant about the power of the red shoes, helpful and withholding. Does her bubble signify her insulation and unreality? And how can Billie Burke, an aging princess herself, with her silly voice, her megadress, and her hypercrown, possibly hold her own against the opposition?

Which is, of course, the incomparable Margaret Hamilton, the definitive Witch, stooped, gaunt, squinty and green with leering, sarcastic meanness. That she is "the Wicked Witch" makes for a wonderful unintentional redundancy: the terms are etymological cousins whose great-grandmother, the Anglo-Saxon *wicca*, means to bend or shape. In a culture of straight lines and right angles, what is bent and twisted is *wicked* — that is, belonging to the province of women. In Margaret Hamilton Hollywood gave us our clearest image of *wicca* turned against itself: the image of what we will become if we're not All of the Above: the unlovely, unloving, unloved, unlovable woman. Whom we all love, dearly.

Her relationship with Dorothy is the most layered in the film. As Miss Gulch, she is the force working to deprive Dorothy of Toto and what he represents. From the film's first shot, it draws its life from the antagonism between her and Dorothy; in fact, Rushdie reads the tornado as generated by the "feelings unleashed between Miss Gulch and Dorothy."[14] In Oz, the antagonism and pursuit are complicated by a new element: Dorothy has something the witch is after, but it's not Toto; it's those shoes. If she will fork them over, she and Toto are free agents, off to see the Wizard. And then there is Dorothy's counterpursuit: it's not the witch she is after, but the broomstick. They are locked together not in personal antagonism but in mutual need. Their antagonism seems somehow situational rather than essential or personal. Their opposition is vaguely sororal, especially since Dorothy enters Oz all too literally *in place of* the Wicked Witch's sister, flattened by the Gale house. Her ruby slippers simply appear on Dorothy's feet, as if by inheritance. The fury of the Witch of the West is that of a woman suddenly sisterless, confronting a *rival*. The Munchkins *and* Glinda assume that Dorothy is a witch (or, if not, that Toto might be); the question is "Are you a good witch, or a bad witch?" Faced with that reductive dualism, Dorothy opts out: "I'm not a witch at all." But I wonder. Some have greatness thrust upon them. Dorothy, in her blue pinafore, is suddenly wearing witch shoes: red, sparkly, sexy heels.[15] She finds herself in a place where she is, as Rushdie points out, treated as an adult. In other words, adult womanhood, in the totemic form of those shoes, is upon her. But nobody knows how it works.

How lucky that Hollywood thought red had more screen appeal than Baum's original shoe color, silver. The potent red of menarche and passion is repeated later on in the baffling poppy-field episode, which begins to make wonderful sense if we hear its echoes of "Sleeping Beauty" and "Snow White." In both these tales of female adolescence, the virgin confronts redness at the threshold of womanhood via an encounter with a witch. In "Snow White," it's the apple offered by her *wicked* step-mother. In "Sleeping Beauty," the witch is the thirteenth fairy, uninvited to Aurora's christening, and the red is the blood that appears when she pricks her finger according to the fairy's curse. Then, in both stories, the princess falls into a death-like sleep.

As does Dorothy, sinking under the spell of the bright red poppies, which here, in departure from Baum's text, are the work of the Witch. The journey to womanhood involves unconsciousness: this phase bears multiple and contradictory readings. One is that traditional femininity demands unconsciousness. Another is that the sleep is preservative, staving off the "growing down," the "death" of the vibrant girl-self. Or is the sleep instead the symbolic death all heroes undergo in the process of transformation and rebirth, the descent of Persephone (or Odysseus) into the underworld prior to the attainment of the goal — which, in the *Odyssey,* as in *Oz,* was to get back home?[16]

Why is it the witch who precipitates this fall? On the more literal level, she seems jealous of a rival power, the enormous raw power of the adolescent girl. But symbolically, if the journey underground is a necessary phase of the hero's passage, then the witch acts her part as a guide, just as the fairy-godmother/"good" witch acts hers in awakening the hero.

It is Glinda who originally sends Dorothy to the Wizard; the Witch keeps yanking her off course; and Aunt Em keeps calling her home. Their messages seem so contradictory, unless they are seen as a trinity, operating archetypally on a number of levels. They represent the adolescent's mixed feelings about womanhood. They present three cultural options: good woman, bad woman, and victim. They offer three versions of the Mother: Good Mommy, beautiful but elusive, magical and kind; Bad Mommy, punishing, depriving, incarcerating, denying; and Real Mommy, harried, exhausted, worn, pragmatic, impatient. But finally, they are the three faces of the Goddess: Virgin, Mother, and Crone, representing sequential phases of woman's traditional biological life as well as coexistent dimensions of her being.

This explains what was always for me, as a child, the most frightening moment in the film. Dorothy, captive in the witch's castle, sees Aunt Em's face emerge in the crystal ball, calling her name. Beating on the glass, Dorothy tries to answer. Then suddenly the worn, doughy face of Aunt Em blurs and melts into the green hatchet-shaped mask of the witch, cackling maniacally and turning to the camera, which moves into tight close-up. And the witch mocks Dorothy's own cry: *"Auntie Em! Auntie Em!"* The lines of identity and typology get as fuzzy as the crystal:

Aunt Em turns out to be the witch? The witch is calling Aunt Em, who is calling Dorothy, who is calling Aunt Em? The witch is a gruesome parody of Dorothy *and* Aunt Em at once?

In this context of fluid, overlapping female imagery, the "liquidation" of the Witch becomes an even more resonant moment in the unfolding of Dorothy's mythic journey. Even in this climactic scene, Dorothy does not intend to harm her antagonist. In an interesting departure from Baum's text, where Dorothy explicitly throws the water at the witch, Judy's Dorothy throws it at the Scarecrow, whose arm is on fire; it hits the witch accidentally. Here, as elsewhere, Dorothy's heroism is instinctual, unreflective, protective of a friend rather than aggressive against an enemy — as when she becomes the only one to stand up to the lion, slapping him on the nose when he goes after Toto. The Land of Oz keeps precipitating her into crises where her loving, brave nature and allegiance to the under*dog* (pun intended) get the chance to manifest themselves *effectively* as they never did in Kansas. When the witch disappears under a steaming heap of black cloth, Dorothy, in classic female style, begins apologizing. Like a true girl, she has trouble accepting that despite her best intentions, or even because of them, she will wind up doing harm. Once again, she's killed a witch unintentionally; once again she is thanked for it. But the difference is that here, at least, she has acted.[17] She is able to vanquish the witch at this moment precisely because, after an extended period of passivity — captive in the castle, weeping, watching the red sand run out in the hourglass — she suddenly becomes active, an agent in her own salvation. She takes her power into her hands, but for the sake of something weaker than she, her stuffed friend.

And her power is that most fluid, multivalent natural symbol, water. In historical terms, it suggests the baptismal water no witch could tolerate, or the old trial-by-water used to condemn women as witches. But it is also the source of life, the generative element of transformation. "As the Wicked Witch of the West 'grows down,'" Rushdie concludes, "so Dorothy is seen to have grown up."[18] True, but in doing so she also absorbs that shrinking figure as she absorbed the Witch of the East earlier. The broomstick, that ordinary implement of housewifery that provided the witch's transportation, is the tangible symbol of the transfer of power, as the ruby slippers were before. With a difference, once more: whereas the slippers simply appeared on Dorothy's feet, she actively achieves and requests the broomstick. And armed with it, as the questing knight was always armed with the magical weapon or emblem, she starts back toward her final challenge, the one that comes when you think your troubles are over, and your road is clear, and your enemy is dead. Confronting the witch, which Rushdie defines as Dorothy's moment of maturity, is indeed a triumph, but only because Dorothy subsumes the witch's power, which is to say that she *realizes* (in both senses) her own power, her *wiccadness.*

As she's melting, the Witch poses one final question: "Who would have thought a good little girl like you could destroy my beautiful wickedness?" But Dorothy is no longer a Good Little Girl. Having gone beyond Good and Evil into Wiccadness, Dorothy marches back toward her ultimate battle, the one that's been waiting at the end of the Yellow Brick Road. She's off to see the Wizard.

4. The Great and Powerful

Our first glimpse of Emerald City, from the edge of the woods before the poppy field, is a cluster of tall, skinny, pointed, metallic-looking spires, a medieval castle crossed with a 1930's futurist fantasy. In short, a phallic cartoon, very different from Denslow's lower, rounder Oz. Rushdie ignores Emerald City in setting up his paradigm of the geometry in the film — the simple, regular shapes of "home and safety" versus the sinuous, twisty, bent shapes of "danger and evil."[19] What he needs is a paradigm shift, away from moral dualisms toward an older set: the regular is male, the sinuous and "wicked" female. Thus Glinda's "perfect, luminous sphere"[20] has less to do with goodness than with patriarchal constructs of feminine virtue. But if we shift the paradigm again, setting neither good against evil nor regular versus irregular, but linear versus curving, then we bring Glinda back into the female realm, along with the tornado. The Yellow Brick Road, which begins, as Rushdie notes, in a "perfect spiral," becomes rectilinear, but then "splits and forks every which way," which he reads as its entering the evil realm.[21] In fact, what it enters, and takes Dorothy into, is the realm of choices, asking that she cease the literal, obedient "follow, follow, follow, follow,/Follow the Yellow Brick Road" that initially had her walking in circles in Munchkinland. She must choose her direction. The necessity for choice also leads her into the encounter with her first ally, the Scarecrow, who represents her own brain, her ability to make choices.

That this road leads ultimately to a cluster of phallic spires is pretty ironic, but so accurate: the girl in us thinks the final authority will be the Daddy/God who is "a whiz of a wiz, / If ever a wiz there was." He can answer any question, supply all wants, solve any problem. He is also the patriarchal authority underlying all the female authorities in Dorothy's world, and in our own. For most of the film, all we, and she, know about him is that he is Great and Powerful, "very good," Glinda puts it, "but veeerrrrry mysterious!" And that's the crux of the matter: his power *is* his mystery, his unknowability, his transcendence. Thus is it that when Dorothy & Co. reach the city gates, they are told: "The Wizard? The

Wizard??! Nobody sees the Wizard!!" Indeed: so maybe "seeing" the Wizard is precisely the point. Maybe Dorothy needs to "see" the Wizard more urgently and for different reasons than she knows.

And what is this Wizard, revealed after all in his inner sanctum? A giant disembodied bald head, surrounded by a lot of pyrotechnics. (In Baum, this is but one of his manifestations.) During which of my adult viewings of the film did I suddenly remember Virginia Woolf's wonderful deconstruction of male intellectual authority in *A Room of One's Own,* where she likens the domed reading room of the British Museum to a great bald head? If we now recall the Wizard's Kansas persona, this all makes delicious sense: *Professor* Marvel, an unemployed university man, who knows all and sees all, familiar with the "Crowned Heads" of Europe. He is academic patriarchy, the Realm of the Intellect, the Mind of the Fathers, the "brain center" for the whole enterprise, the Head of the Corporation. He is "purely academic," an abstraction, "detached," divorced from the body: the patriarchal ideal of intellect. He knows what girls want better than they do: "SILENCE! THE GREAT AND POWERFUL OZ **KNOWS** WHY YOU HAVE COME!" And as Professor Marvel, he has already been exposed, though not to Dorothy, as a charlatan. We saw, if she didn't, that over the exit from his wagon hung a skull — another disembodied head, signifying death.

Dorothy's first encounter with the Wizard, before she is sent to vanquish the witch, contains all the ambivalence of her adolescent femininity. In response to his Jehova-like introduction ("I AM OZ, THE GREAT AND POWERFUL!"), our hero inches forward and presents herself as follows: "If you please, sir," (curtseying) "I am Dorothy, the . . . Small and Meek." That she is anything but small and meek has been evident from her first moment onscreen. This leftover from Baum rings highly ironic. The next time she confronts the Wizard, she will know better. For now, she does what we all learn to do in the presence of intimidating male authority: she grows down, makes herself small, and meek. But when the Head bellows at her friends, Dorothy rises to the occasion, true to form, and tells him off, accusing him of the worst sin in her book: bullying those smaller and weaker than himself. The true indictment of a girl-child. As always, it is in embracing and defending the Small and Meek that Dorothy reveals herself to be Great and Powerful.

Sending them out after the witch's broomstick may simply be the Wizard's cheap way of getting rid of these interlopers who might blow his cover, for they will surely die trying. But he wins either way, for if they succeed, he is rid of a formidable adversary — maybe his only real adversary, given his eagerness to eliminate her. If Oz is patriarchal power at its most mystified, what would it fear more than the archetypal figure of female power, the Crone? What he doesn't know is that the little girl who brings back the broomstick carries its power as well. Like the Good Girl she is still trying to be, believing truly in the Fathers, Dorothy curtseys and lays the emblem of power before the Head. At this altar she will sacrifice if only he will send her home again.

Nowhere is the dissonance between the forces whirling in Dorothy clearer than at this moment: the will to be "good" versus the will to power; self-diminution versus self-assertion; Dorothy the Small and Meek versus the Hero, the Bust in the Munchkin Hall of Fame. The turning point comes when the Wizard tries to put off the petitioners, telling them to "COME BACK TOMORROW!" so that his giant cerebrum can figure a way out of this. Another adult weaseling out of a promise; another power figure exploiting the weak, who have risked life and limb. "Tomorrow!" Dorothy wails, outraged. She steps forward, literally "out of line": "But I want to go home today!" Her fine sense of justice joins forces with her desire. And this synergy seems to set Toto in motion. Acting *for* Dorothy, not so much on her behalf as in her stead, he resolves the impasse by drawing back the curtain with his teeth (in Baum he merely knocks it aside inadvertently), unmasking Power itself in its innermost recesses.

"PAY NO ATTENTION TO THAT MAN BEHIND THE CURTAIN!!"

Ah, how often have we heard that one? But once we've seen him, we can't unknow the awful truth: the Great Mind is but a man; the Head has a body; the Great and Powerful is a composite of technological smoke-and-mirrors. This is where we realize we've seen him before, and not just as Professor Marvel. He was all over the Emerald City, as the gatekeeper, the coach driver, the lugubrious palace guard. In other words, these authorities, these officials who control access and movement, the Powers that Be — they're all him. He's everywhere. When Dorothy calls him "a very bad man," his response — that he's a very good man but a very bad wizard — not only amounts to hair-splitting moral evasion but classic patriarchal compartmentalizing: self from role, personal from public. Dorothy, whose "nose" for the truth is represented by her dog's, is on the money: a good man who pretends to be omnipotent, manipulating everybody through deceit and fear into obeisance and danger, becomes a bad man. And in unmasking and then naming him, Dorothy has done the ultimate Women's Work, braved the dragon every questing girl must finally confront. She has exploded the myth that kept her in thrall.

As an academic, it makes perfect sense that the Wizard deals in symbols and trappings: diplomas, testimonials, ribbons and medals. The Scarecrow does a wonderful parody of academic self-delusion: given his diploma, he is suddenly brilliant, reciting a mathematical formula (which, by the way, turns out to be incorrect). But Dorothy has wanted something for which there is no tangible replacement or signifier: Home. She falls once more for the Wizard's promises, and Toto's final subversive act is to prevent her going with him. When the balloon breaks loose, the Wizard confesses incompetence once more: "I don't know how it works!" No professor, wizard, balloon, bubble, or broomstick will get her home. Nothing will get her home now but her own two feet in their witchy shoes.

5. No Place Like Home

But Home — what's that? Surely Rushdie is right: the end of this film is a terrible betrayal of its heart. In the terms of the myth of female identity, Kansas is an awful, tragic/ironic ending to Dorothy's quest: she circles back to Aunt Em, whom she will become. She returns to domesticity, drudgery, the death of imagination and desire, to the place where girls aren't believed and their over-the-rainbow dreams translate into homiletic cliches worthy of the parlor wall sampler: "Oh, Auntie Em, there's no place like home!"

Is that all there is? Well, maybe so. Maybe the filmmakers just got themselves into a corner with the film's subversiveness and had to weasel out, like the Wizard, domesticating dangerous Dorothy — not only bringing her back to Kansas, as in Baum's original, but reducing her entire journey to a dream or hallucination, of which there is no hint in Baum. But maybe not. There are alternate ways to read the return that ends the film.

One of them has to do with the circular/linear paradigm mentioned earlier. In that context, Dorothy's return makes complete sense. In all those ancient quest stories, after all, the object is to return — to Camelot, to Ithaca, to wherever one started — but to return changed, enriched, worthier, wised up. In Baum, this element is missing entirely. In the film, when Scarecrow asks Glinda why she didn't tell Dorothy that she had the power to return all along, Glinda says, "Because she wouldn't have believed me. She had to learn it for herself," prompting the big question: "What have you learned, Dorothy?" Dorothy is the one whose quest has not resulted in a tangible Grail, so her prize must be intangible, internal.

But for women in particular, I think, her return, not to mention her consistent yearning for home, makes a kind of psychic/emotional sense. Our quests tend to be in two directions at once — outward and inward, away and back, toward independence and toward relationship. That we develop toward adult autonomy *in the context of our affiliations* has been amply documented. We seek self-determination, but through connection and commitment. Cutting our ties to Aunt Em is too big a price to pay for reaching our Emerald Cities. We don't wish to become Aunt Em, but we don't wish to disown that weary old femininity from which we come. We owe her. She's Home.

Our developmental quests, then, are deeply ambivalent, especially in adolescence. We (and those who theorize about us) tend to see this ambivalence as problematic — a conflict to be resolved. But perhaps it isn't. Perhaps it's our way. Perhaps we are always singing a double song: "If happy little bluebirds fly / Beyond the rainbow, why oh why can't I?" and "Auntie Em! Auntie Em!" Perhaps we only move forward, and up, by circling backward, and down. Perhaps the cyclone is the most telling image in the film after all.

What happens to the problematic ending if we see Dorothy's entire journey as covering internal landscapes? If Scarecrow and Tin Man and Lion find their hearts' desire within them, and if they are in turn parts of Dorothy, and if Dorothy discovers that the power to take herself home was within her all along, then wouldn't it make sense to conclude that "home" is also internal? That Dorothy's desire to go home finally has less to do with Kansas and the "real" Aunt Em than with the groundedness of self-knowledge? Doesn't Dorothy return to the black-and-white Real World possessed of her own brains, heart, courage, and witchery — the Greatness and Powerfulness of Oz?

But wait: according to Dorothy, what she's learned is that if she ever goes searching for her heart's desire, she won't look any further than her own back yard. And her back yard is definitely Kansas. Except that Oz has been a sort of psychedelic version of her own back yard. What does she say to all those concerned folks clustered around her bed when she wakes up? "You were there — and you, and you — you were all there!" Even Miss Gulch was there. Oz is populated by the characters from her own back yard. It is a re-imagined "real world," or, as she maintains to the faithless, "It was a place, a really real place!" So she who wanted escape, yearned to go "somewhere where there isn't any trouble," got instead a place where there was nothing but trouble, larger than life: witches and winged monkeys, malevolent trees playing hardball and drug overdoses and disembodied heads. What she got was the colorized version of her own life. She got what we all get when we dream, not escape from trouble, but a reconfigured encounter with our own psychic "back yards."

Rushdie's conclusion is that "once we leave our childhood places and start up our lives, armed only with what we know and who we are, we come to understand that the real secret of the ruby slippers is not that 'there's no place like home,' but, rather, that there is no longer any such place *as* home."[22] But of course there is: it's simply migrated inward. This is what Dorothy has learned: home is where the heart is, and the brains, and the courage. And there is, in fact, no *place* like it. It is Oz, a "u-topia" ("no-place").

Whatever "home" we carry around inside us, whatever smarts or heart or guts, we must join the world of untrustworthy or incompetent adults. For Rushdie, this is the travesty of the ending. For him, remembering the film through a boy's eyes, the film tells us that in "ceasing to be children, we all become magicians without magic, exposed conjurers . . . ."[23] Well, not quite all of us. We girls did not usually imagine growing up to be wizards, defrocked or otherwise. That was not among our options. We knew, with the untutored instincts of girlhood, that wizards are humbugs and when they get rid of one, they replace him with a straw man, brainless as he may be. We girls grew up to be Auntie Em, or worse, Miss Gulch (the "miss" telling the whole sad story). Some of us, the girls I couldn't stand, could become Glinda, eternal prom queen. But some of us dreamed of getting on our broomsticks and riding, in smoking circles around our very own castles, black capes flapping in the wind.

Well, we didn't. Or rather, we became All of the Above: drudge, spinster, fairy godmother, crone. But when we watch the film again — and we do, every chance we get — we are reminded that there is someone else in us: a girl, a not-so-little girl, mustering her forces and easing on down the road, full of possibilities. Still and always, we are Dorothy.

(And her little dog, too.)

5

Letting it Be

"Dear Mr. Freeman,

The three girls in your photograph are myself, my sister Norma, and our friend Ruth. I've spoken to my sister to refresh the memories for your Beatles book because it's very hard to put into words what we remember . . . . I find it hard to put into words our devotion to them at that time . . . ." [1]

What we remember.

It is finally happening, the consummation devoutly wished since 1970. They are "getting back together," whatever that can mean in the long shadow of John's absence. In this prolonged thirtieth anniversary, between the release of *Live at the BBC* on one end and the "new" album and documentary on the other, there is ample room for retrospective analysis. As I write, *The New Yorker* has done its second. Before this is over, I will have read many more — erudite, judicious assessments of their musical contribution or of the phenomenon itself, titled "Yesterday and Today" and "When They're Sixty-Four." All of them will share a voice, the voice that made Rolling Stone the voice of rock. The voice is hip, highly knowledgeable, full of cool, technical expertise — and always, always male.

If there ever were a phenomenon that demands a female voice, it is the Beatles. And yet I search my memory of the past quarter century (God!) for a critical assessment of Them in a female voice.

So what else is new, right? And anyway, we were never supposed to be articulate about the Beatles; we were just supposed to scream. As the categorical descriptor for us, the media chose a loaded word from our history as women: hysterical. By the end of 1964, sound bites of sobbing, stammering, fundamentally inarticulate girls had become a staple of media humor about "Beatlemania." It was for guys to be analytical and descriptive; we were simply lost in the phenomenon, immured in passion, swept away, unconscious. (Kind of like sex.) Feminine immanence vs. masculine transcendence, etc.

Or was it that we had no words for what we felt and knew, no language to explain their significance, no way to define this cultural tidal wave — so public, so personal — in which we were active subjects and passive objects at once. I still struggle for words. Even talking to myself, I cast language out over the dark water of the past. Is there some kind of shame here, at the root of the silence? Have we learned the contempt the Boys always had for us? Are we ashamed of our obsession, our mania, our "hysteria" thirty years ago? Embarrassed to take our fourteen-year-old selves seriously, we leave them stammering, weeping, fainting away in the past.

Or is our shame more current? In our heart of hearts, don't we still think they are the most important thing that happened in the sixties? Well, yes, but so do a lot of grown-up boys. What is it, then? Is it that, in fact, we've never gotten over Them? That somewhere in us, we're still stammering, weeping, fainting away? Listen to journalist Myra McPherson: "No politician or movie star ever had quite the magic of Paul, smiling in recognition and asking my name as I covered the Beatles' final day in Washington."[2] Now that I can relate to.

Thirty years. And it is time to hear from the Girls.

September 5, 1964

All of life, for the past six months has funneled to this point. This is the longest span of intense waiting I have ever done.

It is a hot night. The other five — my friends Jessica, Carol, Bonnie, and Connie, and my cousin Rhys — are at my house, sleeping over. Was this slumber party sanctioned on grounds that it would be easier to transport us all downtown if we were all at one place? Or was it that somehow my mother realized we had to be together on this night? She has shown other instances of surprising insight, for someone who cannot fathom what has happened to her mature, academically gifted, generally well behaved and responsible daughter, known for her superior attitude toward the vagaries of her peers. Something in my mother comprehends, enough that on the rainy, chill day in March when tickets went on sale, she agreed to drive downtown and stand in line for us. When I got home from school, she had them, six tickets. Six tickets that really said, "The Beatles."

That was the day I learned that there is something more wonderful than a dream coming true: the luxury of knowing it is going to do so.

My mother and stepfather have graciously retired upstairs, leaving the family room to us. Naturally we play the albums over and over. In a mere seven months, between British and American record companies, they've managed to crank out five albums: "Meet the Beatles"; the piecemeal American product "Introducing the Beatles"; the soundtrack from "A

Hard Day's Night"; "The Beatles' Second Album," which isn't (it's only their second for Capitol Records, another slapdash American attempt to get songs from British Beatles albums out as quickly as possible); and finally the very recent "Something New," released at the end of the summer and containing the rest of the cuts from the British soundtrack album plus other stuff uncollected in America. As a group, we know most of these albums by heart by now. But I know them perfectly, note- and letter- perfectly. At the end of one song, I can begin the next before it starts, at the right tempo and in the correct key.

Like all Beatle fans, we have Beatle identities. Me with my visual sweet tooth, I'm a Paul. So is Connie. My cousin and Carol, who empathize deeply with underdogs, are Ringos. Bonnie, the mature, ironic one, is a John. And Jessie, independent and iconoclastic, belongs to that strange breed, that interesting minority, the Georges.

One of the ways we get through and also revel in the hours is by playing What Will They Sing? There are certain givens: "I Want to Hold Your Hand," "She Loves You," "A Hard Day's Night," "Can't Buy Me Love," probably "Twist and Shout." Then there is a wide, delicious range of debatables. We propose and argue and insult each other ("Are you kidding? They can't do 'I Wanna Be Your Man'! They'll never let Ringo sing in public!" "Oh, really? Well, maybe they'll do 'Til There was You' so we can all hear Paul say he 'never SORRRRRE them winging'!"). But I'm drawn to the less obvious songs, least likely to be done in concert. Like "Things We Said Today," my private song, with its funky, stuttering guitar intro and its moody modulations from minor to major. But it's a nowhere song, buried on "Something New." Paul will never do it.

The evening passes in a sustained, ecstatic silliness. As the dark comes down, near ten o'clock as it does in Michigan in late summer, our excitement intensifies. When we are not listening to albums, we are listening to WKNR, Keener 13, which is, of course, playing lots of Beatles, running a contest to win tickets and a chance to meet Them, and issuing regular Beatles Updates. They are flying in tonight. Sometime late in the night, eleven or midnight, we are outside, in the backyard, watching the sky. The others run back inside, overflowing with nervous energy. But I stay out, watching planes come in toward Metro Airport from the east, thinking, "That could be them. That could be them. This is as close as I've ever been."

It's about as close as I'll ever be, too. When we reach our seats at Olympia Stadium, Home of the Red Wings, we are miles from the stage. But we're there, we're together, and it's going to happen. The idea of using a sports arena for rock and roll singers is unheard of, laughable. But we understand: this is what the album advertises, something new. This is a first rock concert for all of us, so we're unprepared for the fact that there will be other acts besides the Beatles. We assume, therefore, that the two *hours scheduled for the concert will be entirely filled with Them. So when the Cyrkle comes out, any fondness for their hit, "Red Rubber Ball," dissolves in outrage. When Jackie de Shannon follows them, we are agonized. How can this be happening? Every moment seems stolen from Them.*

And then a long, terrible intermission, several delays and false alarms, and then they are there, small stick figures running onstage. The screams rise to a sustained, impermeable wall of sound. Of course, it is all completely unreal. I'm anxious, troubled; I can't grasp what is happening, this thing that has centered my life for most of 1964. It is only edged in reality by the sound of Paul's wonderful voice, doing the announcing and patter, and by the music. The music, the music. I discover that if I cover my ears, the screaming is muted but the singing is clarified, or so at least it seems.

But almost as soon as it starts, I realize with a shock something that has eluded me for six months: it will be over. I am beginning to learn the dark corollary to the other lesson about anticipation: what it is to anticipate loss, to know absence before anything is gone.

And then suddenly I can't believe it but it's true: "Things We Said Today."

"For me," I think. "This one is mine."

August, 1993

One of my infrequent housecleaning binges has taken on a momentum of its own. I have ventured into closets I've avoided for years. Perhaps it's this spirit of confronting the long-buried and braving what Bonnie Raitt calls the "tangled and dark" that one night leads me to the basement to get the Scrapbooks.

They are in the storeroom, stacked on the third shelf near the door. There are six of them, big and packed to overflowing. They are also a mess. When I first moved to this house, I had them in a carton on the floor. When the basement flooded, the albums got wet. By the time I got to them they were muddy, mildewed, moldy, edges turned to mush. I dried them as best I could, stacked them on this shelf, and left them. Since then, I have taken them upstairs once — to show them to Peter, a former student who was writing a play about Beatles fans and wanted to know what it was really all about. We sat up one night until four a.m., playing the albums and thumbing through the scrapbooks. We made it as far as "Abbey Road," but only as far as Scrapbook Volume Four.

Now, I say to myself, is the time to rescue them from oblivion, clean them up, throw out what's irreparably damaged, and move the fragile newsprint articles and clippings into photo albums with plastic sleeves for protection.

It is time to remember, and to remember what I wished to remember in filling these bulky, messy scrapbooks. It is time, too, to ask why I kept them. What was I keeping? For whom? It's occurred to me that these albums are probably worth a whole lot of money to a collector. But then, aren't I a collector? And could I really part with them? What would it mean if I did? What would be gone? Why do people collect, apart from monetary reasons? Why did I collect, with staggering assiduousness and compulsive thoroughness, this mass of paper — photographs, news clippings, interviews, fan mag articles, every scrap of paper that mentioned the Beatles, from 1964 well into the seventies?

The job is physically unpleasant — dust, mildew, aged Scotch tape gone orange, its adhesive dried up, falling in my lap; scraps of paper all over the floor. The job is also difficult: to save space, I taped entire articles onto one page, with other articles and photos taped to pages and spaces that didn't deal with the Beatles. So with almost every page turn, there are layers upon layers of Beatles to unearth. It is a virtually archeological undertaking. The job is also embarrassing: I had no discrimination whatsoever. Significant news articles, lengthy, intelligent interviews, and rare childhood and family photos couple promiscuously with the most obvious schlock from *16 Magazine* and *Tiger Beat* — apocryphal interviews ("What Kind of Girls the Beatles Like!"), fraudulent journals ("Paul's Very Private Dreams!") and letters from London ("George Tells YOU About His Wild Nights!"), photos of the Beatles' heads on cartoon bodies, accounts of "feuds" with the Dave Clark Five or the Rolling Stones. But the heterogeneity of it all may finally be part of its point. What I begin to see is the vast Beatles Industry; and beyond it, the Beatles Phenomenon; and beyond that, the Beatles Years, a pivotal, dramatic time in the life of this culture, this century. That time, that phenomenon, that industry, was indeed heterogeneous: the schlock came with the soul, the dross with the gold. The Beatles were a great leap forward for the marketing/media industries that would, in the next twenty-five years, masticate the culture almost to pulp. The Beatles were also the most important musicians of the second half of the century, transformers of their culture and their art form. In Tony Kornheiser's words, "What we know as the sixties was as much their doing as anybody's."[3]

And yet the Beatles Years, as I saw them chronicled in the Scrapbooks, existed on a smaller, more private scale as well. They were a time in one life, my own, that is marked more voluminously than any other. Beyond both the marketing/media phenomenon and the cultural revolution, the Beatles' significance lies in another place, harder for me to reach at this distance of years, harder to describe honestly, without embarrassment: they were powerful agents in individual lives, more particularly individual girls' lives. Mine was one.

Four people I never knew — and were these scrapbooks my effort to "know" them? Does this mountain of unfiltered data constitute some kind of scholarship, some knowing, or its opposite? Four people I never knew, who (say it) affected me as deeply as anyone I've ever known, as deeply as some people I've loved.

January, 1964

Under the four- to five-month blanket of greying snow and dense cotton sky, Michigan goes to sleep. It is as if the world has gone silent and still after violent lights and colors, sounds and motions.

I have no context to understand what an astonishing year it has been in the United States. Almost daily, dramatic images from the south, accompanying tales of savagery and grace. Then, on November 22nd, the unimaginable.

That's the backdrop to the stage of my own life. In June I completed seventh grade, the first year of junior high, my first year at a new school, in a new suburb, wealthier than anywhere I'd ever visited, much less lived. After school I came home to a new house, where we had moved when my mother married my stepfather the previous fall. I turned thirteen that summer and wore a tight-bodiced, royal blue and kelly green satin dress with a "bubble" skirt and my first heels — sharp-toed kelly green silk — as a bridesmaid at my new stepsister's wedding. In September I started eighth grade. In November my stepfather, a boyish, generous man whom I was learning to love, had a heart attack. In December, my adored older brother was married. And on January 4th of the new year, my stepfather suffered another heart attack and died in the middle of the night.

The best of times, the worst of times. Excitement, laughter, astonishment, mourning. But above all, change. After the comfy stasis of the fifties, the sense of a world passing away, the crush of the new. The new flamboyance of things: new colors and shapes, more hair, more make-up. The new music, the second generation of rock-and-roll just announcing itself, and the new, intense flowering of r&b down on Grand River Boulevard, a sound called after its label, which is called after the city: Motown. For me, above all, a recognition, bewildering at that age, of how swiftly things, and people, could appear and vanish.

For instance: I had spent sixth grade in my "old school," the vine-covered elementary school in the village of Franklin, Michigan. I knew everyone, I had grown from five to the monumental age of eleven there, and everyone knew me. They knew me as smart, funny, moody, talkative, a writer, a singer. I edited the school paper, I wrote huge reports on China and epic poems on Italy, I adored horses and "Bonanza" and music, I had a best friend and an array of other cohorts and collaborators. I worried about popularity, but not profoundly. I began to set my hair at night, but just barely. I had crushes on boys, but briefly.

Then, all at once, junior high. Bloomfield Hills, home of Ford and GM executives, home of Governor Romney himself. Girls in make-up and ratted hair, expensive sweaters, narrow straight skirts and Capezios. Tight, formidable cliques. Entrenched, immutable modes of carrying one's books, walking, speaking, behaving in class, a tacit code wholly intolerant of deviation. Parties to which I was not invited. Rumors of making out and going all the way. Rumors of drinking and smoking. Femininity, annoying and frightening as ever, but suddenly in the foreground, imperative. I am no more than five miles away from Franklin, but I might as well be on the other side of the planet. I am wholly lost that first year, flailing for bearings, desperately seeking a group, a being of my species. Or more accurately, a species which will accept me.

And then, incredibly, the reason for our being in Bloomfield Hills has vanished. I come home from school on those winter days to a quiet house. My stepfather's childlike delight in surprise and silliness is gone. My mother's grief is dark grey, like the days. My brother, my stepsister are gone.

I crawl inside myself to think, to play, to indulge unorthodox or unacceptable feelings. I cultivate a private world, dreamy and expansive, dramatic and intense, comforting and close.

The reconfiguration of my family has yielded me a stepbrother. He is closer to my age than anyone in my family, all of eighteen, and I think him very cool, very funny, very nice. He kids me, is kind to me, talks intelligently to me, takes care of me. And one day in December he comes home and hands me an album. "Meet the Beatles." Four grave, shadowed faces framed with shiny, dark hair.

Now, music is in my deep structure. My themesong at age three was "The Battle Hymn of the Republic," to the point where my grandmother called me Glory Hallelujah. I started piano at seven or eight, showing marked talent and a prodigious ear. I have sung in choirs at school and church for years. My mother was a music major who still sings and occasionally, when no one is looking, plays the piano. On our hi-fi there is classical music or Harry Belafonte, whom I join in duets with Odetta and Miriam Makeba. At this point, my own record collection consists mostly of my brother's folk cast-offs, Kingston Trio, Joan Baez and Peter, Paul, and Mary. This is the first rock-and-roll record I've ever owned, or co-owned.

And it sounds like nothing I have ever heard — not Elvis, not the black groups my brother listened to, not the white groups I kind of like for their harmonies — Four Seasons and Beach Boys; certainly not the pompadoured Frankies and Bobbys currently manufactured for white girls. Like nothing and nobody I have ever heard.

In the next weeks I play the album until I am convinced it has somehow passed into my brain cells, my bloodstream. It fascinates me, mostly by its diversity. Every cut is so distinct, so idiosyncratic. It's an album full of contradiction, light and shadow. The cheerful mooniness of "All My Loving" cut with the spooky, bluesy "All I Gotta Do." The primal chant of "It Won't Be Long" versus the silky three-part harmonic mesh of "This Boy." And the finale, the moody "Not a Second Time," driven by that sullen, lonely piano.

I convince my stepbrother to go in with me on Album Number Two, "Introducing the Beatles." For the first time I know the impatience to hear a new record. Side one, track one: "Please, Please Me" explodes, dancing buoyantly down the scale and back up again and down, a roller-coaster of a song. Then the bridge, and when Paul soars up to"YOOOOOOU" and bounces down on the "whoa, yeah," the hair on the back of my neck stands up and my stomach lurches. Maybe that's the moment it happens. I think the energy is going to lift me off the ground. This frustrated complaint that comes off like the most jubilant anthem.

The penultimate track on the album is a weird, dissonant, echoey number about the secret place in your mind where you can go. It's like listening to the inside of my own head. I hear it in that private internal space where I've found solace.

Within a week, I have the grooves of this album in my skin and hair. I've also reread the liner notes to both albums over and over. I know their entire names, and I know their voices: George's adenoidal throatiness; Ringo's bleat, always a semi-tone flat; John's raspy or nasal edginess, which can subside into softness, a perfect lock in two- or three-part harmonies; and Paul's lilting clarity. I learn what a rhythm guitar is, and how to listen for a bass line. I learn to hear a double-tracked voice. It is the first music of my own time that I listen to, closely and carefully, again and again, until I own it. I know it in the Biblical sense, with an intimacy and thoroughness that feels like a kind of belonging: they to me? I to them? Who knows?

I have been a marginal listener to the music of my peer group. As a student of classical music, I've learned to regard it with contempt, but occasionally something will filter through and grab me. The rhythms of early Motown move me. So do lush, dense harmonies. But this — this is different. The harmonies are different, the instrumentalization is different. The lyrics, with their exotic northern Anglicisms, are different. There is a strangeness about these songs; however harmless they pretend to be at first, they turn on you. They come on like traditional rock, or r&b, and then they take these odd turns: major turning to minor, like bright water suddenly giving up a moody depth; unexpected chord progressions taking you suddenly off the yellow brick road and into the woods; romantic clichés

complicated by syntactical oddities and emotional jolts. In some sublimi-
nal, uncritical, and inarticulate way, I understand that this is a musical
force that is revolutionary.

So by the time they arrive, on February 7th, the chaos at Idlewild
Airport is something that, to my surprise, I can understand. And I'm specu-
lating about what they'll sing on Ed Sullivan. More than that, I'm wonder-
ing how it will be, to see them walking, singing, moving, alive; my relation-
ship thus far has been with photographs. On Sunday, February 9, my step-
brother and I are down in the family room watching when neckless, dour
Ed, his mouth just barely twitching, comes out to face a theater full of
ecstatic, impatient girls.

I find the screaming embarrassing, distracting, annoying — I
always will. But when the Beatles are on, doing "I Want to Hold Your
Hand" and "All My Loving" (close-ups of Paul that make me catch my
breath), I discover in me an intensity, a focused energy that, if translated
into sound, would, I suppose, be sustained screaming. I watch, rapt. For
the next six amazing years, I will be watching, with unbroken attention.
And meanwhile, I will grow up.

January, 1994

Sooner or later, in the daily phone conversations with my best
friend, we will come to the Beatles. From there, the discussion usually
degenerates from some aspect of how great they were right on into what
we call "the John-Paul wars," in which Diane makes supercilious and dis-
paraging comments about Paul's level of talent and depth of soul, and I
observe how facile it is to canonize the dead.

But recently we were talking about what we felt for them as girls,
and we divulged the fantasies we had about them back then. I finally
confessed my secret longing for the first time: more than anything, I
wanted to sing with them. In my visions, I was onstage with them, or in a
hotel room, or at a party, providing a harmony so true and sometimes so
original, not to mention a knowledge of their oeuvre so complete, that
they would be amazed, dazzled by my talent.

Diane's fantasy, meanwhile, was of having them over for dinner,
making them meat loaf and baked potatoes, the white midwestern version
of soul food.

Please notice that neither of our fantasies can be called sexual,
unless you want to be technical about food symbolism. We didn't even
imagine dating them (yet). Now, the fact that Diane is five years younger
than I and thus would have been nine in 1964 makes the asexuality of
her fantasy understandable, if it also makes her desire to cook for them
even weirder. Maybe after all there was something to Dr. Joyce Brothers'

annoying theory that Beatlemania was rooted in maternal instincts.

Probably my fantasy registers as the proto-feminist one. But think again: what I wanted was to join them on their terms, to be one of the boys (I even visualized a collarless grey Cardin suit with a skirt). What Diane wanted was for them to join her on hers, to swallow what she dished out.

My passion for them was certainly a way into sexuality — a friendly, joyful inroad at that. But it was always so much bigger than sex. Sex was not primary, not in the early years. Someone — probably Dr. Joyce — theorized that adolescent girls adored them because they were hermaphroditic (adults seemed universally unable to get past the hair) and therefore sexually unthreatening. As the psychological line of the time had it, the attraction to unthreatening men was regressive, a form of resistance to adult femininity Well, they got one right: we were indeed resisting adult femininity. Left out of the equation, as we learned a bit later, was the need to ask questions about the link between masculinity and threatening sexuality, and about the relation of that threatening male sexuality to female "maturation." Perhaps what we were after, or at least what I was after (and was I alone?), was a different way of being with men, a different manliness and a different womanliness than those my culture prescribed — some tentative precursor of the gender revisions of the seventies. Of course the Beatles weren't the least bit hermaphroditic, but they might well have presented us with — and we may have assigned them — what seemed a new-fashioned masculinity that felt friendlier, in comparison both to fifties constructs of masculinity and to contemporary parallels — for instance, the Beatles' demonic doubles, the Stones. A few nights ago, a male friend and I were listening to the Stones. I had been telling him of my quest into the past to figure out what the Beatles were for me. Suddenly he said, "I know why I didn't get into the Beatles: the Stones were my band." We began to discuss the disparities and common-alities of these two, the archetypal British groups. We spoke of musical geneologies: the Stones came more directly out of black blues, the Beatles out of a diverse spectrum of early rock and r&b. But the next day, replaying the conversation, I saw the duality in different, gendered terms: the Stones were a boys' band; the Beatles were for girls. The Stones rep-resented the mean, destructive side of male sexuality — forget what you've read about Jagger's "androgyny." But the Beatles you could imag-ine singing along with, having over for dinner. It's not that they were more acceptable, though they were certainly marketed as such; it's that they seemed more companionable — funnier, kinder, more vulnerable.

For adolescent girls, one tremendous anxiety is the loss of male friendship. Boys who were your comrades, companions, confidantes become your predators and your adversaries. They become Other, laughing behind your back or to your face with a tight, mean clot of buddies. If they want you, that has its own dangers. If they don't, you're subject to ridicule, insults, and social nonexistence. Between the two there is sometimes little room for friendship to survive. And what's at stake here is more than the boys themselves: the loss of friendship is the loss of a world where boys and girls co-exist as something like equals. The loss of boys' friendship is one of the myriad disheartening warning signs defining the world we enter as women.

When the willful, desiring subjectivity of ten-year-olds gives way, goes under, a transfer of loyalty is taking place. Girls learn to identify outside themselves, negating themselves, because they learn to despise what is female and valorize the masculine. So many cultural forces work to transfer a girl's loyalty from her own heart and her mother's legacy to patriarchy. None of these forces is more potent than the Rock Star. His power as a socialization tool lies in his glamour, his charisma, his sexuality, but his not-so-secret ingredient is his apparent rebelliousness. He makes a remarkably effective agent of patriarchy precisely because he seems so clearly not to be, defying parental authority in defying legal, moral, and cultural authority. From Lord Byron to Sinatra, Elvis to Lennon to Kurt Cobain, he represents himself as an agent of the counter-cultural, anarchic, oppositional impulse the West has defined as crucial to adolescence.

But, like most male-defined revolutions, his merely turns in circles, back to where it started, in the land of the fathers. His rebellion is that of the son against the father, whom he overthrows only to replace. And through him, the little girl who is energetically "disloyal to civilization"[4] at eleven comes to worship at the fathers' shrine by fifteen. It is as if the authentic personal energy, spiritual and physical, that drove her up trees, into deep water, and onto the massive back of a horse at ten is sucked out of her, siphoned into his atmosphere. The distance between herself and the worshipped object becomes crucial, marking this alienation of energy. The classic rock-fan behavior caricatures traditional female traits so clearly that it seems almost a ritual masquerade: screaming (uncontrolled emotionalism), fainting (weakness, loss of "consciousness"), mobbing the stage door for hours (waiting for/upon others), and of course, sexual submission, which needs no translation.

In the late sixties, *Rolling Stone* did a huge feature on groupies. I remember poring over it, fascinated. One girl in particular, very high in the California groupie echelons, stared out at the camera with intelligent, proud aplomb, wearing a touch of irony along with a silky shirt and leather vest. There was not a trace of the bimbo about her. And much as I morally disapproved her particular vocation, I would have sold my soul to the devil to look exactly like her — not just to have the vest, the body, the wavy dark hair, but the look in her eyes.

But the ultimate fascination was the famous Plaster Casters, a group of girls who made plaster casts of the erect penises of rock stars. At the time I thought they were a shocking-but-funny sidetrack on the rock-and-roll road the Beatles had pioneered. Now it seems clear to me that the Plaster Casters weren't marginal at all, but rather absolutely central, and possibly more honest than the rest: they simply literalized the metaphor. They ritualized the general cock-worship underlying the rock industry, and they also represented the deceptive sense of control and power available to girls through worshipping at the phallic shrine. And of course, like me, they were collectors.

While the Plaster Casters pursued their craft, I and my less ambitious sisters holed up in our bedrooms, ringed with posters, listening to the albums again and again, imagining these four cute, funny, smart, interesting, somewhat childlike and fabulously talented friends. We invented them; they invented us. Somewhere in the air between us our projections of desire and need collided with their projections of themselves and turned into the cyclone of Beatlemania, though we never used that media word. We developed a remarkably convincing intimacy with our own inventions; we knew them, we knew we did. We knew them in the individual essences that distinguished them, and we knew them collectively, as Them. The hurricane surrounding them brought constant comparisons with Elvis or Sinatra, but they were distinct, among other respects, in being a group. That mythic number Four, the number of directions, seasons, elements, gospels, Musketeers, Horsemen of the Apocalypse. We often thought of them as four dimensions of one being, devoted to each other, brethren, one for all, all for one. Our fantasy was acknowledged and wonderfully satisfied in the film "Help!", when they are seen entering adjoining row houses which turn out to be one huge room, a kind of nursery/playground/bachelor pad where they all live together in pre-sexual brotherhood. They were the inner circle of a fraternity that included Brian Epstein and George Martin and roadies Mal Evans and Neil Aspinall. And in my dreams, that fraternity would open to me. While Diane kept them fed, I'd be up there on stage with them, laying on another level of harmony that would simply astonish them, even cynical John. One of them, the lefty with the obscene eyelashes, would, of course, fall deeply in love with me. I wanted the love, the passion, the romance, the desire and, more importantly, the desirability; but I wanted inclusion, recognition, admiration, respect, equality. I wanted to be among that exalted sisterhood, the Beatle women, Cynthia, Jane, Pattie, and Maureen, whose hair and eye make-up I studied as assiduously as I studied English novels; but I also wanted to join the brotherhood, to be that mythical personage, the Fifth Beatle.

What a conundrum for a growing girl: to be subject or object? Actor or audience? Hero or "heroine"? That is the question. And in the tortuous passages of female adolescence, that question rephrases itself constantly. It is reenacted in many of the dramas of young teenage girls, and it lurks behind many of their strange, extravagant passions. Put abstractly, the question is this: as a female, what do you do with power? Become it, or seduce it? Embody it, or marry it? Enact it, or worship it?

It's enough to make a girl scream.

June, 1967

"London" has become not a place but a concept. Yardley, who made the soaps I gave my grandmother for Christmas, is suddenly "Yardley of London," featuring British-accented voiceovers and wispy, straight-haired models resembling Pattie Boyd Harrison. A New York Jewish comedian dubs himself London Lee. "Carnaby Street" becomes a brand name. "English Leather" is now worn by teenage girls as well as by their fathers, and their ad, likewise, features a Pattie type with oceans of straight blonde hair, bending down from atop a horse to present a man with a bottle of cologne.

My hair has always been completely straight, so I have 33% of the problem licked. At fifteen I grow it long, and then I lighten it further and further away from what my mother calls "honey-colored" and I call "dishwater." I have mastered eyeliner and pale pink lipstick and false eyelashes by the time I am sixteen. The eyes are crucial: they are eyes to be looked at, not to do any looking. The dramatically emphasized eyes, combined with the paleness of the rest of the face and the long, straight hair, yields a look that is a signifying hybrid of sexual and childlike, a phenomenon that seems to resurface in American culture periodically: it appeared in the twenties; it will return again in the nineties. On one level, of course, it reflects patriarachy's pedophilia and infantilization of women: it wants women who are sexually available, but not grown up enough to make their own choices, sexual or otherwise. On another level, the look perfectly reflects our own dilemma as we wander the border between girlhood and womanhood, seeking out a way to be.

The changes in my life have not slowed. In 1965, just before the release of "Help!", my mother remarries again, and we move away from the Detroit area to Ann Arbor — funky, hip Ann Arbor — just in time for me to start high school there, the huge, nearly 4000-student, multi-ethnic Pioneer High. If I was adrift in little Bloomfield Hills Junior High, I am positively drowning here.

But I learn to swim. The Beatles are the touchstone, the lingua franca, the currency of the realm: I find friends who are more or less

Beatles types too. They are not the popular girls. Here as in junior high it is the marginals, like me, who are Beatles fans. To other girls, they are a really good, even great band. To us, they are a certain way of life, a perspective on things, a force. And they are our knights against dragons of loneliness and exclusion.

Among its other riches, Ann Arbor boasts a thriving rock music scene. Reigning over it, at a benign distance, is Bob Seger, then fronting a band called the Last Heard. But on the lower echelons are a variety of assortments of white boys playing lead, rhythm, bass, drums, and keyboard. Beatle offspring, one and all. And true to our training, we follow them — figuratively and literally. We go to their gigs, we drive past their houses, we sniff out information about them, we resent their girlfriends, we buy their occasional records, we get their autographs. Some of us even sleep with them. Not me; I'm above all that. Beneath it too.

One fine day I am unexpectedly thrust into a dress rehearsal for the big scene of my fantasy: I find myself, along with my usual gang of girlfriends, in Bob Seger's mother's actual living room, harmonizing with the Last Heard while Bob is upstairs changing clothes. And they are truly, genuinely impressed.

Meanwhile, I am taking A.P. classes and becoming a National Merit Semifinalist and investigating colleges. I speak fluent Spanish and have been to Europe and North Africa. I sing in three choirs simultaneously. I think I want to be a journalist.

I achieve like crazy, and I practice subordination with the diligence of a true believer. I assert myself, I abase myself. The dissonance doesn't strike me, or if it does, I tamp it down and go on.

Every six months there is a new Beatles album, summer and Christmas, with sometimes another thrown in to take up the slack between American and British LP lengths. or to compensate for that British innovation, the Extended Play record, or EP. Life simply has nothing better to offer than a new Beatles album, especially in those ripe days just before its release, when CKLW or WKNR is playing its advance copy so you get a sharp, sweet taste that makes you hungrier. The rush down to Discount Records on release day; the private intensity of the hour in your room after dinner when you first play it through. Each is like a lengthy letter from old friends exploring terra incognita: This is where we are now, here's what it looks like. *A new world opens up.*

The summer of '66 sees a windfall: "Yesterday and Today" in June, and the amazing "Revolver" in August, days before the launch of their third U.S. tour. At the time I'm in Spain, studying at the University of Madrid and agonizing over missing their second Detroit concert. I'm blessedly ignorant of the fact that it is also my last chance to see them perform together.

That year there is no Christmas album, an anomaly almost signaling that something special is brewing. The next summer dawns very hot. I'm planning a trip out to Oregon in September, to see my brother and his wife and my little nephew and newborn niece. Where I really want to go, of course, is San Francisco. When I come back, I'll start my senior year. In the meantime, I'll be working a lousy fast-food job which I have to lie about my college plans to get. The greasy young manager is looking for girls who are really committed to wearing green checkered aprons and hats and bagging fries.

But today June is still young. After school I head straight for Discount Records. The new album is in. Only this is no album, this is a musical microcosmos. There has never been an album like this, from the elaborate cover to the cardboard cut-out mustache inside, from the opening crowd-and -orchestra noises to the last endless vanishing chord of "A Day in the Life." Over the next two days I breathe in its surreal atmosphere, learn its textures and tonalities. By the end of the week I am hearing it everywhere. Everyone is talking about it. Every magazine has a review. At every party it's playing. The local band members are breathless, awestruck.

Afterward many people call it the Summer of Love. Around Detroit we remember it as the Summer of the Riots. But in my memory it's the Summer of Sergeant Pepper. And me, I'm the queen of the Lonely Hearts Club Band.

March, 1994

I know by the thinness of the light that it's very early, and I intend to go back to sleep, but the dream is strong upon me, I must get up and record it. Later in the day I call Diane, clutching the scribbled scrap of paper.

"It began as an awards ceremony. Paul was getting some kind of award, and Linda was there, only she had a very short, shag haircut. I was just watching from the rear of the auditorium. Then it changed into a class, my class, and Paul was a visitor. What he said to the students was —" I am laughing so hard I can't read. "Now get this: he said, 'You can draw the most idealistic lessons from the most abject circumstances.'"

For a long minute the phone line goes almost silent with our breathless laughter.

"Can you even imagine Paul McCartney saying anything like that?"

"I can't imagine ANYBODY saying anything like that. So what happened then?"

"Well, the kids wouldn't listen to him. I kept repeating everything he said, telling them it was important, they should listen. But they were totally unimpressed. Not into it at all."

"So you were sort of trying to interpret Paul to them?"

"Yeah, kind of. " I think myself back into the dream. "It felt really strongly like it was about the sixties — like he was an emissary from the sixties and I was his translator, but they weren't having any. He and I were old news."

"What did he say again?"

"*'You can draw the most idealistic lessons from the most abject circumstances.'*"

"In other words," says Diane, "*'All you need is love.'*"

June, 1971

It ain't over 'til it's over, and it ain't over yet.

"The Beatles" don't exist anymore. And yet I have fought my mother for the freedom to spend the summer in England, alone, finding them.

They have given their last concert, five years ago at Candlestick Park. They have sung their last together, on the Apple roof. Brian Epstein is dead. John has announced to both Cynthia and Paul that he wants a divorce. The Four Musketeers are playing what George will call the Sue Me, Sue You Blues. They have put out solo albums. They have gone, as the magazines keep putting it, their separate ways. John is into Yoko and bags and acorns and bed and peace. Paul is into domestic bliss and sheep and Scotland. George is inventing the "Band-Aid" phenomenon, pulling together superstars to sing for Bangladesh. Ringo is making movies and marrying a movie star. Meanwhile, the music-loving world is acting the children in this nasty divorce, blaming the Other Woman (Yoko, or sometimes Linda), hanging on their parents' legs (all eight of them), begging them to get back together, to say it ain't so. But it is. Their last album came out the previous May, titled with resounding finality "Let it Be."

But I can't seem to do it. Later, John will say, "Suddenly, we didn't believe." But our belief, the air cushion on which they rode, went on. I can't swallow the bald fact that they literally don't exist. For me, they will continue to exist until December 8, 1980, which is nowhere in sight right now, high above the Atlantic. And so finally, after seven years, I'm going to find them.

This is probably not a great idea. They have populated a world in my head for a long time; it's not wise to try to find Neverland on a map. But it feels almost like an obligation. I have just finished my junior year at Northwestern. In a couple weeks I'll be 21. The American collegiate com-

ing-of-age ritual known as bumming around Europe merges, in my case, with the imperative of this Magical Mystery Tour. The object of the quest isn't clear to me. What is it I'm after? Perhaps it's just the need to touch it all, to make contact with this other reality that has been a strangely consistent presence in my life for seven years. On some level maybe I understand that this is my last summer before graduation signifies that I'm a grownup and have to leave the Yellow Submarine.

But not yet, not now. Right now, I'm on my way. Turn right at Greenland.⁵

It is an odd, lonely quest, and one that expresses my own incongruity, the doubleness I feel in myself. Along with Big Ben, I find Apple; I go from Westminster Abbey to Abbey Road. I study pictures at the Tate Gallery, and I study Paul's front window through the bars on his gate in St. John's Wood. I have nothing resembling a clue as to what I would do if he actually appeared.

I rent a car, drive into London traffic on the left side of the road, and somehow make it out of the city alive. I head south, to see if I can find the Tudor mansions where John and George currently reside. I have the names of towns and the names of the houses themselves, but when I arrive in their vicinity I realize I have no idea how to find them; I guess I've been assuming that some kind of aura would draw me to them, some magic gravitation. Then I turn north—to Wordsworth Country, Edinburgh, Loch Ness, various battlefields and museums; but primarily I seek the origins of Britain's two great contributions to western culture: Stratford first, and then Liverpool. The former is thrilling. The latter is grimy, grim, and depressing. I have a little spiral notebook full of addresses of houses and schools where one or the other of them did time. I stand on the sidewalk outside the Cavern and try to summon the ghosts, but they won't come. I imagine them walking the wet streets in long afternoons, fifteen, sixteen, in their leathers and oily d.a.'s, full of attitude, full of music, dying to get out. I can dig it.

One sunny afternoon finds me on a windy hill in the Kintyre Peninsula of western Scotland, miles from anything except a little place called Campbelltown. I am looking down on Paul McCartney's farm. And from the road where I've parked there is, by god, a long and winding road that leads to his door.

But I don't take it. I've come a long way; but so has he. I decide, not so much to leave him alone, as to leave it alone — the feeling, the place. To let it be. This is it, I think. This is probably as close as I'm ever going to be.

And for eighteen years, it is.

December 4, 1989

Teaching is its own reward, as they say. But sometimes there are side benefits, unexpected windfalls that in great measure make up for the lousy pay and inhuman hours.

Peter, a former student now living in Chicago — the one who studied the scrapbooks that night — has somehow acquired two tickets to the sold-out Paul McCartney concert at Rosemont Horizon. I don't know what I did to deserve this, but I'm glad I did it. I think that for him this is a kind of anthropological field trip; what it is for me I don't know yet as I drive west to Chicago, listening to Paul's new album, *Flowers in the Dirt*.

When Peter and I pull into the vast parking lot at Rosemont, it's still early. Ticketless souls plead outside the entrances. Inside, I buy two of the thick concert programs, one for Diane, who will make snide remarks about Paul's incorrigible cuteness, which she describes as "getting old," by which she does not mean "aging." Peter insists on buying me a T shirt. I think he worries that I won't get the Full Experience that those six scrapbooks have earned me.

We find our seats, which are considerably closer to the stage than the ones at Olympia twenty-five years ago.

Twenty-five years??

Peter has not even been alive twenty-five years.

But a lot of people at Rosemont tonight have been. Seeing middle-aged faces, fathers with kids on their shoulders, I'm suddenly aware that I've been expecting the audience to consist of teenagers, as if I grew up but the rest of the audience at Olympia has been in some time warp, waiting for Paul's return. It's a tremendous relief, somehow, to see all these old rockers who have made the same pilgrimage to the same shrine. There is an easy, familiar feeling among the crowd, as if we know each other.

No Cyrkle this time, no Jackie de Shannon. Just Paul. Another of Peter's worries has been that our tickets say "obstructed view." We are sitting to the right of the stage and back, slightly to the rear. The only obstruction turns out to be that we can't see the monster screen behind the stage, on which the pre-concert film appears. I know from following the tour in the papers that the film places the concert squarely in a Beatles context. Paul is no longer trying to define himself away from that. His quick, ubiquitous critics say he's desperate and finally acknowledged the great truth that his appeal lies in what happened a quarter century ago. Many seem particularly incensed that he's including Beatle songs in this repertoire. It's as if he's violating dead bodies. The nerve of the man, singing his own music. You'd think they were literally sacred texts in a dead language. And yet I'm almost dreading the first Beatle song. You can't go home again, I remind myself. Especially after you know that "Please Please Me" was really about oral sex.

But what else are we here for? Is this little gathering of several hundred thousand of us something other than a homecoming? We are wandering in from our middle-aged lives at the tail end of a dismal, mean-spirited decade that began, with dramatic symbolism, in the death of John Lennon and the election of Ronald Reagan. What we're looking for is some alternative to our sense of discontinuity and exile. We've come in search of a continuum stretching back into the time that marked us, the time we marked as our own, the time in which we formed certain basic assumptions about the world. This is the need that has brought us here tonight, only superficially described as nostalgia .

Bam, there he is, in his tiger shirt. We are looking down over his right shoulder, but he seems very close. He turns to wave up at us. Why do I never in my life have binoculars when I need them? I can see his graying hair, but I can't see his eyes.

So what did they give me? An addictive escape from the realities of my adolescence, or the rich soundtrack of my troubled times, sustaining me, through the comradeship and the wealth of the music, in my passage? What were they for all us girls? Meretricious tools of gender conformity teaching us to demean ourselves and worship phallic gods? Or subversive cyclones of change, freedom, energy, and creativity who lifted us out of the fifties and brought us down into a new world? Agents of patriarchy, or brothers in the Resistance?

Could they have been double agents?

When the Beatle songs come after all, it's nothing but wonderful. What I feel is relief, as if he is liberating them from museum status into the living present. The only twinges come when he does songs that are less completely his own, songs I associate with the four of them — like the dueling guitars between "Golden Slumbers" and "The End." His current band is solid, tight, but the sweet, brief, three-part harmonic conclusion, that equation about the love you take and the love you make is almost unbearable. From "Love Me Do" through "She Loves You" and "Can't Buy Me Love" through "All You Need is Love," wasn't that the moral of the story? To my right, a forty-ish guy with shaggy (for 1989) hair and a toddler on his lap is swaying in time, singing along. Yeah. Yeah? Yeah.

At his psychedelic white upright piano on the rising platform, Paul is the Fool on the Hill. Then at the gleaming black grand, he becomes the philosopher troubadour. It is the one song in which he — perhaps the most closed, unknowable of the Fab Four, in direct contra-

diction of public persona — gets seriously autobiographical, and of
course it is the song about the Lost Mother, the myth that originally
bound him to his two-years-older mate, John Lennon. I'm chanting along
with him when I suddenly understand that Mother Mary's apparently simple maternal advice is weightier, more complicated, than I've been thinking all these years. "Let it be" means "Leave it alone" or "Let it go." That is
what we had to do as the sixties turned into seventies and the Beatles
"went their separate ways": we had to learn to let it be, turn it loose,
move on. But I wonder if Mother Mary didn't intend something more:
allow it to be whatever it is, or was; don't second-guess it, don't diminish
it. And also, then, a third dimension: let it go on being, let it be alive, per-
mit it to live. There in the dark, high in this huge arena, that's what I do: I
let it all wash through me, as something gone, belonging to another time,
another me; but not dead, never dead, and still inside me just as that
other me is. She is saved with her scrapbooks.

All three implications feel very true to me, very expressive of the
art of living through time, change, and loss. You have to let it go when
it's over. But it was what it was. And it also goes on being what it was, it
doesn't die. What better emblem for the continuance of the past than an
old song? Listening, I realize the songs are myths now, the myths of our
lives, available to all of us — including the man who co-wrote them and
has had to outlive his partner, his brother, his alter-ego, some say his better half, now his albatross, the other half of the equation in which he will
always come up short. Just as I'm awash in my own philosophy, I'm
yanked back by a stuttering guitar chord. It can't be, but it is. "Things We
Said Today." I grab Peter's arm and he turns to study my face for the
source of the emergency, but I can't take time to explain. I am breathless
anyway. Twice in one lifetime? Sure enough: my secret favorite non-hit
Beatle song must be one of his favorites too, one he's carried close to him
over the great divide, as I have.

*"It is hard to put into words what we remember." Collective memo-
ry, this powerful sea in which we all float. All of us here, remembering the
times of our lives. The long and winding road that brought us here, to the
threshold of the nineties and a new century, to middle age, to wisdom or
foolishness, dreams and disillusion, love and loss. And what it feels like,
here, tonight, is that I was right at thirteen: the Beatles represented some
kind of friendship, some bond bigger than sex or even media hype, born of
shared desire and youth and memory, and reenacted every time we sing
the songs in the privacy of our living rooms or the cavernous intimacy of
Rosemont Horizon.*

It's the end again, and probably everyone here knows what song it's going to be. When he moves to the piano and sings that first acappella note, the roar goes up and the lighters come out and come on in the dark and the great body of us begins to sway. I'm thinking about the derivation of this song. It germinated as "Hey, Jule," written as Uncle Paul's response to the sadness of six-year-old Julian Lennon over his parents' breakup. Letting her into your heart: was this Paul's recommendation to Julian concerning his new, strange stepmother, Yoko Ono? Or was Paul translating Julian's anxiety about change into adult terms, the terms of his own life, into which Linda Eastman had come, along with the dissolution of "the lads," which he had fought until it got bloody and he emerged as the bad guy?

"Don't let me down," he sings. Is it an accident that this also happens to be the title of one of John's primal, aching songs about Yoko? When Paul first played "Hey, Jude" for him, John remembered, "I took it very personally. Ah, it's me! I said. It's me. He says, 'No, it's me.'"[6] In the slime and mess of the "divorce," the music returned them for a moment to their telepathic, uncanny brotherhood. The Nurk Twins.[7]

I have to confess that "Hey, Jude" was never among my favorites. To me it always seemed to go on forever, the "Na, Na, Na, Nanana Na" tail wagging a very simple dog. But tonight it's a different song. "Hey, Jude" is an elaboration of "Let it Be": a grown-up song about allowing change to happen, letting the past (the "sad song") be and letting what is to be enter in. As Paul invites several hundred thousand voices to join him on the chorus, something weird happens. It is as if the nonsense syllables become a mantra of sorts for a vast group meditation. I am enveloped by the song — its sadness, its modest hope, its compassion — and by the voices around me singing words we all know by heart. This time no screaming to get in the way of my old fantasy: I'm singing with him like I've done it for years.

September, 1995

I am in the middle of the brief article in the paper before a powerful wave of deja vu stops me: I am reading about a new Beatles album. It will be out by Christmas, full of unheard songs from the past but also new ones. Is that what they are, new songs, these tracks of John's onto which the others have layered their voices and instruments? A collaboration with the past, literally with the dead — what kind of newness is this?

The gush of excitement reminds me of something I am learning repeatedly as I cross this rich terrain of middle age: that fourteen-year-old is alive and well in me. Alive and yearning. John Lahr has referred to the sound of the Beatles as "what passed for hope and Heaven in those bumptious, buoyant times."[8] True; but it was Heaven only in the sense of

the Kingdom that is all around you. They were my parallel universe for a
decade, a place that still exists, where I can still go once in a while; the
rich, intense place measured, in fact, by the power of my own imagination and desire. Ultimately, they were about how much I was, how much
I wanted.

    One Saturday morning within days of the newspaper article, I go
from deep sleep to complete wakefulness in the space of the first three
chords of "I Want to Hold Your Hand," blaring from my clock radio.
NPR's Weekend Edition is doing a short piece on Carroll James, the DJ
credited with first playing the Beatles in the U.S. It was a girl named
Marcia Albert, he remembers, who sent him the record, having carried it
herself from London. A week later, Weekend Edition does a follow-up.
Listeners have written to ask a question that I am ashamed to realize
never occurred to me: why James was interviewed, but not the woman
responsible for his having a place in rock history. I know the answer
before I hear it: Marcia Albert, the American girl who knew a great thing
when she heard it, cannot be found. From Marcia Albert, the vehicle by
which the voice of the Beatles reached the ears of Carroll James, and
eventually my ears as well — only silence.

6

Girlfriend

. . . we were two throats and one eye
and we had no price.

—Sula[1]

February, 1994

I find the road without trouble. It's longer than I expect. It curves
up and around a hill straddling the line between Leverett and Montague,
one of the rough blue hills that are my favorite part of my temporary
home in western Massachusetts. The road's a little slick — almost every
road out here is a challenge in this winter of our extreme discontent —
but not treacherous, and I wind up in front of what looks like the right
house. I creep over the ice to the brightly lit entrance. A woman emerges,
smiling. This must be Donna. And behind her, all brown eyes and laughter, is Julie.

Here we are, next door to each other again, in a sense, forty
years (almost to the month) after we first met. Life is sometimes very artistic.

Donna and I barely introduce ourselves to each other before Julie
and I are in each other's arms, laughing and exclaiming. She is more regal
than I would have expected, but as beautiful as she was as a child. My
first thought is that she is very like her mother, who died this year.
"Didn't I tell you she'd say that?" She turns to Donna for confirmation. "I
told you she'd say I looked like my mom!"

"But you sound like her too — your laugh is just like hers."

"You're kidding! It is?"

And we're washed away in remembrance. Donna and her husband, voluntarily hosting this reunion, seem not only to tolerate it but
actually to enjoy it.

In fact, Donna goads us into reminiscence. She has known Julie a
long time, but as an adult. Over dinner and afterward, Julie and I rush
forward and back in time, bringing each other up to date on our parents

and siblings and cousins, the extended family of our mutual childhood. Julie tells me that my book was the last thing her mother read, and that it occasioned a remarkable conversation. Her eyes flood, and mine do too.

To explain to Donna what we meant to each other, I tell her about the Saturday morning my widowed mother woke me early to show me a square-cut diamond on her left hand. She was going to marry the nice man she'd been dating. And of course, we would be moving away.

I got out of bed, dressed, flew from the house, across the broad suburban yard, down the rise where the property line lay, into the Robertsons' yard and onto their back porch. I quietly turned the door knob and went inside. (My god, I guess we never locked doors, did we?) The house was still. I crept down the hallway to Julie's room and peeked in to see her asleep. I had never been so alone. I left the house and ran down to the river to weep away my rage, my fear of this uprooting, this separation, the first and most drastic of my life.

Either I never told Julie of this, or she has forgotten. She is amazed to hear me describe walking through her sleeping house, looking in bedrooms, leaving again without waking anyone. But where else would I go in my utter despair but to the Robertsons? My alternate family, absorbing me so easily. I probably had a kind of Waltons fantasy about them. During my childhood my much older father was dying. By the time I was ten, he was dead and my only brother was away at college, so I functioned as the only child of a single parent much of the time. Next door there were two parents and six children — three of each. Chronologically I fell smack in the middle, alongside the youngest girl: Julie, born twenty-three days before me.

I suppose the Robertsons represented some ideal of Family Values I was soaking up from "Father Knows Best" and "I Remember Mama." Although I was an introspective kid who needed privacy and aloneness, I had a flip side that desperately needed to belong to a bigger group. In addition to the immediate family next door, there always seemed to be extra kids around, cousins and friends, bikes and dogs, projects and plans. It was a household with a comforting degree of structure — everyone had definite tasks to perform and rules to abide by — in which there was tremendous room for chaos. I was always welcome, and when I stayed for dinner, which was often, Mr. Robertson included me in the grace he said, thanking God for my presence. Is it any wonder that (much to my own mother's amused dismay) I would jump up from our dinner table to rush next door in time to help the Robertson girls do the dishes? At my house you couldn't sing three-part harmony while you washed and dried. And after dinner, anything might develop: a trip to Putt-Putt, a game, a session in the official Girls' Bathroom, where Mary Jane, the eldest and to my mind the repository of endless secrets of femininity, would teach Martha and Julie and me how to roll our hair or apply lipstick, to a background narrative of high school, boys, teachers, dating, parties, friends. "I think it was at your house that I learned about being a girl," I tell Julie.

"You know," she says, after a short silence, "I always thought that what attracted you was my family. But all I wanted was you. Just you." She looks at me across the years.

Did I know that?

Her face dissolves into the one I knew thirty-five years ago. No. Your family gave me something I wanted, but they were an extra. It was really about you. Me and you.

Snatches of feeling come back: jealousy, need, competition. I remember being jealous of her other friends, afraid of losing her, of being usurped as her best friend. But that all came from a deeper place, more tangled and shameful than my love for her. It was my envy. Everyone seemed to love her, from her soulful brown eyes to her goofy humor to her trusting openness. She had this gift, this genius for being lovable. I felt I could never get it. I was a smart, talented kid, who was always at the top of the class and had a remarkable ear for music and always felt confused and complicated. But what I wanted was to be Julie.

When I tell her of this envy, she smiles. "I used to hate it when people compared you to me," she says. "Do you remember? I'd say, 'Come on, let's go,' and pull you away."

Was that my first lesson in loyalty, the absolute allegiance of girl-friends? Envy so deep I can still taste it, alongside this fierce devotion? *I wanted to be you* and *All I wanted was you*, joined in a complicated fugue. Are those somehow, down very deep, the same thing? The same thing that drove us to pick our mosquito-bite scabs and rub our bloody arms together, so that we could be blood sisters?

Julie has photos. Her mother, shortly before her death, put together scrapbooks for each of her six children. Julie's scrapbook is full of me. I'm everywhere — in the ballet class picture, the birthday party picture, the bike-riding picture. It's a kind of confirmation of how constant we were in each other's lives, how merged our girlhoods.

Looking at the photos isn't entirely pleasant. They confirm my memories: I look tense and repressed, my pudgy body ill at ease, my dirty-blonde hair curling sullenly and unnaturally. Julie looks wide open to the world, eager to please, easy to love. A stranger would never pick us out as bestfriends. The ballet-class picture is especially horrible; we both look uncomfortable in our tutus and our tortuously posed hands, our feet twisted into third position.

Suddenly we shriek in unison and point to our knees: "Look!" There we are, little ballerinas struggling within the constraints of femininity alongside our peers and our teacher and an inexplicable cart decked with artificial flowers, and on our knees are huge twin bandaids. Shredded memory: some mutual accident (on bikes?), our mothers laughing at their bandaged ballerinas the morning of the photo. Am I right that we went before the cameras proudly, wearing our badges of honor, evidence of our other life, where we were blood sisters forever?

We come to a photo where Julie's thick chestnut hair is suddenly short. "Remember?" she says, "When I got my hair cut? Remember how upset you were?"

I had been gone, up north with my family, or maybe to camp. I can taste the anticipation of coming home, seeing my room and my toys and my dog — but most of all, telling Julie everything. And there she stood, transformed, her long ponytail gone. I felt betrayed, left behind somehow. We were blood sisters and she had changed, without me. "Yes," I smile. "I remember."

> *At first, as they stood there, their hands were clenched together. They relaxed slowly until during the walk back home their fingers were locked in as gentle a clasp as that of any two young girlfriends trotting up the road on a summer day wondering what happened to butterflies in the winter.*[2]

In the fifties, if you were a girl who read, contemporary girls' books were sort of a wasteland, except for one important figure: a blonde teenager in a red "roadster," whatever that was, who could solve any mystery on earth. There were two thoroughly remarkable things about Nancy Drew. One was that the most important thing about her was her brains. The other was that her boyfriend, the ever-faithful Ned Nickerson, not only never saved the day but was far less important — to Nancy as well as the plot — than her best girlfriends, Bess and George.

Bess, plump and coifed, always wore shirtwaist dresses and was always afraid. George, slim, athletic, short-haired and trousered, could be relied on in any crisis. Any self-respecting girl — certainly myself — admired George, allying herself with what I seem to remember as the authorial point of view in affectionate disparagement of Bess. Together, they fascinated me. Frankly, they were my favorite part of the books.

Did anybody ever contemplate the psychosexual drama being played out for impressionable girls like me via this dynamic duo? A bona-fide femme-butch team, flanking Our Hero, Nancy, in all her endeavors. I contemplate the shelf full of books in my memory, trying to see what was going on: were Bess and George dimensions of Nancy, her capable, bold side versus her timorous, gentle side? Or was Nancy supposed to be the hero precisely because she presented a golden mean between the two extremes of female identity? Was their polarity directed at me, the reader, to show me the two ends of the spectrum of feminine possibility? Am I right that the author deprecated the lily-livered Bess as much as I did? And if so, does that mean that the various Carolyn Keenes were doing a serious critique of femininity, fifties-style? Did my contempt for Bess reflect a healthy contempt for constructions of feminine incapacity, or did it reflect my pre-feminist contempt for the female and valorization of the male, embodied in the muscular, lean-and-mean George?

But the very thing about Nancy was that her spirit was bigger than mine: she loved them both. Bess was useless in an emergency, but Nancy loved her all the same, as she loved the not-cuddly George. They were girlfriends. Mysteries in locked rooms and secrets in old clocks come and go, as do alliterative boyfriends. Girlfriends remain. Among the awful lessons I took from the various propaganda that passed as children's literature or schoolbooks in the fifties, I took this salutary lesson too: the secret places of girlfriends accommodate all of you, everything you are and fear and know.

I loved them, that invincible trio. I loved their jokes, the teasing of good buddies. I loved their loyalty to each other. Through the Bess-and-George paradigm I was certainly working out my own gender identity and sexuality. Maybe I was also using it to ponder my girlfriends, my bestfriend, my own role as a girlfriend. Your girlfriend so often seems to be that dimension of yourself you can't quite own, or don't get to acknowledge. She is at once your absolute Other and your mirror image — that is, your self reversed, possibly distorted. She is what you crave and what you disown, what you wish to be and what you deeply are.

I wanted to be you.
All I wanted was you.

Their friendship was as intense as it was sudden. They found relief in each other's personality. Although they were unshaped, formless things, Nel seemed stronger and more consistent than Sula, who could hardly be counted on to sustain any emotion for more than three minutes. Yet there was a time when that was not true, when she held on to a mood for weeks but even that was in defense of Nel.[3]

"Chloe liked Olivia." This unprepossessing sentence, said Virginia Woolf, is the most astonishing line in English literature.[4] From here she begins her ironic, twisting road toward her point: that one thing women's literature gives us is a view of female friendship, a phenomenon sentimentalized, deflected, obscured, omitted, deformed and derogated in most men's writing down the ages. And as usual, Woolf is precisely right: one of the first things one notices in a serious immersion in women's writing, from earliest times, is the presence of other women, as allies, models, lovers, and friends. Sometimes it takes a shift of perspective to see it: from a traditional vantage point (that is, one framed to foreground the masculine), Jane Austen's novels are all about women trying to get themselves or others married. From a woman-centered vantage point, however, the scene shifts fairly dramatically: the hymeneal finale is a concession to literary traditional and socioeconomic necessity that affords an excuse for women to spend time with their sister-friends, talking through the complexities of their lives, characters, and choices. Take *Pride and Prejudice* : the question may be whether Elizabeth and Darcy and Jane and Bingley will ever get together, but meantime what makes the novel go is Elizabeth's generous, intelligent relationship with Jane, her tangles with Bingley's dreadful sisters, her reflections on the embarrassing women in her own family, and the subtleties and shifts of her interactions with her own bestfriend, Charlotte Lucas, whom she must learn to respect enough to embrace her difference, allowing Charlotte her own legitimate (if appalling) marital choice.

But back up further — say 150 years. Katherine Philips, known to a small but admiring public as "the Matchless Orinda," writes to her sister-friend Anne Owen in 1667:

> I did not live until this time
> Crowned my felicity,
> When I could say without a crime,
> I am not thine, but thee. . . .

"[N]ever had Orinda found / A soul, till she found thine," she wrote; "I've all the world in thee."[5] The poem argues the speaker's joy as superior to the "bridegroom's [or] crown-conqueror's mirth" (an interesting pairing!) and ends with an assertion of the women's "innocent . . . design." Whether this is a lesbian poem or not, it is unquestionably a testament to the primacy of female affiliation in women's lives. The innocence she protests may be sexual (especially given the earlier reference to crime), but might it not also suggest girlhood, so that this friendship partakes of, embodies, the love between little girls?

"I am not thine, but thee." I don't belong to you; I am you. Her relation to Anne is something more profound than mere connection; it is complete identification. She lacked a soul until she found Anne's. They form an entity in which individual boundaries are blurry — the pre-sexual, fluid unity of little girls. I am not thine, but thee. (I want to be you.)

I've all the world in thee. (All I want is you.)

But what of girls themselves? Where are they? As complex central characters they are rare in literature before the Romantic revolution of the late eighteenth century, when childhood became a focal point of intense interest. With that interest in childhood comes the bildüngsroman or novel of education and development. It gives us David Copperfield and Pip — with little girls appearing as anxious, long-suffering sisters and cousins. Unless a woman is writing. In that case, the subject often becomes — to borrow a phrase — little women, presented and explored in contexts where their relations with one another, as sisters and friends, are crucial.

If you haven't read *Jane Eyre* for a while, you might be surprised to recall how much occurs before we meet the Byronic Mr. Rochester. Jane has a very significant girlhood before she frightens his horse on the icy path to Thornfield, bringing him down to earth for the first of many times. I generally spend at least three class periods talking about what happens before Rochester. The first third of the novel covers only a short period in Jane's miserable young life, during her eleventh year, but its events carry the psychic weight and metaphorical import of primal experiences — including a girlfriend.

Helen Burns isn't with us for long: she appears, reading *Rasselas,* in chapter five and is dead at the end of chapter nine. But she is Jane's bestfriend. Actually, she's Jane's only peer friend in childhood. If I want to generate a hot class discussion, I ask about Helen. At least half the class will loathe her. And indeed, she is one of those characters about whom Brontë makes it very difficult to share Jane's feelings. Her saintly transcendence is only slightly less annoying than her stoic endurance and her moral righteousness. As thirteen-year-olds go, Helen is a real drag. In terms of her symbolic impact on Jane's evolution, the question of whether she is a figure of infuriating feminine submissiveness or of courageous resistance entirely depends on one's point of view. In fact, I think Jane is a little confused on that point: she is awed by Helen's ability to submit unflinchingly to unjust punishment, but her awe is one part admiration and one part horror.

Soon, all she wants is Helen: she would gladly submit to any physical torture, she proclaims, in characteristic hyperbole, for some gesture of love from Helen. And she wants to be Helen as well. Helen "burns" with exactly the fire Jane needs at this juncture: not the self-immolating conflagration of Jane's own passionate nature, but the "hard, gemlike flame"[6] that will allow for peace, dignity, and hope. She wants not only Helen's power to endure pain and injustice, but her mind and her and articulate voice. Helen represents a kind of intellectual power and spiritual liberty that are entirely new, and dazzling, to Jane, whose intelligence and spirit have brought her only trouble.

From Helen Jane draws the foundation for her future survival. Perhaps her most important message comes after Jane's own public humiliation before the entire school. "[I]f others don't love me, I would rather die than live," Jane says, and Helen responds: "If all the world hated you, and believed you wicked, while your own conscience approved you, and absolved you from guilt, you would not be without friends . . . . you think too much of the love of human beings . . ." (VIII). A hard, bitter, and nourishing truth: Jane will need to be less dependent on others' responses, more reliant on her own resources. The gift of a girlfriend: the strength to live without her.

But the simple event immediately following this exchange may be even more important than anything they say to each other: "Resting my head on Helen's shoulder, I put my arms round her waist; she drew me to her, and we reposed in silence" (VIII). The intensity of their verbal interaction folds into this silent physical intimacy, in which they are found, rescued, by the benign Miss Temple. These two preternaturally articulate miniature adults all at once reveal themselves as children — girlfriends. It is an evocative scene: two orphan refugees from patriarchal tyranny find each other and then, as if by some strange causality, are united with the maternal presence for which both of them are starving.

This embrace prefigures another: when Jane wends her way through the typhus-riddled school to find Helen, who is wasting with consumption. Jane crawls into bed with Helen and, after a dialogue on the afterlife, falls asleep in her arms. When Miss Temple finds them, "I was asleep, and Helen was — dead" (IX). The chapter ends with the word inscribed on Helen's gravestone: "Resurgam" — "I shall rise again."

And does she? The embrace in which Helen dies is suggestive, for Helen in one sense dies into Jane. The "disciplined and subdued character" who appears at age eighteen in the next chapter has internalized aspects of Helen, as well as Miss Temple. The furious child of the first nine chapters vanishes, almost entirely, and the dignified, ascetic, stoic personage who takes her place bears more than small traces of Helen. Much of what readers don't like about Jane — her repression, her self-denial, her martyr impulses — is a Helen bequest, along with some of what we admire — her self-reliance, her self-control, her integrity.

But Helen might be said to rise again in another, more obscure, diffuse form. That first and last embrace between girlfriends is mythic, a critical imprinting. It predates the problematic, dangerous (hetero)sexual embraces of adult life (and Rochester's and Rivers' embraces will be fraught with peril for Jane). This earlier embrace between sister/friends ratifies a primal bond, a unity with the self represented in the union with other girlwomen. In the entry into the domain of the fathers through adult heterosexual womanhood, female loyalty shifts, or is shifted, to the male object; the embrace of the sister is broken, the mother is lost. Helen dies just as Jane enters puberty; Miss Temple marries just as she emerges from it. But in our lives as "governesses" in the master's houses, we recover the lost mother/sister in our figurative embraces of other women. In Jane's career, these will include not merely the easily lovable — kind Mrs. Fairfax, needy little Adele Varens, the impressive and endearing Rivers sisters — but the repellent and unwelcoming, the "monstrous" women it is easy to despise: the nasty Reeds to whom Jane returns in kindness, and even the horrifying Bertha, Jane's opposite in every respect, whom Jane first confronts as an image in her own bedroom mirror. (XXV)

The fallen sister is reclaimed. If Helen is Jane's "subdued, disciplined" self, Bertha is her desperate, raging self, the wild child locked away in an upper room. Virgin and whore, good girl and bad girl — these patriarchal projections are subsumed by the girlfriend's embrace, disintegrated by the girlfriend's gaze, which looks into the mirror of the other and sees the self. I am not thine, but thee.

Sula lifted her head and joined Nel in the grass play. In concert, without ever meeting each other's eyes they stroked the blades up and down, up and down Nel found a thick twig and, with her thumbnail, pulled away its bark until it was stripped to a smooth, creamy innocence. Sula looked around the found one too. When both twigs were undressed Nel moved easily to the next stage and began tearing up rooted grass to make a bare spot of earth. When a generous clearing was made, Sula traced intricate patterns in it with her twig. At first Nel was content to do the same. But soon she grew impatient and poked her twig rhythmically and intensely into the earth, making a small neat hole that grew deeper and wider with the least manipulation of her twig. Sula copied her, and soon each had a hole the size of a cup. Nel began a more strenuous digging and, rising to her knee, was careful to scoop out the dirt as she made her hole deeper Together they worked until the two holes were one and the same When the depression was the size of a small dishpan, Nel's twig broke With a gesture of disgust she threw the pieces into the hole they had made. Sula threw hers in too. Nel saw a bottle cap and tossed it in as well. Each then looked around for more debris to throw into the hole: paper, bits of glass, butts of cigarettes, until all the defiling things they could find were collected there. Carefully they

*replaced the soil and covered the entire grave with uproot-
ed grass. Neither one had spoken a word.*[7]

This remarkable scene is prelude to another: Sula swings a boy
called Chicken Little around by his arms, out over the river. Suddenly he
slips from her hands, flies out into the water, and disappears. For good.

Forty-three years later, Nel visits Sula's grandmother, Eva Peace,
in a nursing home. Eva says, "Tell me how you killed that little boy." Nel,
aghast, responds, "I didn't throw no little boy in the river. That was Sula."
To which Eva counters, "You. Sula. What's the difference? You was there.
You watched, didn't you?"[8]

Nel is terrified, not only by the discovery of this ancient accident,
but by the mysterious truth of Eva's words. "Just alike. Both of you. Never
was no difference between you."[9] Nel's entire conventional, responsible,
straitened adult identity has been predicated on her difference from Sula
— the amoral, radically disruptive Sula. For Nel, Eva's assertion of their
undifferentiation puts an uncomfortable spin on Sula's own dying words
to her ex-bestfriend:

Hey, girl." Nel paused and turned her head but
not enough to see her.
"How you know?" Sula asked.
"Know what?" Nel still wouldn't look at her.
"About who was good. How you know it was
you?"
"What you mean?"
"I mean maybe it wasn't you. Maybe it was
me."[10]

Sula's suggestion is obscene: it subverts the very conditions of Nel's
being. First, she is teasing Nel's righteousness. Second, she suggests that
she, Sula, the town pariah, might in fact represent a revolutionary brand
of virtue. But third, she intimates that the very categories of good and bad
are tenuous, fluid constructions, especially as applied to women, and
especially as they drive women apart. This final statement fulfills her role
in her community, to call every assumption into question. Her question,
coupled with her grandmother's, suggests to Nel that the radical potential
in their intense girlhood bond disrupts traditional moral alignments.
Questions of virtue, guilt, and responsibility become very tangled, perhaps unanswerable — even, as Eva suggests, irrelevant. Beyond such a
conclusion lies a terrible freedom.

There is a scene in *Thelma and Louise*. The car is speeding
through the desert, at night. The heroes have gradually divested them-

selves of the trappings of their "normal" lives as women — hairdos, make-up, skirts, jewelry. They are tanned, sweaty, windblown. Glenn Frey's love song pulses in the background: "Part of You, Part of Me."

As the chorus soars, their faces dissolve into each other.

For me this is the turning point in the film, its climactic moment, though nothing is "happening." When I think of this scene, my memory of it is sensory: I hear the song, I feel the cool of the desert evening wind on sunburned, sweaty skin. I feel the utter belonging and expansiveness, the safety and danger, of being in a car with your girlfriend (which your parents never understood when you were sixteen and couldn't explain to them what it was you were going to *do*). I feel a terrible sorrow and a kind of ecstasy. And something more: the sense of having gone too far, way too far.

I think this is, in part, the huge appeal of this film for women like me — the ones who went back to see it again and again with their girl-friends, the one whose cars bear stickers reading "THELMA AND LOUISE ON BOARD" (close kin to the women whose bumper stickers read "TAWANDA!" but that's another girlfriend movie). I nearly bought one of those bumper stickers, but I was truly afraid of what kind of attention it might draw on the road. *This movie could get me into trouble.* And the source of the danger is the premise of the film: *What if you followed your commitment to your girlfriend as far as it took you?*

Callie Khouri arranged the incident that generates the flight of Thelma and Louise so that it dislocates moral responses. Louise's shooting of the would-be rapist cannot be excused as self-defense or defense of Thelma (though it probably saves a lot of other women). Thelma is safe when the shot is fired. Louise, in fact, murders the guy. Our affirmation of her act comes from somewhere beyond reason or notions of justice embodied in the law. From that point on, our allegiance to Thelma and Louise, like theirs to each other, comes from another place, a deep place, a place of memory and imagination, where we were girls together, watch-ing the boy sink under the water. The murder precipitates Louise and Thelma into each other and out beyond the pale, into an unmapped bor-derland where everything is up for grabs, all bets are off, all rules sus-pended. They must reinvent themselves entirely.

This situation seems to recall the existentialist's violent liberatory act. But that self-affirmation included "seeing rape as an expression of freedom,"[11] where this violence has been specifically counter-rapist, deny-ing objectification by affirming connection, identification with the victim of violence. It is the connection, not the violence, that is liberatory, and in patriarchy transgressive, making the women outlaws. Gender makes all the difference. Louise's murder of the rapist comes directly from her own memory of being raped, implied but never described in the film. She shoots the guy because in the near-rape of her girlfriend, she sees her own victimization — and vice-versa. In pulling the trigger she yanks her girlfriend along with her over the border into No Man's Land.

"Over the edge," as we say of those who, by whatever accepted measure, have gone too far. I had an interesting argument with a colleague about this film. He argued that it represented a feminist cul-de-sac because Thelma and Louise die at the end. "But they don't," I said. His expression was incredulous. Surely I didn't think the Thunderbird survived the flight into the Grand Canyon? "That's not the point," I insisted, not having thought about it until that moment but absolutely sure I was right. "They do not die at the end of the film." It was impossible to say what I meant; my colleague thought I was talking in literalistic or sentimental terms. What I was struggling to say was that whether they die or not is not the film's issue. The film ends not with their death but with their flight. What happens at the end is that they keep going. They make a very deliberate decision to do so, and not in the traditional male-western terms of liberty-vs.-death, going-down-shooting: in those terms, they would have turned the car around and driven into the army of cops. It is a sudden, simple, joyous decision (Thelma's idea) — not to die, but to keep going. This is what gives the end of the film its tremendous thrust, its transcendence. Having crossed the line initially and kept going, they remain true to that radical commitment to each other: they go way, way too far.

> *It was like getting the use of an eye back, having a cataract removed. Her old friend had come home. Sula. Who made her laugh, who made her see old things with new eyes, in whose presence she felt clever, gentle, and a little raunchy. Sula, whose past she had lived through and with whom the present was a constant sharing of perceptions. Talking to Sula had always been a conversation with herself. Was there anyone else before whom she could never be foolish? In whose view inadequacy was mere idiosyncrasy, a character trait rather than a deficiency? Anyone who left behind that aura of fun and complicity? Sula never competed; she simply helped others define themselves.[12]*

My best mind. It came to me, finally, in those words, that precise phrase. She is my best mind.

When I told her, she said, "Yeah, you too." She always says that.

In the months before I left Kalamazoo for ten months, she was seriously deranged. To my surprise, I wasn't. I didn't feel the sense of

imminent loss and deprivation in her absence that she was feeling. I finally figured out why: "Our friendship is pretty much telephone-based, so
what does it matter if I'm calling you from 800 miles away or four
blocks?" She wasn't buying it.

We "do things" together, as girlfriends do. We go downtown for
double lattés or lunch, we celebrate Winter Solstice and our respective
birthdays and her son's birthday, we religiously attend each other's readings. Once in a while we just cruise around in her van in the summer, air
conditioning roaring, wasting gas and ozone and energy and time and
polluting the air and doing nothing productive.

Except talking. That is our real element: the verbal. And mostly
we do it by phone. This has surprised me, as I am one of the small
minority in this society who avoid the telephone. We have both become
rather hermetic in our advancing middle age. She's positively eccentric
about it, but I'm not far behind. We don't entertain or go out a lot; we do
strenuous, high-stress jobs and we come home and hide. And call each
other on the phone. People who know us sometimes assume that we see
each other constantly and are incredulous when I say that weeks go by.
But if more than a day passes without the sound of her voice, I think
she's mad at me. If more than a day passes without the sound of mine,
she thinks I'm dead. We think this says just about everything about our
similarity and our difference.

Of the seventeen years we have known each other, we have
spent two (not successive) not talking. It's interesting: little girls say
they're "having a fight," teenage girls say they're "not talking." The sudden, overwhelming estrangements between girlfriends, at a certain age,
are defined in terms of verbal deprivation. It's completely apt: what was
horrible, during those years, was the silence, the ringing silence on the
other end of the phone line. What's perhaps even more interesting is that
we have never discussed those two not-talking periods. I honestly don't
know if that's because we're afraid to go near them, or because we truly
don't need to: those were our silences, between our talking, and they're
over. We talk now.

My relationships with men became easier when I finally figured
out the basic and absolute gender difference around "talking." When you
go to a man with a problem — let's say a struggle at work or a fight with
your mother — he becomes either Handyman or Superman. He wants to
fix it, to save you. The talk in which you engage has a purpose, a goal
line: to solve the problem. Now, if you're pursuing this discussion like a
true girl, what you do looks to him very much like resisting solution: you
respond with "Yeah, but" and "On the other hand" until he's exasperated
and depleted. What you are actually resisting is closure, and the reason
you're doing this is that solving the problem is only part of your goal.

First, and most important, there is process. The process — talking it through, considering angles, speculating, analyzing everyone involved, departing from the subject and returning to it renewed — precedes any reliable solution, for you. But the process also has inherent value. It satisfies a need all its own.

That's where your girlfriend comes in. Between girlfriends there are two levels of experience: what happened, and talking about it. What happened quite literally hasn't been experienced fully until you've talked about it. People are real when you've talked about them. The world comes into being when you talk. (This is what patriarchy calls women's proclivity for "gossip.") This is the epistemological dimension of girl-friendship.

The ethics of a real girlfriend conversation are subtle but important. Your girlfriend always takes your situations seriously. She may tease you — in fact, that might be one of her important tools — but she never condescends, minimizes, or dismisses what concerns you. For her, the import of an event or situation is not what it means to her but what it means to you: this is what she listens to hear, your meaning. If your meaning seems destructive to you, she revises it, suggests an alternative. Above all, she has a certain you in her mind. The you she has in her mind is the best you — the worthiest, the smartest, the ablest. She gives this you back to you when you have lost it. Her thinking is your own best thinking, at times when perhaps you can't think your best because you're scared or tired or discouraged, your head crowded with other voices, other versions of yourself. Then you need her, your best mind.

a conversation with herself
Neither one had spoken a word

Those times, it's like digging down into the earth with two sticks. There are other times when the motion is reversed: upward, spiraling into the stratosphere. Like juggling while flying.

This happens to us usually late at night. It begins at what we think is the end of a phone call, when we have sifted through each other's days, untied our knots, unloaded our shit. We think we're moving toward, "Well, call you tomorrow." We're both tired and have other claims on the rest of our evenings. And then something happens, some trigger is pulled, some catch released. It's like what rising in a hot air balloon might be like, I imagine. Often there's a familiar vehicle — the meaning of particular scenes in *The Wizard of Oz,* or the respective talents of Lennon vs. McCartney. Reliable mythic vehicles from the culture that formed us, you understand. Vehicles that take off and go. The fuel is often laughter, a very peculiar laughter that resides deep in a primordial well that only she can plumb. It starts as a chuckle, swells to a cackle, and then breaks its chain and runs wild, until we're breathless, cramped and gasping, then shrieking like banshees. I am having visions, insights that astonish me — or are they hers? (You. Sula. What's the difference.) We are prodigious. We are invincible. Our enemies — whatever fools are giving us trouble, undervaluing our brilliance, insulting our magnificence — are in for it now. Our laughter is the cauldron in which they cook, until they're shriveled and bloodless. Our laughter is the explosive that blows our demons, past and present, to smithereens. We are brave and beautiful and bold and brilliant, and no one can touch us.

> *I want to be you*
> *All I want is you*

I feel the edge coming before I see it. Then it is under us, and then we are gone, out into the air, high above our lives. The stomach lurches. The head expands. We have gone way, way too far.

> *Suddenly Nel stopped. Her eye twitched and burned a little.*
> *"Sula?" she whispered, gazing at the tops of trees. "Sula?"*
> *Leaves stirred; mud shifted; there was the smell of overripe green things. A soft ball of fur broke and scattered like dandelion spores in the breeze.*
> *"All that time, all that time, I thought I was missing Jude."*
> *And the loss pressed down on her chest and came up into her throat.*
> *"We was girls together," she said as though explaining something.*
> *"O Lord, Sula," she cried, "girl, girl, girlgirlgirl."[13]*

Long-distance isn't the same, but it works. Six months into my year away, we're talking and suddenly she says, "I got my hair cut."

"You did?"

"Yep. Changed the color, too."

"What?!"

"Yep. You should see it."

"Wait a minute, what's it look like?"

"It's straight and red."

"RED!" My stomach clenches. "Wait, you're not supposed to do that!"

"Do what?"
 "Change without me!"
And we start to laugh.

7

A New York Minute
On the Death of John Lennon

> . . . the anniversary of a death, . . .
> a betrayal, a deep humiliation, can year after year
> extrude its splinters, almost to the day,
> into the scar tissue of the well-annealed self,
> determined to obliterate, to go on without looking back.
> . . . We can come to respect the recurrence, meet it halfway,
> not as interruption, but as a kind of repetition
> by which (time is the school) we learn.
>
> —Adrienne Rich[1]

1. Everybody had a hard year, everybody had a good time . . .

December 8, 1994. . . . In earlier times, death was marked by a black border around stationery. In our memories, death marks and is marked by borders of a different kind, the kind we construct to order the narrative of our lives. We use deaths to close or to distinguish chapters in this narrative. Private deaths, public deaths — the ends of others are put to our own ends, to mark our own ends . . . and thus, implicitly, our beginnings.

To come of age in the sixties was to walk a landscape of dramatic chiaroscuro. The lightning, the psychedelia, the sunshine of that time owe their vividness in part to the ubiquitous shadow of death. There was the blanket carnage of Viet Nam, rendered intimate by technology; there were the stunning casualties of the civil wars — the shocking deaths of the civil rights movement, the singular debacles of Kent State and Jackson State Universities; there were the rock-and-roll deaths, the Altamont side of Woodstock Nation; and there were the stellar deaths, that rapid fall of leaders.

Vaclav Havel has said that while many of his — our — generation cite as the most momentous day in their lives November 22, 1963, he has always felt John Lennon's death to have left a more profound mark on him than John Kennedy's. I was slightly shocked when I heard this, but it was the shock of recognition. Was it that John embodied the force, the energy that touched my formulating adolescent self most deeply, most intimately? Yes, but more: it was that somehow the deaths are related. JFK was the first, the cataclysm that — no matter how you felt about him — blasted the world open; in some way John Lennon was the last. Not the last momentous, sudden, premature death we will live through, but the last of those. After John, something was really over.

We had kept the faith through the seventies — our twenties, that weird, inchoate time. The Beatles were no more, except as a Byzantine (or Dickensian) ongoing lawsuit. In August of '77 the King was Dead, victim to his own mythology. But the War was finally over, Nixon had gone away, and how long could polyester leisure suits last, realistically speaking? Then — a month before John died, I remind myself — Ronald Reagan was elected. It was the eighties, and John's death clinched it, showed us just how mean and crazy it was going to get. After John, we were all grown up, as we swore we never would be, as we were constantly accused of refusing to be, as we somehow thought we wouldn't have to be. Finally his death left us no choice.

The "where were you" game is a generational favorite: seek out the historic moments (usually disastrous) and hook them into your own life. We play this game so that history may magnify our lives, and so that our lives may give substance and reality to history. We anchor individual memory in the collective, and vice-versa. These moments function as buoys in the sea of time; we clutch them to recall our lost selves from the deep. I have played along with the rest, except when it came to December 8, 1980. That night I have not wanted to revisit. Until very recently, I have failed to acknowledge how much was there, of irony, of innocence, of loss. I know — and I think perhaps I knew at the time — that I was crossing over, from one life to another. It is time to turn back.

2. Is there anybody going to listen to my story . . . .

It is exam week at the end of a long fall term at Kalamazoo College, where I am beginning my fourth year of teaching. I am also completing the second year of the most profound romantic relationship of my life, with a man who touches me so deeply on so many levels that I feel myself a swimmer in a vast ocean, alternately and simultaneously delighted, empowered, terrified. The second year together has often felt shaky; I have sometimes sensed I was willing myself not to be still and look around. Finally, in October, the whole edifice gave way in the most humiliating cir-

cumstances. *For me, it was like one of those Twilight Zone or Avengers episodes where people die according to their own worst fears. The Other Woman stepped in, the whole world knew before I did, the man did one of those sudden, absolute shifts of direction of which men seem much more capable than women, and I am living out a private nightmare of abandonment, rejection, obsession, and endless, cycling pain.*

I can accept neither the simplicity nor the ordinariness of what has happened to us. I feel virginal; nothing I went through at sixteen or twenty has prepared me for this; I have no referent. Consequently, the pure intensity of sixteen couples with the complexity of thirty, two antipathetic fronts producing a kind of tornado in the middle of my life. I attempt repeatedly, in vain, to encompass it with my intellect. The persistence of the tumult frightens me, so that the primal pain is overlain with fear, of how much I can hurt and for how long. I begin a year-long slog through the wilderness. I feel raw, reduced to primary components. The story of my life, the plot I have been unfolding in my bright new adult professional existence, has wandered off into babbling chaos.

One of the many simple truths about the loss of love of which I am ignorant is that it lasts a long time. It is a process, not an event. But I don't know this. I keep crashing on the rocks and thinking, "Well, this is finally it, the bottom, the worst." And, of course, it isn't. On into December we go.

On the evening of the eighth, we are sitting in my living room, going back through the sloughs and thickets, but more deeply than ever. Through the curtain of pain I see myself and him clearly, and I see the end, irrevocable and empty-eyed. I feel myself being born, yanked into an adult womanhood I can only guess is somehow necessary, or at least inexorable.

At eleven o'clock, the phone rings.

My friends don't usually call at this hour, but I don't think about this as I go quickly into the bedroom to answer. I am preoccupied, I want to be back in the living room, near the vortex of my existence.

"Grif?" Marigene is my oldest friend in Kalamazoo. Apart from him, she is the only one who calls me by that name. Both of them came to it independently of each other, not knowing that my dad was never called anything else in adulthood, and that my older brother uses it as well.

"Listen, have you got the news on? John Lennon's been shot in New York. He's dead. They've got the guy who did it."

I remember emitting the requisite "ohmygod" and getting a brief rundown of the known details. But what I remember most clearly is a lone, clear, sad thought: "Of course. Of course John is dead. I am losing my life. It figures." At that moment, John's shattered skull, his blood staining the pavement outside the Dakota, Yoko's screams, Sean's little lonely face are all secondary details in the drama of my life. I cannot see over, under,

110 Season of the Witch

around, or through anything as large as this pain.

It is almost as if John's murder is a crashing chord in the opera of my tragic love, just as he and the other three have provided the soundtrack of my life since 1964, when Paul became my first love. Not that the soundtrack was incidental or trivial; quite the contrary: it was integral, as in a good film. Literally or metaphorically, for the past sixteen years there has always been a Beatles song in the background of my life. And now, when that life has veered off the edge into meaninglessness, John's life has oozed out onto a cold sidewalk in New York. John's monster has caught up with him: the adoration that wishes to possess and devour; and mine — the terror of abandonment — has found me out as well.

I walk back into the living room and say, "John Lennon's been killed." This means next to nothing to the man I am losing. We dive back into our mutual maelstrom and the night goes on. As for me, John's is a loss I cannot register now; there is no room for it. It waits until this cyclone has left my earth cool and quiet.

3. Strange days indeed . . . .

I have gone back to John's death since. I have put myself on the sidewalk outside the Dakota while the shots were fired — fired, after all, by one of us, one of those who loved him, enough to sign John's name in a motel registry; one of those who so deeply connected John with certain ideals that the notion that John had somehow "sold out" had actually fueled the decision to shoot him. I have heard myself call to John, warning him, as he moves from the car door to the building. I have reached, in imagination, to grab Mark David Chapman's sleeve as he rises from the curb, Salinger in one hand, gun in the other. I have made the small motion that might have saved us this. I have stood, in my mind, over John's body; I have felt grief, pity, shock, but most of all anger. A sharp rage that refuses to accept. Not so much that John should have died at all or died violently, but that he should have died then.

For John's life was taking a graceful shape by the fall of 1980. His particular pilgrimage was bringing him out of the woods into daylight, I think. The prematurely embittered Liverpool kid — no working-class hero at all but a quite middle-class boy whose deprivations were mostly emotional (the absent, indifferent father, the absent, mythic mother run down in the street) — had become the reluctant, cynical star, obsessively given to jokes about "cripples" and analogies with Jesus. The wit was not merely rapier-like, but poisoned at the tip and, like Hamlet's, destined for himself. The light brown eyes could go utterly flat, opaque; and then they could betray leagues of tenderness and hurt. In one of his later interviews he said that the first serious song he ever wrote was "Help" — a strange choice, until you listen again.

It is that James Dean quality, of course, the wounded child behind the sullen exterior, that male as well as female fans found so compelling (for John was the Beatle that boys liked). There was no hurt we could bring to him that John wouldn't understand. For us girls, that reservoir of sadness, loneliness, was enough to draw our attention away from the violence, the misogyny of the man who'd rather see you dead, little girl, than to see you with another man. Robert Bly would identify the problem here as the unhealed wound inflicted by the absent father, and surely the appalling Fred Lennon was enough to wound any son irreparably. But for me, where there is such woman-hating, there is a loss of mother, literal or figurative. "I lost her twice," John said,[2] once at age five, when she left him to Aunt Mimi to raise, and again at seventeen, when she died. The bitterness and misogyny of the boy thus "abandoned" bespeak the Mother's exile from his psyche. Paradoxically, it is he who then finds himself exiled, and his quest must be to rediscover the motherland.

Paul (motherless himself at fourteen) has said that John was the one who tried everything first and right away. The liminal pioneer, the fantastic voyager. I think this is why he was the most important to people. They lusted after Paul (I certainly did anyway), admired George, loved Ringo, but revered John, the quester. The vicious hybrid of racism and sexism that whirled around Yoko Ono at the time of her appearance in his life — and that lingers today in comedians' routines and journalists' asides — was not only a cruel insult to her and the worst return his admirers could have made John, but was also obtuse, wildly so, in failing to grasp him. Every quester has a guide. And when you move out beyond Beatles, you are really at the edge of the world.

In his song to Julia on the White Album, John said that Ocean Child called him. Yoko's name means "ocean child." Seven-and-a-half years John's senior, she became the guide over the waters of memory, the doorway back to his mother, the lost, beautiful Julia. He began to call Yoko "mother." And on their voyage, one of the most significant things to which she opened his nearsighted eyes was the worldwide oppression of women. There was to be no maternal embrace, no return to the warm womb, without a grown-up man's acknowledgment that more than cars run women down on a daily basis.

With Yoko, the conceptual artist, he began a process of deprogramming, shedding layers of attachment to the world's ruses, stripping himself down to some kind of existential core. But in this quest for authenticity and integrity, John, like every hero, had to undergo his season of wandering in the wilderness. True to her role as guide, it was

Yoko who kicked John out. Knowing he was not ready for her yet, that he had to live out his self-destructive nightmares until they were over, she banished him from the Dakota into the desert of L.A. and some years of symbolic death. And then the return, the reunion, confirmed by Sean's birth on his father's thirty-fifth birthday, in his mother's forty-second year, after several miscarriages. Finally, the most radical transformation of John's life, his five years as full-time father, his guitar hung on the wall, while Yoko ran the show and took the flak. For the first time in years, he called his first son, the lonely Julian, to his side. What he learned in this immurement in the "personal," he said, was what women's lives are like. Well, hardly. But it was a start.

Intense fulfillment punctuated by panic attacks: what if he never recorded again? What if everyone forgot him? Who was he if his name was not in Billboard? But artistic creativity returned along with everything else. "Double Fantasy" is the record of and testament to this time of renewal. You can hear John's new universe in "Beautiful Boy" and "Woman," in which he whispers, under the opening guitar chords, "For the other half of the sky." It began to look like John Winston Ono Lennon had found something like peace. Not the absence of conflict, but the presence of something he had never known. A profound reconciliation with "the little child inside your man," as he put it in "Woman."

He was forty — the absolute horizon for the sixties imagination — and life was better than the Beatles and much more real. He had grown real enough to do, over the years, embarrassing things in public — bags and acorns and primal screams and billboards. But when I read, in huge print above a highway, "WAR IS OVER IF YOU WANT IT. LOVE, JOHN AND YOKO," I almost believed it, as I had almost believed that all you need is love. He deconstructed his own power, as one of the Fab Four, by insisting on ours. "Who on earth d'you think you are?" he asked in "Instant Karma":

> *A superstar?*
> *Well, alright you are!*
> *Well, we all shine on . . . .*

It wasn't going to be half bad, growing up, middle age, growing old, because John would be there, liminal voyager still but now one of us, embarrassing himself, daring the most sophisticated naivety, testing the margins, confessing, metamorphosing, full of possibilities, making us believe. And always rocking on. "The sixties were just waking up in the morning, y'know," he said, "and we haven't even got to dinnertime yet, and I can't wait; I just can't wait, I'm so glad to be around."[3]

———— ·—·❧·—· ————

That it was at this moment that he was blown out like a candle still seems outrageous, grotesque. The night he died, one of the emotions rolling through me was a kindred sense of injustice. I, too, had earned my happy ending, I believed. I had done my stint in the wilderness: five numbed-out years in graduate school, family disintegrations, romantic cul-de-sacs, immobilizing depressions. I had a memory of curling in a ball on my bed, wishing to God I had the courage to swallow a lot of pills. As John had found daylight again, somewhere in New York City, I had found myself in Kalamazoo, Michigan, of all places. In my new professorial incarnation, I had felt the shock of rebirth. A job that took everything I could give and made ample return, supportive friends and colleagues, publications, a growing, inspiriting feminist consciousness . . . and then, love, big and deep. Love, the brass ring. And hadn't I earned it all? I approached thirty as a sunstruck precipice from which I could look benignly out over my redeemed life. And then in a New York minute, "chaos is come again," as Othello says.

The lesson I began to learn on the night of December 8th was a hard one: that life has no respect for the meanings we construct for it. Life refuses to be a novel. It has no plot we haven't written for it and rewritten in the face of its digressions, and no respect for our notions of justice or merit, teleology or earned endings. As for love, that turned out not to be all we needed, in New York or Kalamazoo. Any stranger on the street could walk into your life and send it reeling off-course. Any hand could blow it to smithereens. And life, in all its terrible indifference, would do its usual thing: life would go on. Obla di, obla da. There was nothing you could do John had told us — but you could learn how to be you inside, it's easy! Yeah, well, maybe not so easy.

Most of all, in calling back that cold December night, I think of a loss of faith that was for me personal, generational, mythic. My shattering loss of faith in the man I loved and in myself as a lovable person was part of a vaster loss of faith in life's benignity and integrity. And that faith had something to do with the intensity and passion of adolescence, echoed in the music to which I "came up," the music that shaped me — their music, which, even at its most mournful, ironic, or poignant, was always deeply vital and on some level joyous.

It is easy to trivialize this loss of faith as a post-sixties clash with what is called "reality" — unless you happened to live through it. Most of us did. One of us was Mark David Chapman. He says he went after John because he believed John had "sold out" on the promise and promises of the sixties. Like ours, his faith and its loss somehow came to center on John Lennon.

The dream is over, what can I say?
I was the walrus, but now I'm John,
And so, dear friends, you'll just have to carry on . . . .

4. We all shine on

In an interview just before his death, John said of his new album, "I was visualizing all the people of my age group. I'm singing to them. I'm saying, 'Here I am now; how are you? How's your relationship? Did you get through it all? Wasn't the seventies a drag, y'know? Here we are; well, let's try to make the eighties good . . . .'" [4]

Oh, John, they turned out worse. Most peculiar, mama. Talk about a drag. Amnesia settled in like thick cloud cover. It was lonely. A driven, exiled, bitter time. We all got older, some of us got old, many died. One of them was the man who was leaving me that night. A plague came, and he was one of its sacrifices. As the decade slogged on, I missed you more, I felt your loss more intimately. I wonder if it's you I'm mourning or some idea of you, some nostalgic fantasy, some notion of what died with you. I want to do you justice, to grant you the individuated, single life that the unparalleled fame refused you, but maybe that's impossible.

Sometimes I think I see you around the corner, smiling your Buddha smile. What a terrific old man you'd have become. I imagine you on a talk show with Paul, at 72, cackling and reminiscing, giving each other shit. And there I am, 62 or so, on the edge of my chair, drinking it in with my Scotch. I guess I'll never get over you guys.

I thought I'd never get over him, either, in December of 1980. And while I eventually stopped bleeding internally and found love again, I turned out to be right, in the main. Maybe that's one of the few pieces of middle-aged wisdom that have come to me since that night in December: you never really get over anything; you take it all with you. Everyone you've been stays inside you. If you live long enough, you become like a tree, rings within rings, or like a matryoshka doll. And what you get, instead of endings, happy or otherwise, is something less dramatic but possibly more interesting: you get life going on, bringing those odd fraternal twins, Continuity and Change. You get the alchemy that occurs when the new stuff slides into the mix with the old. That's also true of music, as you knew, and of love.

Our lives didn't really intersect that night. You were condemned to die by a random hand; I got a life sentence. I had to live on, past love's devastation, into the rhythmic, pragmatic understandings of midlife. Just like starting over — and over and over and over. The curse of eternal loss and circularity, and also the ultimate reprieve, the blessing of passage and renewal.

You were right, we all shine on. Here in the dark, when I look up, I still see you, brightest of all.

Part Two

The Space Between
On Teaching

The boundary is the best place for acquiring knowledge.

—Paul Tillich

This perception invites us to refuse to run the classroom
like a conveyance, designed to transport children
from the private to the public world,
but to make it instead a real space in the middle,
where we can all stop and rest and work
to find the political and epistemological forms
that will mediate the oppositions of home and workplace.

—Madeleine Grumet

8

On Not Knowing What We're Doing
Teaching as the Art of Faithful Failure

Florence J. Lucasse Lecture[1]
Kalamazoo College
May 16, 1990

In late February, I found myself on a hilltop in western Virginia, at a bucolic paradise called the Virginia Center for the Creative Arts. Both my bedroom and my studio looked out to the Blue Ridge across miles of fields, pines, dogwood, redbud, and black-and-white cows. The silence was luxurious. Yet within a few days I was having tortured dreams. One went as follows:

> *I'm teaching in a huge Greek amphitheater, packed with students. They are raucous, wild, utterly contemptuous and defiant. I am frantically moving from the back of the space down to the front, trying to locate a position of authority from which to gain control, but the chaos goes on. I turn to speak to the one sympathetic student about the situation, and when I turn back, the room is empty. The students have walked out. "That does it," I mutter. "I'm going to see the President right now. I'm resigning. I don't have to take this."*

The next morning at breakfast, I was telling my fellow artists-in-residence about this dream, from which I had awakened with heart pounding. The others listened with genuine sympathetic interest. One woman said, "You mean teachers have teaching dreams, like students have exam dreams?" I assured her that we did, but mine, I said, usually beset me back in Kalamazoo, the week before a quarter starts. Another woman, obviously moved by my confession, leaned toward me and said, with palpable concern, "And are your students hostile to you?"

That's when I began to laugh. Realizing that some explanation was in order, I explained that I'd just received the college's award for teaching.

As I walked out of this building last September, after being notified about the Lucasse Award, I vowed to myself that it would bring me respite from the unremitting self-doubt and self-flagellation that accompany me as a teacher. And it worked — for about a week, as I recall. Then it was business as usual inside my head: the amphitheater resounding with contempt and then suddenly empty.

I had another thought as I left the building last September: *Oh, God — this means I have to give a lecture about teaching! And I don't know how to do it yet!* Lest you think I'm being falsely modest, I ask those of you who teach to ask yourselves whether you could look into a mirror and say, "Yep, I've got this thing licked. I really know what I'm doing in a classroom. I know how to teach." I might be wrong, but what I hear around the faculty tables in the Snack Bar and in this room during our pedagogy workshops is how miserably we're all doing, how incorrigible this or that class is, how impossible and hopeless is this task for which we are paid, and how little we know about it.

My friend Norma Bailey, class of '69, a legendary teacher, when asked what she teaches, says, "I teach kids." And there, friends, is the rub: once we make that shift from thinking of ourselves as teaching some*thing* to thinking of ourselves as teaching some*one*, we say goodbye to any hope of those comforting certainties we think we ought to have about method and about "doing it right." If what you teach is people, your "subject matter" is never static, or coherent, or homogeneous. Students have this annoying habit of being alive. And like other living things, they drag their whole experience into the present moment in our classrooms. Of course, the other part of the equation is the teacher: we're alive too, and along with our texts and notes and slides and stacks of graded papers, we tote into the classroom our entire lives.

It's unspeakably risky business.

And so it goes: you come out of fall quarter trailing clouds of glory, bearing evaluations attesting to your worthiness for sainthood. Then comes winter quarter and within a week you're a disgrace to the profession and your classroom is a scene from *Night of the Living Dead*.

My colleagues, it really is quite an absurd profession we're in. For one thing, it's the only one I can think of for which the practitioner is not trained. It never ceases to amaze me that we spend four or five or more years and a lot of money accruing letters after our names and becoming proficient in all aspects of The Profession save the one for which we will be hired: teaching. Given the consumer mind-set of our students these days, it's probably a good thing they don't think a lot about this or we'd be in court most of the time.

For another thing, no matter what the "assessment" fanatics tell you, ours is a profession in which the results are only minimally and very superficially measurable. Is our success best gauged by a standardized test on the last day of class, or at the end of four years? By graduate-school placement rates, or earning potential? By a two-a.m. conversation in a residence hall that we'll never hear? Or by some obscure moment of truth in a student's life five or ten years away from this place?

And finally, ours is a profession where no two practitioners can seem to agree on the objective. Professor A wants to establish competence in the discipline. B wants to develop critical intelligence. C wants to stimulate personal growth. D wants to impart a firm grounding in Western culture. E wants to instill basic skills. F wants to insure professional success. And G wants to deconstruct patriarchal racist Eurocentric heterosexist capitalist hegemony. Of course, it's also true that if we ask any randomly selected group of students, we'll get a similarly diverse array of responses.

So here we are in these ivied halls, the students paying far too much and we being paid far too little to engage in an enterprise for which we haven't been trained and which nobody really understands, towards ends about which nobody really agrees and results which cannot be reliably measured. But we gather in classrooms at the beginning of each term, knowing that something's going to happen, that something's going to change — or we hope so. And once in a while, everybody goes away smiling, agreeing that it's working: something's happened, something's changed, and we're all better for it. And once in a great while, something very big happens, something profound and moving, and the students actually believe it's worth twenty thousand, and we wonder why people do anything else with their lives.

Talk about your leaps of faith.

In January of 1984, Ian Oliver, then our Assistant Dean of the Chapel, gave a sermon in which he defined ministry as "The Art of Faithful Failure." As he spoke, I found myself substituting "teaching" every time he said "ministry," but we might as well substitute "learning" too. It is the art of faithful failure in which we are engaged here, all of us — the ceaseless discovery of how much we don't know, how bound we are by the circumstances of our lives. Or, as T. S. Eliot put it, "each venture / Is a new beginning, a raid on the inarticulate / with shabby equipment always deteriorating."[2] Sisyphus might have said that the rock seems to be getting bigger every day and the angle of the hill steeper every term.

So here I am accepting an award for the faithfulness of my failure in this very dangerous enterprise of mucking around inside young heads. I considered — very briefly — recounting tonight my most memorable failures in the classroom. There was the women's studies seminar that left me feeling that perhaps the conservatives on the faculty were right. There was the Expository Prose class where one day I felt something snap in my head and the next moment I was hurling the chalk to the floor and bellowing, "If I'd wanted to teach high school I wouldn't have bothered getting a Ph.D.!" There was the Victorian Lit class that began slow, went straight downhill, and reached its nadir in a near free-for-all with a student on the sidewalk outside Dewing Hall. There was the Intro to Literary Study class where it suddenly came to me in a blinding epiphany that the explanation for the unaccountable array of D's on the most recent set of papers was that I had asked the students to demonstrate skill in something I hadn't yet taught them how to do.

Alternately, I considered rifling through thirteen years of evaluations and pulling the real prizewinners to read to you tonight, beginning with the one inscribed diagonally across every inch of the page in close-packed, angry scrawl, telling me in rich detail (and of course telling the Provost and Personnel Committee as well) how utterly intellectually deficient and pedagogically corrupt my course had been.

That way madness lies. So I'll try another direction: Have you noticed that the most inarticulate student, who could never in a million years give you a definition of good teaching, can always tell you instantly who his or her good teachers have been? So I thought that instead of discoursing upon teaching, I'd tell you about teachers — some of my teachers.

My first, greatest teacher was the woman who gave me words. It was she who delighted in the words I invented and imaginary friends I brought home and the inner life I narrated. It was she who smiled whenever I was reading, whatever I was reading. It was she who thrust the entire thousand pages of *Gone With the Wind* into my hands the summer I was ten and bored, and *Jane Eyre* when I was fifteen. It was she who taught me what feminism was about long before either of us knew what it meant. It was she who thought that becoming a teacher was the finest thing I could do with my life, and it was she who first told me that I was a writer. Her name is Barbara Hamel and she's my mother.

After her there were many. At Bloomfield Hills Junior High there was Mrs. Sonneborn, who greeted us in Japanese every day, and who withheld the gleaming 100% for which I lusted on sentence-diagramming quizzes because I could not get the damned indirect object right. It was exquisite torture, but even at the time I knew somehow that she understood my drive to comprehend the workings of words and that she was withholding not *from* me but *for* me the small, deep thrill of getting the indirect object right.

At Northwestern University there was John Margolis, who taught a weekly three-hour evening seminar in Victorian literature, who leaned forward in genuine excitement and encouragement when I fumbled to explain why Tennyson's grief for a dead friend should mushroom into an extended poetic search for God, and who then quoted me for the rest of the class session. To this day I can quote verbatim his glowing comment on one of my papers.

There was also Jeff Prince, who taught the Senior Honors Seminar on Keats and Shelley. He made "Shelley" plural — a great rarity at the time — so that we could read *Frankenstein* too. My utter immersion in the two huge seminar papers I wrote for him is perhaps my dearest memory of my senior year, which he turned into the intellectual thrill that sent me spinning toward a career.

And also toward his alma mater, Mr. Jefferson's University in Charlottesville, Virginia, where my two most significant teachers were, ironically and aptly, not officially my teachers at all. One was Janice Carlisle, an untenured woman who befriended me and let me audit her Victorian novel course. It was while watching Janice in the classroom that I first knew for sure that I wanted to do this, and while watching how she fared in the department that I first had an inkling of the prices women pay. The other was Suzette Henke, whom I barely knew, but who was the sole member of that department who openly worked on women writers. When I recall avoiding her classes and ridiculing her feminism along with the other graduate students in order to blend seamlessly into the fabric, I cringe. I would like to thank her now, wherever she is, for the courage it must have taken, and for planting seeds, however indirectly, that would germinate here in Kalamazoo. They say that when the student is ready, the teacher is there. Suzette was there, but this student, though needing her desperately, wasn't ready, and I'm sorry for that.

That brings me here. The student was ready by then, and oh, were the teachers there, in abundance. Many are no longer among us — gone from the College; gone from this earth. Many are here tonight. My most significant teachers have been the Kalamazoo students, who teach me daily what it is I ought to do the next moment, or the next day, or the next time I teach the course, or for the rest of my life. This has been one of the great surprises of teaching: that along with teaching what you already know, you also wind up teaching what you're on the verge of knowing, or want to know, or need to know, and that some of your best, most satisfying teaching comes at that scary precipice. I thought this was a peculiarly personal truth until I read Audre Lorde's words: "Teaching is also learning. Teach what you need to learn."[3] My students always bring me to what I don't know, so that I can learn it. Thanks to them I have unofficial degrees in crisis counseling, feminist therapy, and political organizing. In fact, it is largely thanks to them that I know anything about

women's studies at all. My best teachers have been the students in struggle. Those who struggle with words teach me how difficult language is,
and how powerful. Those who struggle with feminism clarify my own
struggles. Those who wrestle with a novel or poem make me wrestle with
it beyond my teacherly certainties and controls. In talking to those moving through their own impossible lives, I have found ways to navigate my
own.

Another surprise has been how much teaching and learning
depends upon relationship: the relation of teacher and student, and the
relation of knower to known. Our educational system is geared to pro-
duce what the authors of *Women's Ways of Knowing* call "procedural separate" knowers:[4] those competent, cooperative students proficient in the
terms of our disciplines, replicating our discourses and methodologies as
distinct subjects mastering discrete objects. In recent years my own obser-
vations and conversations with students have led me to believe that there
is a deep, echoing void at the heart of this kind of knowing, not felt by all
students, perhaps, but sensed by many. I have heard the void in papers
written in that competent, highly intellectual, and highly alien voice —
papers which, regardless of the grade they receive (often high), leave the
author alienated and depressed. Often I have discovered that a "writer's
block" is in fact a shutdown after a long season of procedural separate
knowing — a refusal to participate, as it were. I have heard the void as
well in discussions where students tell me, with simultaneous contempt
and sadness, how easy it was to get an A in a given class once one
learned how to play the game. They may brag about their proficiency in
the game, but there is often a deep disappointment beneath the cynicism.
When speaking of other courses brings a light into their eyes, you'll hear
a different story: they will say they changed or grew in that course, or
that they felt valued or freer to speak. They will speak of the class — the
teacher and the other students — with nostalgia. The course became a
complex relationship, a temporary community. Whatever the grade —
and it is often not an A — they know the material in a way that procedur-
al-separate success stories can't approach. They will talk about the course
material as if it belonged to them. Which it does. They were drawn into
relationship with it.

To enter fully into the relationship called teaching is to assume a
terrible power. I think that above all I have learned from my students
how powerful I am. The power has sometimes thrilled me when I've felt
I've used it well, frightened me when I've used it or seen it used badly or
negligently, and at all times chastened me. In classroom discussions of
educational process, I have often wished I could transport all of you into
the room, invisibly, so you could hear how powerful you are: how deeply
they value the time you listened so carefully to them in class, as if what

they said was important, or the time you seemed enlightened by a point
they'd made, or the time you pulled a lecture out of what had been said
in discussion the day before. You used your power to make them feel
their own potential.

I believe that education as a relationship that empowers has
never been more critical. Our students are up against a culture that
defines power as conquest, willfulness, or ownership, that atomizes and
disintegrates, that batters them with ugly noise and vicious imagery, and
that inculcates cynicism as a shield against vulnerability. I have joined as
heartily as the next person in railing against how hopelessly warped their
values are, the children of this culture. But if we peel away the top layer,
what they really are is hungry. It's that void again, that place whose
echoes tell them, like a growl in the stomach, that nourishment is wanting. What they want is connection — with themselves, with us, with others, with the past, with ideas, with the world. Western culture as currently
operating won't do much to assuage that hunger; it's a culture of consumption, but an hour later you're hungry again. Our students need
more. Theirs is a hunger that often they cannot identify or name for us.
It's buried under that protective cynicism, waiting until someone comes
out of the intellectual closet to tell them that hunger is the beginning of
wisdom and to offer them an apple.

Joseph Campbell said, "If you really want to help in this world,
what you're going to have to teach is how to live in it."[5] That's the conclusion I came to round about 1972, and that is why I am here. I believe
that whatever our students might say they want — an A, less writing, med
school, to be left alone — what they are really looking to us for is some
inkling of how to live in this world. And I believe that whatever it is we're
teaching — George Eliot or molecular biology — we have something to
tell them that will help them move further into the power of their own
hearts and minds. If that's what we're trying to do, faithful in our constant
failures, then even in this ridiculous profession where we don't know
what we're doing, we're doing all right.

9

The Lone Ranger and his faithful Indian companion, Tonto, were fleeing a Comanche war party, which was rapidly gaining on them.

"Faster, Tonto, faster!" cried the Masked Man, and Tonto replied, "Yes, Kimosabe."

The Lone Ranger spotted a turn-off into a small canyon. "This way, Tonto!" he cried, and Tonto replied, "Yes, Kimosabe."

But the Comanches made the same turn. Just as he felt an arrow whiz past his ear, the Lone Ranger looked ahead and saw that the other end of the canyon was a solid wall of rock, with no possibility of escape. "Tonto, it looks like we're in trouble," said the Masked Man. And Tonto replied . . .

Who's "We," White Man?

April 26, 1991
Stetson Chapel, Kalamazoo College

Do you remember the name of the actor who played Tonto? Jay Silverheels. I remember his name because it's so beautiful, but also because he was the only Indian on television, or certainly the only one in a major continuing role — the role of a man whose name, in Spanish, means "stupid," and whose virtue lay in his fidelity to the white man and his alienation from his own people. That is, a Good Indian.

Next year we celebrate the 500th anniversary of the so-called "discovery" of this continent by the man who, in fact, by means of his own geographic confusion, made Tonto an "Indian." It was his followers who made the concept of a Good Indian necessary as an exception to the rule — the Indian who was inherently vicious. Who is the "we". who will celebrate this arrival?

That question was drawn up to the surface of my mind last week by a seemingly unlikely hook: a conversation with a relatively new colleague about the inauguration of the College's new president. I was bitching and moaning about how my weekend would be eaten up before it started. "And of course there's the Inauguration tomorrow."

She whispered conspiratorially, "So don't go."

What I felt was akin to shock, a small, sharp electric shock. Don't go? To the inauguration of the President of Kalamazoo College?

"Oh," she nodded sympathetically, "you feel like you have to."

"No, no," I assured her, "I'm tenured, remember? I want to go."

Now, I hope President Bryan doesn't take this personally, but that was not quite it either.[1] I did want to go; I thoroughly enjoy ritual and what my college roommate called "pompous circumstances." But thinking about the conversation later, I realized that the issue was not simple personal predilection. The fact is that I was committed to participating in the inaugural ceremony because I was part of it. It was mine. A major ritual in the life of this college took place in this space last Saturday afternoon, and this college is a "we" that includes "me."

Which is pretty ironic, since every day I am palpably aware of the extent to which the language, the structures of knowledge, the behavior, the traditions of this college marginalize me. For example, in late April we mark Founders Day with a formal convocation here in the chapel. The April in which the college was actually founded was in 1833. But until thirty-seven years later, this college did not even award degrees to persons of my gender. Whose Founders Day? Founders of what?

Last Friday we heard a fine chapel talk on the spirit of professionalism,[2] as contained in the original meaning of the verb "to profess": that is, the spirit in which one takes solemn vows, committing oneself to a higher purpose and power. This impulse, this spirit, is one in which I can participate; that is what my "profession" feels like to me, and what professionalism means to me personally. However, the verb "to profess" has several other traditional meanings, including "to own" and "to claim." And the history of professionalism and of the four so-called Professions — law, medicine, the clergy, and teaching — is deeply imbued with ownership and the staking of claims. It is difficult for me to separate the spirit of professionalism from its historical reality, in which a minute group of people laid claims to ownership of knowledge while others — anyone poor, anyone black or brown or red or yellow, anyone female; in fact, the vast majority of the human race — were barred from membership. Who's "we," professional man?

Until very recently, the practice of law was no-woman's land, and so far as I can see the spirit of the law remains so; otherwise it would not have such tremendous difficulty defining and punishing sexual harassment, battery of women, and rape. As for the clergy and medicine, those were ancient female professions professionalized right out of our hands and utterly transformed away from our image so that even when we have fought our way back into them we find ourselves strangers in a strange land.

That leaves teaching — always women's work, from time immemorial. Except, of course, at colleges and universities, which originated, after all, in monasteries, and where teachers are called professors, often do more professing than teaching, and usually get paid a lot more to do it. It is this knowledge that makes the walk down one of these aisles, dressed in the polyester descendent of a monk's robe and a hood bearing the colors of a state university which refused to admit women until 1969 an extremely complicated act for me. In fact, now that I think about it, perhaps one of the reasons I like to do it is because it brings the submerged contradictions of my life up into my immediate awareness. When I put on the outfit and take the walk, there is a passage I always recite to myself. It comes from Virginia Woolf's advice to women in 1938:

> Let us never cease from thinking — what is this 'civilization' in which we find ourselves? What are these ceremonies and why should we take part in them? What are these professions and why should we make money out of them? Where in short is it leading us, the procession of the sons of educated men?[3]

In other words: Who's "we," white man?

Ah, you say, but that's history, that's the past. Now, anyone can be admitted to the club. Which sounds generous, humane, and liberal, doesn't it? How surprised — understandably surprised — are these sons in this procession, then, when they learn that we draw a line between joining and assimilating; that we join in the wholeness of ourselves, with our own traditions and priorities, and with no particular need to drop those and adopt theirs. In fact, our particular need is often to do just exactly the opposite. How hurt they seem, or sometimes outraged, when we indicate that we have other loyalties. How stunned they appear when we say that their standards and traditions, which they have always genuinely regarded as objective and universal, are subjective and particular; that what they have never doubted to be reasonable and just appears to us unreasonable and unjust. How nonplused they are to discover that some of us, some gifted, talented ones of us who were their number-one draft picks, do not thrive among them. How skeptical and defensive they are, always, when we indicate that we feel our difference from the prevailing "we" on a daily basis, in the simplest of interactions, in the classroom, in the office, in the hallways, in the language spoken, the body postures assumed, the habits observed. This difference is apparently so elusive to them that they accuse us of "finding" discrimination everywhere. We shake our heads: far from finding it, we try to find some way to escape it, but it finds us every time.

In short, how distressed they become when they have our common experience: they hear a "we" and know it doesn't include them. To assert another "we" in contradistinction to the prevailing "we," the dominant "we," if you will, is considered divisive. What it does, as the Chinese say, is to "break the roundness." Kalamazoo College, like other small communities (including families), is a very round place. What it does, our Other "we," is to disrupt the unity that has been asserted to exist. What it does is to acknowledge the differences that have been there all along, sometimes buried in the understandable but futile attempt to avoid what is scary, sometimes ignored in that pernicious confidence, so beloved of academe, that "we" know what is transcendent, what is important, what is "universal," what is worth attention. But sure as I'm standing here, those who will be accused, not of calling attention to this rupture of an otherwise harmonious and homogeneous group but of causing it, are those who ask, "Who's 'we,' white man?"

———

Who *is* "we"?

I am going to venture the claim that this is the most pressing, painful question facing us here at the end of this century. As individuals, as Americans, as world citizens, as students, as intellectuals, we face the crucial challenge of identifying the unities we need as human beings in order to think and act and live together and to make the world intelligible, without denying or effacing the multiplicity and heterogeneity which constitute the human landscape.

In the academic world, this challenge is extremely pronounced at the present hour. It kind of feels like Matthew Arnold's post-Darwinian darkling plain, where "ignorant armies clash by night." An admittedly confusing array of "knowledge claims" has driven one army backwards, into a nostalgic retreat toward an academic world where the boundaries were clearly defined: disciplines were distinct and pure, canons of cultural literacy told you what was important to know, and objective tests told you what you'd learned (or taught); God was in his heaven, all was right with the world, and when somebody said "we," by golly, you knew what he meant: "We as opposed to They," or, more recently, "We, which includes everybody, as long as they're like Us or at least willing to do a convincing imitation."

The mighty "we" of that intellectual establishment has been shaken to its soul in the last twenty years. But it's still standing. The Ideal of Culture struggles to withstand the imperative of multiculturalism, exactly as the ideal of unity struggles with the claims of diversity. The masked man knows he's in trouble, and when he calls on what he thinks is his closest companion, he gets that awful question. I am, on one level, truly sorry for him. It is a hard thing to feel the verities on which you have built your life eroding. But the question must be asked and must be answered. Tonto's survival depends upon it. And if he only knew it, so does the Lone Ranger's.

As it is in the intellectual world, so it is in our society, in our neighborhoods, on our campus, in our departments and classrooms, and inside our busy heads. This year, in my own department, I have learned not only how hard it is to answer Tonto's question, but how hard it is to ask it — and ask it, and keep asking it. My English Department is a "we" in the midst of tremendous transition. It is a "we" that has failed to ask itself many necessary and painful questions. It is a "we" to which I belong deeply in many ways and have never belonged in others. It is a "we" on whose margins I have worked like a scout, riding around looking for possibilities and dangers. I am the central pivot in its turning, and I am also the loose wheel about to fly off, according to some assessments. To ride out these contradictions while continually asking Tonto's question is dizzying and exhausting.

Sometimes I reward myself. For instance, this quarter I am teaching an upper-level women's studies seminar on the works of Toni Morrison. From the beginning of her first novel, *The Bluest Eye*, to the close of her latest, *Beloved*, Morrison is passionately concerned with the concept of "the village" — the neighborhood, one's people, the folks, the "we" that African Americans have forged out of the dissociations and dislocations of slavery and its aftermath. Morrison is neither naive nor idealistic about villages and the complex workings of the word "we." In the excruciating final passage of *The Bluest Eye*, its narrator, Claudia McTeer, confesses that the unity and cohesiveness of the black community of her childhood depended upon the victimization of one of its members, a little girl cast into the role of pariah and scapegoat. Among other things, *The Bluest Eye* is a relentless analysis of the way "we" usually implies, and requires, a "not-we."

The response of my nearly all-white class upon entering Morrison's world has amazed, intrigued, gratified, and saddened me all at once. Instead of leaping into the novels, they have been hanging back, waiting. Partly this is attributable to Morrison and the strange magic she conjures. But it is also due to the whiteness of fifteen of my sixteen students, not the whiteness of their skin but the whiteness of their minds. This is surely the first course they've taken where all the material is by a black author; it's certainly the first I've taught. As white readers we are accustomed to reading about ourselves, of course. We think we're reading about "people," but we're reading about white people most of the time. In my seminar we find ourselves confronting a world about which we cannot so easily say "we." In Toni Morrison's world, we are "They." "We," the white folks, are out on the margins, in the wealthy homes along the lake where Claudia and her sister timorously venture to find their friend, whose mother cleans and cooks in one of those houses. White people appear as neurotic, deluded, unsanitary, dependent, mean, foolish, incompetent, controlling, and above all, *peripheral*. The center, the heart of the world, is the black community.

That displacement frightens us white readers, makes us feel excluded. Of course, black students experience this alienation every day of their lives here, but we aren't used to it yet; we're just learning, or refusing to learn, how to endure not being at the center for five minutes. I believe "we" must learn this lesson, the lesson of seeing ourselves not as Universal Human or Generic American, but as distinctively White — and as marginal to many American realities. At the end of this painful self-consciousness, if we can endure it without retreat or rationalization, lies wisdom.

Because the students in my seminar are, for this campus, relatively sophisticated in racial consciousness, they know that it is wrong for them to assume they can quickly or fully comprehend African American experience. They want to respect the Afrocentricity of Morrison's work, and they want to be honest about their ignorance. But this leaves them in a bind as readers, whose job and whose delight is usually to enter fully into the author's world, to become its denizen. Many of us in the seminar have been renegotiating our relationship with what we call "course material" and our roles as readers. We are trying to find a way that this material can be ours without falsely appropriating it. I don't know whether or not we will succeed by the first week in June. But I do know that although the course has been harder than I'd anticipated because of these issues, I think we are doing exactly the kind of struggling necessary in people who would call themselves educated. In the collectivity of class meetings and in the privacy of our reading, we ask ourselves, "Who's 'we'?"

———

I have had to revise most of the lessons I was taught in my childhood, one of which was that harmony and unity ought to be easy. As long as we maintain that fiction, we will always mystify discord and difference, shaking our heads and wondering why they should exist. The fact is that discord and difference are quite natural, making harmony and unity the hard part.

I believe that, but frankly, as the well brought up middle-class white girl that I am, I find difference and discord excruciating. Peace is at a premium in this world. The most obtuse, arrogant, offensive human being has feelings and reasons and a story to tell. For those not included in the dominant "we," it is so tempting, on some level so easy, to disappear into the roundness (to the extent that we're able), to take care of business as usual, to swallow the hurt, the unwelcome insight, the alienating knowledge, the rage that rises in our throats. But we do so at our peril. Each time we choose not to speak our "we," we go a little crazy, die a little bit. Most of the women I know are, on some level of their being, angry. The people who, by definition, are not part of the prevailing "we" — gay and lesbian people, people of color, female people — keep a lot hidden in order to protect it, and we are all the poorer for what they keep from us.

For those of us who feel threatened by Otherness in whatever form it presents itself, it is very tempting to return, as they used to say at the beginning of "The Lone Ranger," to those thrilling days of yesteryear, when We were We. It is harder, more frightening, and much more intellectually daring to leap forward, instead of back, toward a vision of a spectrum of color that does not reduce to white, to a music that does not resolve to a single song or even to simple harmony. It is hard to conceptualize, even harder to live. And it is absolutely our only hope, Kimosabe.

10

The Bluest Eyes

Teaching African American Literature in White Classrooms[1]

> *I think that the hard work of a nonracist sensibility is the boundary crossing, from safe circle into wilderness: the testing of boundary, the consecration of sacrilege. It is the willingness to spoil a good party and break the encompassing circle, to travel from the safe to the unsafe. The transgression is dizzyingly intense, a reminder of what it is to be alive.*
>
> —Patricia J. Williams[2]

1. Where the Blood Is

Of all the explosive topics in the arguments about cultures and curriculum currently raging through academe, none is more likely to generate more heat (usually without light) than the question of who gets to teach whose literature to whom. The level of energy around this question is understandable; not only does it involve large abstractions like Identity, Intellectual Property Rights, and Freedom, but it involves people easily outraged by even the whisper of a limitation on their potential expertise. This argument interests me, but only on a rather abstract level. For me, these large questions often come disguised as practical dilemmas in the daily life of teaching at a small college.

Like many white people, especially white feminists, I am deeply engaged by African American writing. And like many white people, for a long time I regarded my love for this literature as evidence of my depth of soul and breadth of intellect. Then one day, talking to an African American colleague, I mentioned with barely suppressed pride that I intended to "devote" my upcoming advanced women's studies seminar entirely to the work of Toni Morrison. To my surprise, my colleague looked not the least bit impressed. In fact, I thought I detected suspicion.

Some weeks later, after her return from an interesting literary conference, I asked her how it had gone. She shook her head. "There sure are a lot of white folks giving papers on Toni Morrison."

And this was not a Good Thing?

Her skepticism returned to me the following spring when, for that very seminar, I was rereading *Beloved*. In that novel, the protagonist, Sethe, who has fled slavery across the Ohio River to Cincinnati, is haunted by many demons. But the worst of them is not her white owners, not her white rapists, but the white brother-in-law of her owner, whose ongoing practice it is to take notes on the slaves' habits and to measure their heads. Sethe knows him only as Schoolteacher. In previous readings of the novel, I had identified unreflectively with Sethe, as a reader identifies with an intensely sympathetic, heroic protagonist. This time, with an awful jolt, I realized that my most authentic surrogate was the educated white man studying her subjugation, notebook in hand.

Such moments of discomforting recognition precipitated me into an ongoing and unresolved examination of my relationship to African American literature, as reader, critics, and "schoolteacher," one who introduces this literature to other, predominantly white, readers. A little observation of the current litcrit scene, paired with some consideration of history, especially academic history, clarified for me the question of why African Americans should regard the massive white appetite for their literary tradition as less a compliment than a threat. bell hooks has explained this phenomenon better than anyone I've read, in a context of white (especially feminist) academic fascination with the Other:

> Often this speech about the "Other" annihilates, erases: No need to hear your voice when I can talk about you better than you can speak about yourself. No need to hear your voice. Only tell me about your pain. I want to know your story. And then I will tell it back to you in a new way. Tell it back to you in such a way that it has become mine, my own. Re-writing you, I write myself anew. I am still author, authority, I am still the colonizer, the speaking subject, and you are now at the center of my talk."[3]

This is the voice of Schoolteacher, too. Katherine J. Mayberry has argued that "any white scholar writing about a work by a black writer may come perilously close to this same offense."

> We take a powerful and brilliantly rich text set within a history of racial oppression that implicates us all, and we

organize it, master it, impose upon it a language and perspective utterly foreign to the culture from which it
issued. No matter how good our intentions, how knowledgeable we may be about African-American literary theory, I do not believe it is possible for white critics simply
to leave their perspective, growing out of their white
privilege, at the door when entering these texts. . . . Our
training carries risks: It instills in us a false sense of our
own power and of the docility of the texts that we claim
to master.[4]

So it was that my colleague was less than overjoyed to see a
writer like Morrison — that is, a writer deeply situated in African
American tradition, culture, and community who, in *Beloved*, has told the
unspeakable story at the origin point of African American history —
turned into an industry by white academics, often with precious little genuine understanding of the cultural context of Morrison's work, not to
mention wholly unexamined assumptions (like mine) about their competence to understand and "right" to teach anything they happen to enjoy
reading.

Yet I believe that at least part of the white appetite for black literature involves a genuine hunger — not mouth hunger but stomach
hunger; not voraciousness but the need for nourishment. This hunger is
worthy of attention. In part, I believe, it is a hunger of the spirit at the
dead end of European patriarchal and colonialist paradigms. In part it is
also the yearning to attend to the long-festering gash in the national psyche. Discussions of multiculturalism often come down to black and white
because in this country, that's where the blood is. Or, to quote a colleague of mine several years ago, accounting for the new prominence of
African American literature in American literature curricula, "That's the
national wound!" Indeed it is. When teaching approaches such wounds
— the areas of our collective life buried in confusion, pain, and yearning
— it can assume a breathtaking power.

Thinking back over two decades in the classroom, I recall classes
on African American literature with a particularly complex, fructifying
sense of struggle, encompassing both glory and devastation. It is that
struggle I wish to understand. Above all, I remember charged silences,
thick with fear and loathing, anger and confusion. How difficult it has
been for me and my students to speak about race. It is that silence that I
want to explore, and to break.

To break it requires the most shattering word of all, the word
most often left unspoken in the discourse of race: white. I want to begin
to think about, and to teach about, African American texts as lenses

through which we whose vision is compromised by white privilege can come to see our own whiteness more clearly. In the course of this process of re-vision, I have come to a new view of my role as a white professor, particularly in relation to my white students. I see the black text where we meet as the site of our confrontation with ourselves as white people, placing ourselves in history and within, not beyond, the discourse on race in this country.

2. Reading Through Racism

> The power of that room . . . is the power of racism as status quo:
> it is deep, angry, eradicated from view, but strong enough
> to make everyone who enters the room walk around
> the bed that isn't there, avoiding the phantom
> as they did the substance, for fear of bodily harm.
> They do not even know they are avoiding; they defer
> to the unseen shapes of things with subtle responsiveness,
> guided by an impulsive awareness of nothingness,
> and the deep knowledge of witchcraft at work.
>
> —Patricia Williams[5]

For a variety of reasons, I have taught Morrison's first novel, *The Bluest Eye*, with great frequency. I know this brief, brilliant, terrible novella almost by heart. But the more I teach it, the more forbidding it becomes. It is a work of awesome emotional power: I know no novel so full of despair, from its narrator's first words of repression and blocked potential — *Quiet as it's kept, there were no marigolds in the fall of 1941* (which Morrison has cited as her favorite of her first lines) — to the final words of abandoned hope: *At least on the edge of my town, among the garbage and the sunflowers of my town, it's much, much, much too late.* As in many of Morrison's novels, the abuse, sexual and otherwise, of children is common. The novella's episodic structure is complex, especially since the episodes often involve strange, violent collisions. All of this makes for its beauty and power, as well as its difficulty. Its real danger, in being taught to white students as it so often is, lies in its exposure of dimensions of race and racism that are enormously subtle, little discussed, little known to white people.

Like much of Morrison's work, *The Bluest Eye* concerns itself almost exclusively with a small black community. White people are peripheral, though of course very powerful. Interactions between white and black are rare, and devastating. Such a novel presents two big diffi-

culties for white students. First, they are wholly unaccustomed to literature in which whites are not only not central, but not even present. And
second, they think of black only in relation to white and of racism only in
terms of white interactions with blacks, rather than as an encompassing
system that circumscribes black reality whether white folks are in the
immediate vicinity or not. Morrison depicts the tragic Pecola Breedlove
and her community as studies in the penetration of racism, like some vir-
ulent dye, into the African American psyche. But this reality is so completely obscured from insulated young white people that when it is
brought before them, they often literally can not see it, or if they do, it
comes with too great a shock to grasp.

Precisely for these reasons, *The Bluest Eye* has been a sharp, dangerous teaching tool — but only when I abandoned the white liberal fantasy that mere exposure to fine black literature is an antidote to racism.
The longer we sustain that illusion, the oftener we will despair over our
white students' responses. In a statement that never fails to shock and disturb, Morrison's narrator, Claudia MacTeer, asserts at the end of the novel
that Cholly Breedlove, who rapes his daughter Pecola, nonetheless was
one of only two people who loved her. "Love is never any better than the
lover," Claudia explains (2183).[6] Well, to paraphrase: a reading is never
any better than the reader. Instead of asking black literature to do my
work for me, I'm learning to assume that it will function as a touchstone,
revealing much about its white readers that I need to know to make the
interventions and translations that can liberate the novel's power, to clear
away some of the web of distortions, omissions, and outright lies about
African America in which many white students are stuck, and to dislodge
the ignorance of themselves on which racism depends.

When I speak of the racism of my white students I will refer primarily not to conscious or overt antipathy toward African Americans, and
I will define it primary not as an attribute of individuals. The racism I am
concerned with is much larger, more complicated and thus more dangerous. I will use "racism" to refer to the vast system I mentioned earlier,
which has shaped my white students' thinking, as it has shaped my own.
This system reveals itself in structures of thought and belief, unexamined
assumptions, linguistic constructs which, more often than not, my students have no idea are racist in nature. In speaking of my students'
racism, then, I speak of them as conduits and as products of racism, more
than as agents. It is in watching them struggle to process African
American literature with the wholly inadequate tools given them by education, family, and culture that I have gained tremendous understanding
of how racism is passed on by unwitting collaborators such as my com-
passionate, just-minded, socially concerned white students.

Yet the reason this process is crucial to me, as an educator, is that

I know how easily the unwitting carriers become agents of racism and other systems of oppression. Ignorance is not passive or benign. And, as Malcolm X said, ignorance and power make the most dangerous combination of all, and my students are situated quite powerfully in this society, though they rarely understand or believe it. I see my role as intervening at the points where this ignorance collides with the text in provocative ways, places where it might begin to become self-awareness.

Through years of papers and classes, I have kept a mental list of assumptions I have heard, explicitly or implicitly, in white students' discussions of *The Blues Eye* and other work by Americans of color. This list contains nothing new: these assumptions are as fundamental and ubiquitous in news media and the Congressional Record and adult dinner-table discussions as they are in my students' papers and classroom comments. I have learned to attune myself not just to what the students "see" in the text, but to what they are bringing to it, the baggage that is obscuring or blurring the text. The racist assumptions do not, of course, articulate themselves openly or directly; they are tacit assumptions that appear slowly, like a photographic image, gradually revealing the whole picture. For the sake of clarity, I've distilled them here to their solid essences. The first three are deeply entangled:

• *Black families are unstable, unloving, and violent, and it is they that cause black children's problems adjusting to "society."* White students readily take the disastrous Breedlove family as normative, rather than deviant, as it is clearly presented from the first. The MacTeers, then, instead of representing the moral norm, radically different from the Breedloves, are seen as pretty much the same, only somewhat less violent. The care with which narrator Claudia MacTeer reconstructs her childhood sense of her family's strength and enveloping love must be equally carefully highlighted in order for young white readers to see it. Otherwise, all they see is poverty, sickness, a cold house, a mother who is strict and often angry.

As a byproduct, this assumption allows students to attribute Pecola's almost wholly painful, victimized girlhood exclusively to her "dysfunctional family," without regard to the social and historical forces shaping that family. Pecola's tragedy can thus be contained within an idiosyncratic local system instead of a vast societal one. In other words, if bad black families are the cause of black children's suffering, then we needn't discuss racism — not in my class, not in the U. S. Congress.

• *Black mothers are strong but unloving, harsh, punitive, dominating.* Powerful maternal figures are common in African American literature (I suspect that is one reason why so many white feminists love it).

But white students' assumptions about motherhood are usually deeply informed by nineteenth-century white, middle-class constructs of domestic femininity — Mother is supposed to be gentle, enduring, patient, consolatory. Add to this a little poisonous trickle-down from the Moynihan Report (which most have never heard of) and some current rhetoric about "single" (read "black") motherhood, and you have a recipe for misreading. So the ferocious brand of maternal attention of characters like Mrs. MacTeer, or Maya Angelou's grandmother Annie Henderson, is read by white students as harsh, uncaring, abusive. Its context is missing: a tradition of active, powerful womanhood, and above all a hostile environment where a child's very survival is the primary issue.

A scene near the beginning of *The Bluest Eye* can be counted on to raise these issues. Rosemary, the Italian girl living next door to the MacTeers, calls out to Mrs. MacTeer that Claudia and her sister Frieda are "playing nasty." What they are doing, in fact, is burying Pecola's underpants, stained with her first menstrual blood. But Mrs. MacTeer can't see that. She tears out of the house in a righteous rage, cuts a switch from the bush, and starts in on all three girls: "I'd rather raise pigs than some nasty girls," she says. "Least I can slaughter them!" (2038)

In this scenario, white students often see two data only: loathing of sexuality, and physical violence. They are usually extremely severe on Mrs. MacTeer; for them, her behavior puts her in the Breedlove category. There are other data in this scene that they suppress: Mrs. MacTeer's quick about-face when she understands the situation; and her gentle nurturance of Pecola, whom she takes into the house and gives a warm bath. But still other significant data are unseen altogether — implicit to most black readers, invisible to most white readers. Here is where the teacher's role is crucial, and where her own limitations may have serious consequences. For several years, I explained to my students that because African American girls and women were traditionally hypersexualized by the white imagination and were constantly prey to white male sexuality, a black mother was likely to be extremely strict in supervising her daughter's sexual development. It wasn't until I talked this scene over with an African American colleague that the final piece fell into place. "That's true," she said, "but also, we're taught to be very careful in what we allow white people to see. Remember, that Rosemary girl next door is watching the girls play." Notice how I, the teacher, failed to "see" the white girl, poised powerfully on the margins of the scene, in the position of translating to Mrs. MacTeer what was going on in her own yard? Notice, in effect, how I failed to see myself?

Such failures of vision on my own part help me comprehend them on my students'. For instance, when she calls Mrs. McTeer "unloving," I sometimes open the book to this passage in which Claudia remembers lying in bed with a cough:

> Love, thick and dark as Alaga syrup, eased up into that
> cracked window. I could smell it — taste it — sweet,
> musty, with an edge of wintergreen in its base — every-
> where in that house. It stuck, along with my tongue, to
> the frosted windowpanes. It coated my chest, along with
> the salve, and when the flannel came undone in my
> sleep, the clear, sharp curves of air outlined its presence
> on my throat. And in the night, when my coughing was
> dry and tough, feet padded into the room, hands
> repinned the flannel, readjusted the quilt, and rested a
> moment on my forehead. So when I think of autumn, I
> think of somebody with hands who does not want me to
> die. (2072)

I have read this stunning passage to classes and looked up to see very
confused white faces — students asking themselves, "Did I miss that
part?" The privileged students I teach have minimal sense, if any, of love
that must be tough or fierce so that a child might live.

Confronted with their default assumptions about motherhood,
most white students, especially white feminists, will deny them. I try to
ask them to define precisely what a character does that they define as
Bad Mothering, and then ask them why. Sometimes I see flashes of recognition. Sometimes I suggest — gently, patiently, good mommy that I am
— that perhaps their notion of Mother comes straight out of the very
Dick-and-Jane primer that literally structures and is ruthlessly deconstructed by Morrison's novel. My classes always critique this myth as unreal,
sanitized, and stereotyped, but usually they resist naming it as white or
middle-class, owning this myth for their very own.

• *Black fathers are absent, weak, or criminal.* In keeping with
the selective/repressive pattern I'm defining, white students see Cholly
Breedlove as the "present" father — debauched, vicious — and erase Mr.
MacTeer from the novel, or speak of him as "dominated" by his wife. In
contrast, here is what Claudia actually says of her father:

> My daddy's face is a study. Winter moves into it and pre-
> sides there. His eyes become a cliff of snow threatening
> to avalanche; his eyebrows bend like black limbs of leaf-
> less trees. His skin takes on the pale, cheerless yellow of
> winter sun; for a jaw he has the edges of a snowbound
> field dotted with stubble; his high forehead is the frozen

sweep of the Erie, hiding currents of gelid thoughts that
eddy in darkness. Wolf killer turned hawk fighter, he
worked night and day to keep one from the door and
the other from under the windowsills. A Vulcan guarding
the flames, he gives us instructions about which doors to
keep closed or opened for proper distribution of heat,
lays kindling by, discusses qualities of coal, and teaches
us how to rake feed, and bank the fire. (2100)

(n.b.: White students may comprehend the reference to the wolf at the
door, but they probably need a translation of the hawk that comes in
under the windowsills.) Mr. MacTeer is also described working in the garden with his wife, smiling at his daughters' play, and violently ejecting
from his home the boarder who molests them. That he is given heroic
warrior attributes here because he is fighting for his family's survival goes
straight over my white students' heads. Again, the love that must of
necessity express itself in struggle, resistance, fighting for life, is alien and
indecipherable to them.

   • *Black women are either puritanical or promiscuous.* It's not
really surprising that students have trouble conceptualizing any kind of
healthy active sexuality, given the cultural data bombarding them. But
when race enters the picture, their default assumptions take over, even at
the risk of outright contradiction. Raised in a culture that regards modesty
or dignity about sexuality as "puritanical," white students (good little post-
Freudians that they are) tend to see any discouragement of sexual display
as "repression." On the other hand, if a black female character is sexually
expressive, that is also particularized to her race.

   In a first-year seminar in autobiography, in which the reading list
was multicultural and an understanding of cultural difference was one of
the primary goals, we were discussing *I Know Why the Caged Bird Sings.*
The students began to speak of Marguerite's mother, the sophisticated,
sexy Vivian Baxter, as "promiscuous," so I intervened to ask what they
meant — these children of nineties for whom all sexual boundaries have
supposedly fallen! One student, sensing my dismay, quickly said, "But
that's just part of their culture." An old racist notion, masquerading under
our enlightened discourse of cultural "difference"! I countered by asking
them how, if black women were culturally permitted to be more sexual,
they could explain Annie Henderson, Marguerite's grandmother, whom
they had been complaining about for the entire preceding week as too
"puritanical"!

   • *Black (or any non-western) spirituality is "superstition."*
Consequently conjurers like M'Dear or Soaphead Church in *The Bluest Eye*

or Pilate in *Song of Solomon* are often wholly unintelligible to my students. But I learned the hard way that without addressing this issue head-on, Maxine Hong Kingston's *The Woman Warrior* or Amy Tan's *The Joy Luck Club* is a complete muddle. In Kingston, my confused first-year students told me, everyone is always talking about ghosts, so doesn't that mean that Chinese culture is very superstitious? At that time I was just learning the technique of asking for words to be defined, and I asked what was meant by "superstitious." "Well, not rational, not scientific," said one young man. And then, in a burst of inspiration, I told them it was Story Hour and I wanted to share a superstition from another culture. Without using names, I proceeded to narrate the virgin birth. One of my favorite teaching moments.

 • *Black communities and culture are defined by what they lack.* Many liberal white students have learned to think of African Americans as absolutely defined by oppression — that is, by white people's movements and institutions. They interpret black characters exclusively as victims or victimizers, never as agents or creators. To begin to study black culture as presence rather than absence, especially as a healthy, thriving presence, requires a huge paradigm shift for most. Because in many cases my students' notions of black community consist almost entirely of negative, violent images, it is difficult for them to make room in their minds for the healthy dimensions of black community actually presented by black writers: the humor, the traditions, the tolerance of deviance and iconoclasm, the interdependence, the morality and spirituality, the imagination, the devotion to children and education. For example, it almost always escapes my students' notice that as the novel opens, the MacTeers, struggling as they are against the wolf at the door and the hawk at the window, have taken Pecola Breedlove in when her family has collapsed. My students criticize Mrs. MacTeer's priceless monologue on Pecola's inordinate milk consumption: she is being a "bad mother," begrudging milk to a child. They tend to overlook not only its tremendous humor, and not only Mrs. MacTeer's quite legitimate worry about where the next quart of milk is coming from, but the transcendent fact that she has taken this surplus child into a home where milk is a luxury. They speak of "everybody" rejecting and despising Pecola, totally "backgrounding" the way she is embraced and protected by the MacTeers.

 • *Racism's victims are racism's agents. The Bluest Eye* is the best fictional depiction of internalized racism I know. Most of the novel's tensions are generated by colorism within its black community. I have been amazed to learn how few white students are even aware that within black communities, physical attributes nearer to Caucasian have been valued —

or, more importantly, why they have been valued — over African features. The role of Maureen Peel, the "high-yellow dream child," is a mystery because they do not know what "high-yellow" means — or signifies. White students may even read black hatred of blackness, epitomized in the nearly universal disparagement of Pecola, as racism, and to conclude that black people hate black people as much as white people do.

It becomes my role to interrupt these conclusions in the making, directing attention to the larger fabric in which Pecola's brief story is one broken thread. This is the moment to have white students list the images of whiteness that corrode black self-esteem: Shirley Temple and other white movie stars; Mary Jane on the candy wrapper; the white men with the flashlight who vitiate Cholly's sexual initiation; the little Fischer girl whose parents employ Pecola's mother. Which brings me to the final, most devastating assumption:

- *If whiteness isn't visible, racism doesn't exist.* Because white people remain on the fringes of the novel, or on the bottom of drinking cups, white students can ignore white racism, though it sometimes requires interesting maneuvers. I have listened to analyses of the effects of racism that did not once mention white people or institutions. I have heard class discussions and read papers in which the suffering of Pecola and her community is explained in terms of family dynamics, psychological development, self-image, economic class, sexism, cultural ideals of beauty, the media, and God, without ever mentioning race or racism at all. Now, recall the title of this novel: such an omission requires that the pervasive central metaphor of blue eyes be treated as if they had nothing to do with white skin or white power — a truly daunting feat of denial. A vast white silence, like snow, comes down over a complicated, vibrant black text.

The teacher's job is to break that silence, whether it comes from denial or ignorance or both. A white teacher in a predominantly white classroom has much less to lose than her colleagues of color in asking the questions, making the interventions, that disrupt racist readings of black tests. Sometimes these interventions consist simply of foregrounding elements of the text that a racist reading has filtered out. Sometimes, on the other hand, my role is to provide context implicit in the text but invisible to my students because of their ignorance of African America. A third common type of intervention is to ask for a definition of terms in statements like these: "She's not a very good mother." "She's kind of promiscuous." "The father isn't very responsible." A fourth type comprises ques-

tions aimed at flushing out confusion or unexamined assumptions —
tricky work, best accomplished in the interrogative mode. The questions
tend to be variations on two basic themes: What do you not understand
here? and What are you assuming? Such questions turn textual issues back
on the reader, so that reading a black text becomes, in part, an exercise
in white self-awareness. For above all, teaching African American literature taught me how difficult it is for white people to conceive of their
own whiteness — as a limitation, as a power, as a history, as a potent factor in their experience of the world of the text and the world beyond it.

     But I also find myself acting as the counterweight in a constantly
shifting, delicate balance in my students' evolving confrontation with the
humanity of the "Other." Undergraduate white Americans, especially
younger ones, tend to conceive of human beings in either radically indi-
vidualistic or radically collective terms; they see the particular and the
general as distinct and oppositional. They have great difficulty moving to
a third, more realistic position, where the collective and the individual
inform each other, where the particular and general interpenetrate. Within
a given class, discussion will swing between two frustrating poles: on one
end, everything about a black character is explicable in terms of her
blackness. Her humanity is engulfed by her race. On the other end, her
race doesn't exist; she is generically human, free of the imprint of culture
or history. Contradictory as they may seem, these poles often coexist in
the same mind, just as they coexist in white American thinking: on the
one hand, blacks are inaccessibly Other, alien, essentially different; on the
other, race shouldn't be "dragged in," people are people, we're all
human. I often feel mired in this contradictory and falsifying subtext in a
classroom. One moment finds me trying to offset the alienating, dehu-
manizing effect of the particularist point of view ("They're Different.") by
emphasizing empathy with the situation of an African American character;
the next moment I'm shifting to the other side, problematizing trans-racial
generalities by emphasizing particular features of black experience and
culture at work in a character's behavior. Always I see my work as
unearthing the genuine complexity of the human drama, the satisfying,
gratifying complexity that my white students have been enculturated not
to see.

3. In the Passive Voice: the Grammar of Racism

     As Ruth Frankenburg has written, "Whiteness, as a set of norma-
tive cultural practices, is visible most clearly to those it definitively
excludes and those to whom it does violence. Those who are securely
housed within its borders usually do not examine it."[7] To white people it
"has no name and few distinguishing marks and thus is not, apparently, a

cultural space."[8] One hears this assumption confirmed in the popular cultural discourse, where "ethnic" or "racial" implicitly means "non-white."

The obliviousness is a function of privilege, analogous to the difficulty that the best-intentioned men have in seeing modes of their being as gendered and masculine. It is less usefully regarded a moral flaw than as a harmful byproduct of illegitimate power and the illusion that one's own assumptions about "reality" are either peculiar to one's individual self, or else a-historical, transcendent, "natural," and universally human. Hence the seeming paradox Frankenburg notes by which white people see whiteness "simultaneously as generic or normative and as an apparently empty cultural space,"[9] functioning "as both norm and core, that against which everything else is measured, and as residue, that which is left after everything else has been named."[10] Similarly, "The category of 'American' represents simultaneously the normative and the residual, the dominant culture and a nonculture."[11] So privileged white people see themselves simultaneously as "everything" and as "nothing." This interface of arrogance and a weird sense of exclusion or inferiority explains a great deal about the difficulty whites have in peculiarizing whiteness, removing it from the "everything/nothing" duality. "Naming 'whiteness,'" Frankenburg writes, "displaces it from the unmarked, unnamed status that is itself an effect of its dominance." And, I would add, that then becomes a cause of its continued dominance. "To speak of whiteness," she continues, "is, I think, to assign everyone a place in the relations of racism."[12]

To speak of whiteness: easier said than done. What I have learned is that like me, my students can much more easily think and talk about black people and racism if they do not have to assume a particular place by thinking of themselves as white. The most frightening vision is always the face in the mirror. The invisibility of whiteness to my students is visible to me not only in the content of their comments and essays, but in the very form of their writing. In fact, their whiteness becomes visible in its invisibility, just as so often the issue of race is present in its absence in public and private discourse in this country: it is what we don't say, cannot say. It is the repressed. The ear must be attuned to the sound of absence to hear the grammar of racism, to master its rules:

Rule 1: "We" is White

Explaining the function of the Dick-and-Jane primer excerpted at the beginning of *The Bluest Eye,* a white student wrote the following: "This portion of the story represents the educated, respected white person and their vision of normalcy and acceptance." And later, in the same paragraph: "This portion of the book represents us, the reader and society, and our view of the world." "Us," then, "the reader," is "the educated, respected white person." The implicit "we" or "us" in white students' papers often is.

Rule 2: "We" are the World, We Are the Normal

Note that the coded white "we" in the preceding example is also "society." In my white students' papers, "society" often functions as code, an unconscious synonym for "white." "Society" — a comfortable abstraction as well as a universal villain of adolescence — allows them to avoid defining that part of society to which they actually refer: the white part, which includes them. Another student wrote that, whereas the worldlier Claudia "knew it didn't matter what color her eyes were, because people would notice the color of her skin first," Pecola "was innocent to the ways of society." In this double-whammy, not only is "society" white, but so are "people"! In refusing to mark constructs like "society" or "people" racially, a writer simultaneously aggrandized whiteness ("everyone" becomes white) and erases it: everything and nothing, once again.

Similarly, the concept of normalcy is invoked to describe that which is white, as in the example quoted above, where "white" and "normal" are implicit synonyms. In Frankenburg's terms, whiteness becomes "an unmarked marker of others' differences — whiteness not so much void or formless as norm."[13] Responding to Maxine Hong Kingston's recollections of growing up in the Chinese immigrant community in San Francisco, a student wrote: "Normal everyday Americans are reduced to loud, 'red-mouthed,' white 'ghosts.'" Here, very clearly, "Americans" represents "white Americans," just as "normal" does. The sentence captures its author's incomprehension of a non-white perspective on white people: how could white Americans be seen as anything other than "normal"? In her confusion is something close to hurt, or insult, caught in that word "reduced." White people have been made smaller!

Rule 3: The Case of the Invisible Agent

The passive voice is an invaluable tool in avoiding whiteness, for the same reason that English teachers decry it: it eliminates agency by turning object into subject. Effects can be discussed apart from causes. We can talk about the struggles of black people without ever implicating white people or institutions, and thus ourselves. For instance, a white student's paper will introduce racism in the following terms: "Blacks were perceived as inferior." Who actually perceived them that way is left blank, as if the perception were floating in space, emanating from nowhere and everywhere. In this syntactical construction, whites are indeed everything and nothing, all-powerful but unnamable, blameless. (This is not to mention that racism reduced to a matter of interpersonal "perception" loses a great deal of its power.) The alternative, active voice, would mean a painful level of specificity: "Whites perceived blacks as inferior." (The passive voice functions to obscure agency in other dangerous linguistic confrontations too: almost always we cite sexual violence in terms of how many women "are raped" every however many minutes, instead of how often men rape women.)

Sometimes a sentence comes so webbed with grammatical and ideological convolutions that it's difficult to see what's being said and what's left unsaid: "At a time of white supremacy," wrote another student, "Toni Morrison, in her novel *The Bluest Eye,* draws attention to Black Americans and gives compassion to those that were deemed unacceptable." Is the agent of the "deeming" clearly implied in the opening prepositional phrase, or does that phrase relieve the pressure to define the "deemers"? And further: to what does that prepositional phrase refer? Grammatically it refers to the time of Morrison's writing of the novel; but it is probably intended to refer to the time in which the novel takes place. This blur is convenient, as historical displacement (racism used to exist a long time ago) is another tool students use to distance the implications from themselves.

To intervene in the grammar of racism, our best teaching tools are, again, interrogative, rather than declarative or accusative. The interrogative is the truly educative voice, for it draws out (educes) what is unexamined and inarticulate. In the margin beside the sentence telling us what "we" believe, we can ask, "Who's 'we'?" Further on, alongside the sentence that tells us what "society" does to black people, we need to ask two questions at once: "Aren't black people part of society? Do you mean a particular part of society?" And finally, next to the sentence that says black people were or are deemed inferior, we can ask, "By whom?"

And we can answer these questions ourselves — out loud, in public. We can own up. We can teach our students to be less afraid of questions than of the silence that racism feeds on.

4. Voices from the Porch

Spring, 1992. The seminar topic was the construction of selfhood in writing by African American women from the eighteenth century to the present. In the small room in the below-ground floor of the library, the white silence had become almost palpable. I could smell the nervous self-censorship, see the apologetic, guarded gestures. Actual silence — that is, the absence of speech — was rare; this was the terrible silence of constraint. No wonder: there were only thirteen students, and three were African American women. At Kalamazoo, that constitutes a rare critical mass, and they knew it, the trio. They liked each other, they trusted me to some extent, the material was theirs by right, they had Voice, and they used it.

Finally the dynamics became so pronounced (or unpronounced) that I had everyone answer some questions, in writing, about their feelings about class participation. Not for my benefit, I already knew what I'd get, but to raise the white students' level of consciousness about class process. Sure enough, the primal fear was of "being perceived as racist," and the fear collected around one of the black students in particular, Rosie, with her hip-hop style, her wicked laugh, and her fierce, bright eyes.

We scheduled a discussion about it. On the day before it was to happen, the verdict in the Rodney King case came down in Simi Valley. I began by talking about how white fear operated in L. A., and then I shut up.

Some of the white students said they thought the main problem was their fear of disagreeing with a black student. One of the trio, Geneva, said, "Listen: If you disagree with something I say, tell me; I can deal with it. And if I disagree with you, you'll know it."

Ah, I thought, that's exactly what those white students are afraid of, the forthright, emphatic black speech that feels, to white kids from middle-class homes, combative or abrasive and that plays into twenty years of fear of angry black people.

Then something seemed to catch in Geneva's eyes.

"What do the white students in this class have to be afraid of, anyway?" Her voice become more impassioned. "I mean, I don't get it. You all are sitting here at a white college, with a white professor to support you." She gestured toward me and Rosie murmured assent from her corner. "Black students at this college are always nervous in classrooms."

"That's it," Rosie testified from the sidelines.

As the days went by and the fires burned out in Los Angeles and our class got back to "business," some of the white students clearly resolved to "get a spine," as the students say. But now Geneva went silent, sad and resentful. "I hated that damn discussion," wrote Rosie in her journal. "Now look what's happening to my girl Geneva. She used to be a big part of this class, and now she doesn't say anything."

In the ensuing weeks Geneva came part way back, but never fully. And the white silence was still there, a vast iceberg. So now there were two silences working against each other and against all of us. I finally had to accept that I couldn't make it OK again for Geneva; that her exasperation and frustration were her own. It took me a longer time to accept that white silence, though it presents pedagogical challenges, may be a "natural," even necessary element of a multicultural classroom: white people are going to be scared, ill at east, off-center when the center is no longer themselves. Theirs is the voice that has dominated academic discourse for centuries. So if, in one seminar, the African American voice got heard more clearly, so be it.

And there was one day when its power left us gasping. In self-selected groups of three, the students were to make presentations to the class on one of the authors, and to conduct discussion. I lay down ground rules, beyond which, I said, they could be as innovative as they wished. Rosie, Geneva, and the third African American, Martha, instantly constituted themselves as a group and chose Zora Neale Hurston. That meant that their group went first.

They were armed with discussion questions on *Their Eyes Were Watching God*, submitted by the rest of the seminar. One frequent question had to do with "the Porch," an institution that appears in much of Hurston's work: the townsfolk of Eatonville, Florida, the all-black town in which Hurston herself grew up, who collect on the porch of the General Store to play the dozens, tell tales, and signify on their fellow townspeople. The Porch, which often yanks the "plot" to a dead halt, becomes a collective voice through which moral and ethical issues are worked out, community life is mediated, and the cultural backdrop is filled in.

Well, when we came in to class on the day of the group presentation, lo and behold they had constituted themselves as The Porch. Rosie introduced the exercise: "We were surprised that a lot of you didn't understand about the Porch. That's really familiar to all of us from our childhoods, people sitting around on the front porch or the front stoop and talking. When you're a kid, you mostly listen. That's one way kids get educated, by listening to the adults on the porch. It's how the culture gets passed down."

Glimmers of dawning awareness in the white faces around the room, my own included.

"So what we're going to do is talk about some of the main questions about this novel as if we were on the Porch. What you'll notice is that in our culture, a lot of disagreement is allowed. People can disagree with each other violently on the Porch. That's the place for it. But everybody's still included."

And off they went. One of the trio would pose a question about the novel, using her normal "student" voice. Immediately the trio moved into vociferous argument, in an entirely different voice — full-throated Black. Assertions were made without qualification or concession; opinions were decried outright or enthusiastically embraced. Voices overlapped constantly. The issues were never resolved; the differences were allowed to stand. When the dimensions of the issue had been aired, there was a return to class persona and a new question was introduced.

And when the hour was done, the room erupted in applause. The white students were delighted, impressed, and put on notice that they had a hard act to follow. I went back to the office chuckling and marveling, bragging to my colleagues about what had happened in my classroom, and thinking about academic "discussions." Instead of talking *about* the Porch, my students had talked *from* the Porch — that is, from a site within African American tradition. And they had offered us, wittingly or not, another strategy, another metaphor, for discussing ideas. Had the class somehow been able to adopt it, the white silence might have been broken for good.

The African American students had asserted their authority, in the true sense of the word, very clearly: this literature comes from a familiar place to us, they said. We know this, on an entirely different level from the way of knowing we are cultivating together in this classroom. We can help you to understand this work. In another rather magnificent assertion of authority, Rosie determined, without consulting me, to write her papers in a perfectly beautiful, clear, expressive Black English—not an affectation or an imitation, but a very authentic personal voice, the one she used in her real life. I deeply regret not keeping copies; she let me hear my mother tongue singing a song I hadn't heard before, lit crit in a new and illuminating key.

And it was also Rosie who, when some of the white students had been giving me some kind of resistance, said after class, to Geneva, in my hearing, "They shouldn't give Gail trouble. She's one of our elders." At the age of forty-two, I didn't know whether to laugh or cry, but I went still inside, and then warm. It was almost like being invited up onto the porch for lemonade.

5. Learning to Fly

Accepting white silence doesn't mean affirming it. For me, as a teacher, accepting it means that I have stopped regarding it as a terrible failure, a matter of individual student "reticence" or "discomfort," or a problem that demands quick resolution so I can get on with the course. Instead, I am learning to regard it as a pedagogical challenge that belongs to a course on, or including, African American literature. In short, I have normalized it. White students have every reason to resist speaking about race. First, they are fearful and confused, again with good reason: aren't we all? And second, they have been given precious little knowledge or vocabulary in which to speak about race.

In negotiating their own relation to racism, white students are often caught in what Ruth Frankenburg has called "a contradictory equation from which there [is] no exit," in which they are "able to argue only 'I am entirely responsible for racism' or 'I am not at all responsible for racism.'" [14] The former option strikes most of my liberal-to-radical students as outrageous, the latter as inadequate to their sense of injustice. The option of being responsible *to* racism is rarely articulated.

Embedded in the question of their relation to racism is the issue of their relation to race itself, in its cultural dimension. If they have grown up in predominantly white homes, neighborhoods, organizations, and schools, they do not think of themselves as "raced" at all. So when race becomes the issue, it is someone else's issue, someone who "has race." But when race becomes the issue, they also suddenly become White, "othered," an uncomfortable, disconcerting metamorphosis. It feels like exposure or diminution at best, indictment at worst. It feels clumsy, because they have so little experience thinking and speaking in terms of whiteness. Regarding themselves as belonging to no particular culture has, in Frankenburg's terms, a "double-edged effect on the question of identity," such that the students "at times view themselves as 'empty,' yet at other times as the center or the norm. . . ."[15] Emptiness, norm: whiteness is nothing, whiteness is everything.

If whiteness is everything, then white culture is simply "normal." But if whiteness is nothing, white culture is no culture at all. The sense of being, "empty," culturally void, deprived, or excluded, is part of what drives white Euro-Americans to the literature of those they see, in distinction from themselves, as "ethnic." But these conflicting constructions of whiteness as "normal culture" and "no-culture" are further complicated by a third: the tendency of liberal-to-radical whites to see whiteness as "bad culture," in Frankenburg's terms, precisely because it is "a space defined only by reference to those named cultures it has flung out to its perimeter . . . ." It is "a relational category"[16] where the relations have been those of dominance, exploitation, and destruction, as most of my students know. Whiteness, then, is distinguished as a construct by its "slipperiness": "it shifts from 'no culture' to 'normal culture' to 'bad culture' and back again."[17] To white students engaged in seeking a place to stand in a multicultural world, there seems to be no dry ground to stand on.

Psychologist Beverly Tatum, working on racial identity development, provides another way of looking at my white students' confusion. She argues that "there are really only three major models of whiteness readily available with which students might identify," each of them hopelessly inadequate and counterproductive. These she defines as the "actively racist white supremacist," the oblivious or "what whiteness?" position, and the "guilty white" model.[18] Clearly the Frankenburg and Tatum models can be juxtaposed: the white supremacist regards white culture as normal (and other cultures as deviant or deficient); the oblivious white regards it as no culture, and the guilty white regards it as bad culture.

This white cultural dilemma expresses itself variously among college students. The most radical are often the ones caught in the "bad culture" trap. One common expression of their "ethnic envy" is the cultural impersonation that quite justifiably infuriates people of color. It is embodied in the white student who wears dreadlocks and African clothing, speaks black slang and listens predominantly to black diasporan music. For this cultural impersonator, the answer to the dilemma of whiteness is to attempt to abandon it — or, in other words, if you don't want to beat 'em, join 'em. It is difficult for such white students to see this cultural appropriation as other than a form of respect; when black people see it as another form of slumming or "going native," white students are appalled and hurt. But it's even harder for these students to understand the dangers of self-denial in these affectations of Otherness, the way they are, in fact, using cultural disguise to cheat the mirror, mediating or avoiding confrontation with their whiteness.

For me, these tangled questions came together in the Toni Morrison seminar — the one my black associate wasn't nearly as impressed to hear about as I thought she should be. Morrison had just won the Pulitzer for *Beloved*, students were catching on to her in droves, and I had long relished the notion of a total immersion: we would read all her novels, plus any other of her words, including interviews, that I could lay hands on. All the secondary material would be by African American critics.

The seminar included one African American woman and some ten white students, including two men. It was very rough going. First of all, Toni Morrison is a difficult writer. She is "magical," funny, and often thrilling, yes; but she is aesthetically and morally complicated and not given to gratifying easy reader expectations or political assumptions. Second, we hit the White Wall early on. No one in the seminar — including the teacher, by the way — had ever been in a classroom where 100% of the course material was by African Americans, about African Americans. We white folks were uncustomarily thrust into the margins and rapidly thrown back on ourselves, our whiteness — and where was that? Morrison's deep cultural specificity left us, literally, dis-located, Strangers in the Village, to borrow Baldwin's term. All the baffling problems of cultural identity came quickly to the fore, in the usual form: silence.

Such a situation raised fundamental questions about reading for us to ponder and negotiate. Common to these questions was the notion of "belonging." To me, reading is an interpenetrative act: reader enters text, text enters reader. In heinous contradiction of prevailing literary theories, I tend to encourage students to cultivate belonging when they read, to get to the point where the text belongs to them and vice-versa. But

how can black literature "belong" to white readers without their coloniz-
ing or appropriating it? And how can they "belong" to a fictive world that
comes from foreign cultural soil, one in which images of them are generally appalling and alienating? How can white readers find a relationship
with the text that will allow the deep and delightful immersion of literary
study, without totally annihilating critical racial self-awareness?

I saw the white students as caught between their love for
Morrison's work — the desire to "give themselves" to her — and their
self-consciousness as whites, which held them back, guilty or just confused and hesitant. At the time, I understood very little of all this in these
clear theoretical terms. But by the third or fourth week, I felt a kind of
estrangement settling in. I see in retrospect that they were immobilized,
unable to conceive a viable relation to the texts.

Shortly thereafter, midway through the course — at novel #3,
Song of Solomon — I made a discovery. It did not constitute the dramatic
breakthrough that vanquished all these impediments, but it altered the
rest of the course as well as the way I thought about white people reading black literature. Concurrently with the novel we read several interviews and articles in which Morrison discusses the figure of "the ancestor."[19] Often but not always female, this figure appears throughout African
American literature, prominently in hers. The Ancestor represents a collective presence, the spirit of the Old Ones, the enslaved and the free
Africans before them, which informs the present for those with ears to
hear their ancient voices. The Ancestor figure sets wayward youth
straight, illuminates mysteries, displays supra-rational powers, and above
all acts as guardian of what Morrison calls "rememory."

I went into class that day, I remember, assuming that the concept,
lucidly explained by Morrison herself [20] and righteously enacted in our
novel in the figure of Pilate, would be crystal-clear and terribly exciting to
the seminar members. As we began to discuss it, I rapidly learned my
error. All around the room, the white faces were blank or confused.

I slowly understood my mistake. The spiritual traditions that
honor ancestors were not theirs, and the historical reasons for treasuring
the ancestor figure, needing ancestral memory and wisdom, were
unknown to them. I looked around the room again: this time they
appeared to me not so much uncomprehending as deprived. I recalled
something Morrison herself said: "The people who practice this racism
are bereft."[21] These children, struggling so hard not to practice racism,
were bereft of ancestors.

Back to square one. Why, I asked, do those of us in this class
who are white have difficulty with this concept? The answers came quickly. First, as white people, we need not struggle consciously to keep our
heritage alive; it's handed to us on the silver platters of academe and cul-

ture. (As women, though we could begin to comprehend the ancestor much better.) Second, the Euro-American culture that shaped my students is hardly one that respects the past or reveres age. And finally, from another angle, notions of "white tradition" or "white heritage" belong to the discursive neighborhood of the Klan, the neo-Nazis. Our past as white people gives us little to celebrate or to want to preserve.

What about our roots in specific European cultures? From specific religious traditions? What about our past as women? In the terms of Holocaust survival and the feminist excavation of women's past, the Ancestor's face began to come clear. As we circled the Ancestor together, figures resembling her began to emerge from a few students' family experience — second- or at most third-generation Americans from eastern European stock — that is, those who had a stronger sense of cultural identity within racial whiteness. I heard about Polish Nanas and Czechoslovakian Poppis, repositories of power and authority, conduits of heritage and belonging. The WASP students — the students like me — looked on in interest, but also in wistfulness. (The solitary out lesbian wrote in her journal of the novelty and excitement of thinking about a lesbian ancestor.)

I came away with a new and provocative insight into the power of African-American literature for white readers: it can show us our losses, the price Eurocentric culture has paid for its dominance in the deprivation and diminishment of its children. And then it can help us to recoup those losses, by sending us back into ourselves, but deeper. Like all important quests, it involves death and rebirth. We can choose to enter what Minnie Bruce Pratt has called "a positive process of recreating ourselves, of making a self that is not the negative, the oppressor." Pratt goes on to draw the crucial, often elusive connection between the death inherent in white self-awareness, and the birth:

> When we begin to understand that we have benefited,
> for no good reason, from the lives and work of others,
> when we begin to understand how false much or our
> sense of self-importance has been, we do experience·a
> loss: our self-respect. To regain it, we need to find new
> ways to be in the world, those very actions a way of creating a positive self.[22]

I don't pretend that we achieved this goal or even came close to resolving the profound questions raised by our work in the seminar. For me, and I think for most of them, having engaged the questions counted as success. As readers, as learners, as Americans, as men and women, as African American and European American, we were changed by our work together. But I recently came upon some student writing from the end of the term that told me that on their own levels and in their own language, many of them had found germs of answers, and ways of making the questions, as well as the course material, their own. Wanting something more than I could glean from the course-evaluation forms (which are, as one student wrote, "really merely exercises in speed-writing and the construction of incomplete sentences") I had asked everyone to scribble a one-page account of what they were taking away from the course.

The statement of the sole African American, a science major, testified to a kind of literary homecoming that brought that issue of "belonging" into even greater relief for me:

> Experiencing the world of Toni Morrison this quarter has
> been a kind of re-awakening for me, a re-affirmation of
> who I am. . . . Many times while reading a novel or an
> article, I thought, "I remember hearing something about
> that," or "That sounds just like something mother (or
> another relative) would say." At other times, I became
> aware of attributes such as the importance of folklore
> and the realities of slavery. Before reading any of
> Morrison's work, I guess I never really defined for myself
> what it means to be an African-American, and now
> Morrison has given me at least a beginning to this defini-
> tion.

What she didn't write was her experience in the *class* — how her alignment with Morrison and the material positioned her to see our struggles in relation to her own. That narrative remained submerged. That is the story black students are often unwilling to divulge to a white professor. That is the story saved for "family."

The white students, in contrast, wrote directly of complex, confused, painful adjustments and evolutions. But nonetheless, these often ended with a kind of homecoming as well. Their statements comprise a rich store of evidence of the particular value of African American literature for white students, the manifold ways in which it answers that need I cited initially, as well as that lack I discovered when we talked about the Ancestor. But behind the words, between the lines, they also convey a sense of agency and power that radically contrasts the white blankness, immobilization, and entrapment I heard earlier in the term. It is as if, in their unusual, very specific marginality to this particular subject matter, they learned the radical potential of the margin[23] as a space to read, think, and feel anew. Somehow, some of these students seem to have come to a new way of thinking as white people that allowed them to "belong" to

the literature and to absorb its sense of human power and potential without deluding themselves or denying their status as whites.

One white student spoke simply and directly of a new respect for
African America, without a trace of guilt but instead with the clarity of
new knowledge and suggests, in its tone, a sense of responsibility for the
knowledge one gains:

> It is remarkable to me how people adapted and survived
> under such violent and threatening conditions. That
> shows a deep sense of strength which really came
> through in *Beloved*. Mostly, though, I will take away a
> better understanding of the everyday struggles that
> African Americans have in this country.

Another spoke in quite pragmatic terms of Morrisonian concepts she had
valued and internalized for future use. In her directness I hear a respect-
ful, intimate working relationship with Morrison's work that neither
appropriates nor alienates:

> I take away from these books a greater respect for the
> courage it takes to remember. . . . I will also keep in
> mind what it means to be a daughter, as described by
> Ondine.[24] Remember where I came from and take care of
> my people. Morrison's idea of the ancestor is important
> in a country that seems to get more and more detached
> all the time. It made me see how lucky I am to have the
> family connections that I do.

A couple of the white students spoke of what they were taking away in
relation to where they began. They defined a journey: from the solipsism
of racial guilt to richer, more complicated and fulfilling responses to
Morrison's work. One put this development in the terms of a major epistemological shift, from subjectivism to a dynamic, interactive engagement
with the unknown:

> I began overwhelmed with guilt, shame, and bewilder-
> ment in *The Bluest Eye*, then progressed to shock at *Sula*,
> who sent me into a personal abyss of confusion. . . .
> Now, after five novels, I can read Toni Morrison for me,
> but have learned to move from relating it to me only, to
> being able to also open up new worlds of experience in
> myself. The "black" elements of her writing create new
> understanding and experience — the village[25], flying[26],

the community, all have meaning and a place in my
heart and knowledge.

From subjectivist alienation outward, to the world beyond the self — and
then to an enlarged, enriched self. And finally, something like that
belonging I hoped for, a complicated, "post-colonial" belonging where
Morrison's world is known and loved, inhabited and personalized, but not
appropriated or denied its specificity or complexity.

Another student described what I think is the same basic movement, from guilty alienation to a responsible and liberating engagement.
In fact, this student makes a fleeting, barely articulated causal connection
between acknowledging her legacy as a white person and being newly
able to "touch" Morrison's work. Guilt itself — or rather, guilt that is permitted to be felt and explored rather than denied — becomes the medium
of initial contact. But only initially:

> I really do think of this class as a journey — one created
> by Toni Morrison; a journey that takes us down and
> brings us back out. For me it was a journey of truth,
> though there were distinct stages of the recognition and
> attitude toward it. The truth was one that most of us do
> not see, a blindness from our race, experience, and a
> carefully sheltered vision. The stages of truth began at
> shame, embarrassment and guilt; the approach [to the lit-
> erature] at this stage *wasn't* [an approach]: I backed off,
> afraid to touch and feel. The next stage was three big
> steps and two leaps away — the acceptance of the guilt
> — and furthermore the approach is there: I can feel this,
> I am allowed, invited in fact, to touch this with my
> hands, my heart. The next stage — well, I floated into
> this one — not consciously, but once you let go, the air
> will carry you.

A deft touch there at the end, alluding to the final sentence in *Song of
Solomon,* where Morrison discloses the secret of power: "If you surrender
to the air, you can ride it." And that paradox of assuming weighty responsibility in order to be able to let go and soar just happens to be precisely
what Morrison's protagonist, Milkman, learns in the novel. What this student took from Morrison was, in fact, a model for reading her work as a
white reader.

Without directly addressing the debilitating dualisms of traditional
white racial thinking, three students spoke of Morrison's epistemological
and moral complexity. One put it in terms of learning to sustain various

perspectives:

> One major point or thing that I will take away from
> Morrison's novels is the ability to look at more than one
> side of a person or situation. . . . I will take away the
> desire and hopefully the ability to look at people around
> me with a more open eye, and I would hope that I
> would be able to look at myself more openly.

For another, the gift was the ability to tolerate lack of certainty and order:

> Morrison has given me a better understanding of the
> ambiguities of the world — I think of Sula's freedom or
> Milkman's flying. I feel now or feel more strongly that
> the world is not the unified whole I used to think it was.
> Not only the fragmentation of the various communities
> within the United States . . . . but the fragments that the
> ambiguities I mentioned before create. Sula and Son[27]
> disrupt society in amazing ways. I would like to think
> that I have a greater respect for those disruptions, those
> fragments, the non-unity of my world.

How's that for postmodern thinking at it's best? The third interestingly
combined a vision of an expanded, complicated world with a more solid
sense of a "center":

> . . . just as Morrison claims that being black, and being a
> woman, tends to, if anything, make her world larger, it
> does the same for all of us. Think of how many profes-
> sors and students in all fields of study have a narrow and
> incomplete sense of the world through literature and
> therefore of the "real world," too. I think this course has
> saved some of us from being, as Joseph Campbell puts it,
> "spiritually off-center."

That final rejection of monocultural education was echoed in what is perhaps my favorite response. In this one, I hear even more clearly than in
the others the comprehension of the conundrum at the heart of the whole
enterprise: how the pain of white awareness is the beginning of its own
release:

> The college is finally sleeping, yet here I sit on my win-
> dowledge, at 4:30 a.m., still trying to sort out ten weeks

of pain, confusion, joy, surprise, and funkiness. I don't mind the waves which are still coming from *Beloved* to slap against my face . . . my mind . . . my perception of history

They taught me in primary and secondary school that "slavery was a terrible thing" but never gave an honest or even slightly thorough view of that or any other aspect of African American experience. Few people were concerned that my government-required American History class never studied the Civil Rights Movement..

And then there's Toni Morrison . . . she first appeared on my bookshelf during the summer of 1989 to tell me the untold stories — the ones that hurt as well as healed. Morrison stepped into my dreams that summer and told me quite matter-of-factly that I still have a long way to go as far as my education is concerned.

. . . When Morrison reminds me in *The Bluest Eye* that when why is too difficult to handle, we must take refuge in how[28] she is telling me again that all forms of education must be examined.

The stories need to be told and heard by all people.

Amen. Hallelujah and amen. In the most interesting of the responses, I would maintain that the fundamental shift is from a sense of entrapment in whiteness, to a sense of positioning. There is no attempt to deny whiteness; these students acknowledge that, in Frankenburg's terms, "one is implicated in one's racial positioning whether one chooses to be or not."[29] They also, however implicitly, understand whiteness as more a historical than a cultural phenomenon: "That which is most 'given' about whiteness (and indeed about the relations of race in general) is the materiality of its history — the impossibility of undoing what has already taken place."[30] One way to see my white students' struggle is to see them engaged with the terrible "done-ness" of history. But they also learned that history is only the beginning. As James Baldwin wrote about his own people: "To accept one's past — one's history — is not the same thing as drowning in it; it is learning how to use it."[31] From that particular "position," we can all take off and fly.

6. *The Face in the Mirror*

I will probably go on teaching African American literature, interrogating myself all the way, sustaining my uneasy resolution. For me, it still begins where it first began, with love. But in my early years in the classroom I taught it also out of a sense of responsibility to black people. When they hardly ever appeared in my classroom, then, I felt frustrated. I knew the literature was "good for" the white students, of course — a sort of educational vitamin supplement. But I thought of its salutariness mostly in terms of its acquainting white students with African American reality, hopefully deepening their understanding of U. S. racism.

This is still among my motives — perhaps even further in the forefront, as I am now teaching a generation of white students who are more badly informed about the actual lives and history of African Americans than their predecessors of a decade or two ago, primed as they are with the "new" (that is, newly acceptable) racism in U. S. public and private discourse. But I now have another purpose. African American texts have become tools in my own process of self-discovery, lenses through which I am coming to see more clearly not only African American imagination and reality, but my own whiteness. Contrary to the ubiquitous alarms about what will come of deepening our consciousness of difference, the result is that I find myself more able to make genuine, significant contact with the African American imagination, and with African Americans.

In this process I have come to a new understanding of my role as a white professor at this point in academic history, particularly in relation to my white students. We become the objects of our study, along with the literature. In fact, our study — ourselves as perceivers — becomes an important object of study. Inevitably, in a good reading of literature, the reader is forced back upon herself. I try to make African American literature a crucial site of self-discovery for white students, a profound mirror, a deep well that gives back their own faces through the dark water.

In teaching my students to read Morrison, I also try to teach them to read their world; but in order to read Morrison, they must reread the world, including the passages "whited out" in their early education. Their "whiteness" — not in essentialist terms, as skin color or genetic material, but their constructed, lived whiteness, as members of a highly privileged racial group — blanks out much of the complex black text, which must be dug out, revealed. Their very privilege is their worst educational handicap in this endeavor. As white kids, many of them have not had to ask certain questions, confront certain realities, feel certain emotions, or read certain texts that would prepare them much more fully for their "higher education" than any number of elite private schools or SAT preparation courses.

I know this because I speak of myself. Quite literally I know where they're coming from: it's my home town. Their assumptions and presumptions, protections and defenses, confusion and guilt and sheer monumental ignorance have all been mine. Likewise, their recognitions and illuminations, delight as readers, hard-won intellectual progress as a result of wrestling with this literature have also been mine. And until I realized that beneath the blank looks on their faces lay great reservoirs of need and deprivation, I didn't understand that I lacked, and missed, ancestors myself.

Finally, this may be the most compelling reason for a white woman like me to teach African American literature to white students. The bluest eyes in the room are my own.

11

Beware the Jabberwock
Declining to "Debate P.C."

*The conventional wisdom of the Tower of Babel story
is that the collapse was a misfortune.
That it was the weight of many languages
that precipitated the tower's failed architecture.
That one monolithic language would have expedited
the building, and heaven would have been reached.
Whose heaven, she wonders? And what kind?
Perhaps the achievement of Paradise was premature,
a little hasty if no one could take the time to understand
other languages, other views, other narratives.*

—*Toni Morrison*[1]

1. Border Wars

In the academic year beginning in the fall of 1993, I sat on Kalamazoo College's presidentially appointed committee charged with studying the curricular implications of multiculturalism and making recommendations. Now, when the curriculum is the issue, you can be certain that the discussion will be fierce at any moment in academic history, surely in this one. There are those for whom the curriculum is a kind of Fort Knox, a stable, invaluable repository of our cultural wealth. There are others, myself included, for whom it is far less solid and static, though no less important: in Madeleine Grumet's words, the curriculum "becomes tentative and provisional, a temporary and negotiated settlement between the lives we are capable of living and the ones we have."[2]

That fall I also applied for a sabbatical for the following year. I was hopeful of getting it, and the thought of twelve months away, writing and reading, sustained me through the darkening fall afternoons of committee meetings that I left with kettle-drum headaches and a sick spirit. When I departed campus the following September, just after the committee made its tepid recommendations and dissolved, I knew that I needed the sabbatical not merely to write and read, but to crowd certain memories and images out of my head: the icy hostility, the name-calling, the ruptures not only in "collegiality" and "civility" but in actual friendship, the disillusionment, the feeling of futility, the sense of constant miscommunication and failure of understanding, the rage, the shocking discoveries of what people actually thought, the intense backroom politics on which some people thrive but which make me nervous and exhausted. Yes, I too yearn to "rise above" politics.

But there is no rising above. As the song says, it's so high you can't get over it, so low you can't get under it, so wide you can't get around it; you gotta go through the door. Or as some other very wise someone once said, the only way Out is Through. Nonetheless, the Way Through is treacherous and often ugly. What we are "going Through" at this point in academic history is some uncharted, very overgrown, brambly, swampy terrain around a disputed border. As teachers, "intellectuals," scholars, we are engaged in a border war, painful and costly in human spirit. It is taking a grave toll, as all such important, worthy struggles must.

Hardly anyone in my profession would dispute the border war as a fact, but there might be dispute about its implications as a metaphor. The border conflict is usually spoke of in terms of defending a border (the one surrounding white/western/male/heterosexual preserves of knowledge and power) against incursions (by various Barbarians at the Gate). But the conflict might be refigured: what if the motion, the unmistakable energy, is pushing outward rather than inward? What if we are engaged in an *ex*cursion, across the epistemological boundary between the knowable and the unthinkable, the unitary or dualistic and the multiple? On one side lie paradigms of knowledge, truth, and value so entrenched as to be mistaken for nature or culture itself; on the other side stretches a vast, shadowy terrain so revolutionary that it is understandably described almost exclusively in terms of threat rather than treasure.

I try to keep my eyes on that new world. I try not to allow the boundaries of what is to constrict around me. I keep myself rooted in my own truth, mindful of the ways feminist and multicultural studies opened my intellectual frontiers, expanded my mental horizon, vastly enriched my teaching. But such mindful rootedness is difficult to sustain in this crazy weather. These maddening winds blow me senseless and flat.

As somebody once said, gimme shelter.

2. The Top Ten List and the Creature Beneath the Table

I said that this struggle was exacting a serious toll — from academic communities, careers, friendships. But the toll has been raised far beyond what the struggle demands by misrepresentations and caricatures, especially in the media. For this I do not blame academic conservatives. If

we who believe in the opening of the curriculum had communicated ourselves clearly and forcefully beyond academe, the slanders and travesties
we see daily could not have taken hold of the public imagination — or
not so easily, at least.

But within academic circles and texts, too, people promoting
change in the name of multiculturalism and feminism regularly confront
versions of themselves and their positions so reductive and distorted that
we can't laugh for crying. What we see is a grotesque beast, composed
of many incoherent parts. Here, in short form, are its lineaments. Call this
the Top Ten Dangers of Multiculturalism:

10. *It wants to Throw Out Plato.* This is a recurring alarm.
Apparently, Plato is in grave danger from the likes of me.
He'd better watch his back.

9. *It holds that certain racial, ethnic, or gender groups
"own" certain cultural products and won't let anyone else
have them, teach them, or learn them.* This particular
phantasm comes from a distinctively capitalist mindset
that pictures learning as a kind of enclosure system for
the head and assumes everyone else does too. I've been
surprised by how many articles critiquing multiculturalism take great pains to argue that people of color can
benefit from white western male thinkers — as if anyone
ever said otherwise.

8. *It renders all knowledge relative.* Witness a recent letter
to a university alumni magazine: "A university community
that pretends civilization benefited as much from
Australian aborigines and African bushman (sic) as it did
from Egyptian astronomers, Greek philosophers,
European nation builders, Confucius, and Shakespeare is
a university with a political agenda rather than an educational one."[3] This making knowledge relative is a particular source of dismay, especially if the relatives threaten to
be aborigines or bushmen — that is, non-white.
(Egyptians, of course, are honorary Caucasians.)

7. *It's about various groups fighting for a piece of the pie.*
Pastry is a popular metaphor. Once again the male capitalist mind at work: knowledge commodified, rarefied,
and hoarded; knowers fighting like starving peasants for
a potato.

6. *It politicizes education and institutions, causing incivility.* (This is one of my favorites.) The assignment of
causation gets interesting in these discussions. Talk about
killing the messenger on a vast scale! By the same logic,
the woman who files charges against an abusive husband
is causing the rupture in their marriage. In any struggle
for power, including this border conflict, can one side be
called "political" while the other is somehow not?
Apparently when a white man tells a racist joke, he's
merely being "politically incorrect," but when a black
woman calls him on it, she's "causing incivility" and
"politicizing" their relationship, or her institution, or
whatever.

5. *It represents neo-Stalinist/Nazi/McCarthyist thought
control.* The analogies approach the surreal. Proponents
of pluralism and diversity sent to bed with recent history's best examples of tyranny, ideals of uniformity, and
the silencing of dissent. The experience of actual, living
victims of this unholy trio is lost in a terrible translation.
(My favorite recent example: in an address at DePauw
University, filmmaker Ken Burns, defining multiculturalism as threatening a "new tyranny," accused it of sepa-
ratism and drew an analogy with the seceding Southern
states,[4] so that the descendants of slaves were rhetorically
transformed into slaveholders.)

4. *It propounds "feel-good" education (as opposed to
excellence).* The radical notion of introducing students to
widely diverse perspectives is thus domesticated into
some kind of psychotherapy. Those of us who have seen
the struggle that characterizes a genuine feminist/multi-
cultural classroom can sing, in harmony, "If this feels
good, why do I feel so bad?"

3. *It promotes political or social causes at the expense of
intellectual standards and integrity:* it wants to replace
Shakespeare with Alice Walker. He, of course, is no
longer with us, but Walker must have had to cultivate
either a truly wild sense of humor or a virtually Buddhist
detachment to endure this positioning of herself as the
(obviously) inferior, cheap replacement for the Bard. (Is

it my imagination, or is it the case that in this fantasy, the obviously inferior replacements or additions are always people of color? See #8, etc.)

2. *It represents the overthrow of order and the onset of intellectual/pedagogical/institutional/civil chaos.* This takes #6 a few steps further. I have even heard an opponent of multiculturalism say, in a public forum, that the implications of multiculturalism were evident in Los Angeles in 1992. In such a mind, difference is indistinguishable from disorder, conflict, and violence: this confusion testifies powerfully to the difficulty traditional western culture has in comprehending and encompassing diversity.

And the Number One Danger of Multiculturalism is:

1. *It focuses on and perpetuates our differences rather than emphasizing our common humanity.* This one gets first place because it raises perhaps the most serious issue of the entire debate — maybe the fundamental question on which the future of the U.S., or of the species, rests. Like the concepts of equality and difference, commonality and difference are always set in opposition (dualism again), and difference made synonymous with discord. Border war again, instead of border expansion. A tragically dwarfed intellectual imagination that cannot conceive of a new kind of comm-unity, conceived in difference and dedicated to the proposition that all of us are created different, and equal, and capable of finding common ground, common commitment.

I admit to simplifying and exaggerating for my own diabolic ends — but only a little. Any veteran of the border wars will, in an honest moment, admit to familiarity with this hideous beast. It took me a while to realize that this figure represented me, like a grotesque caricature of the Enemy circulated on the Homefront to stimulate the necessary chauvinism in time of war. I think I am not alone in this experience of dissonance, as of looking into a severely distorted mirror.

Never mind the sharp inconsistencies — for instance, the notion of multiculturalism as both a kind of Hitler enforcing a tyrannous mental order and an urban gangster, a source of violent disorder. Instead, just glance at the Final Four once more. They have an important commonality: their reductive, exclusive dualism. For me, this is the hidden enemy in many of the skirmishes along the border.

Last year our committee agreed to read the anthology *Debating P.C.*[5] together to ground our discussions (though to say that such a group might read together is like saying the blind men described the elephant "together"). Why did I override my instant suspicions of both terms in the title? "Debating" grounded the volume precisely in the reductive, adversarial, dualistic (and duelistic) approach dear to the heart of western masculine tradition. I generally find it remarkably unproductive and falsifying. No wonder high schools have teams that compete in it. And then there was that other term, "P.C" — announcing that the debate was a charade; the volume had already made up its mind.

Reading each week's "assignment," I felt a certain dissociation, at first dim and then steadily more pronounced. Not only in the antagonistic, "anti-P.C." pieces but in those where I expected to find, and sometimes did, congenial insights, I kept running up against the cartoon figure, positioned anywhere from the exact center to the far periphery of the argument. This creature lurked around our committee meetings too, snapping its jaws under the table, cackling in corners as we "debated P.C."

In such meetings the mind sometimes asserts its need for respite by taking flight. Sometimes, in the midst of the fray, I would suddenly, inexplicably think of classrooms — classrooms where I have felt that peculiar satisfaction of a truly rich, layered discussion. What I thought of, specifically, was the confused and then delighted surprise of students who have come up with three or four different angles on a literary problem or textual passage when, instead of telling them which one is right, the teacher either pulls the variants together somehow or lets them stand in their diversity, even their contradiction, and moves the class on. The almost illicit thrill of entering the land of many answers. The mystification of realizing that the more possibilities get generated, the more satisfied our minds, the fuller we feel, the closer, in fact, to "truth."

I thought of such classrooms a great deal as the committee jerked and floundered through its uncreative lifetime. True to my academic roots, I often thought about language, because I often felt its lack. I repeatedly found myself without language to describe such classrooms to uncomprehending ears, and no language to refute, deconstruct, or reconstruct the Top Ten List. I returned to an issue that moved to the center of my thinking and pedagogy about fifteen years ago and has lodged there since, the issue of naming (or, if you will, "linguistic construction") and, more particularly, the question of who in any system is empowered to name and define reality. Sometimes a name can transform the thing named. Sometimes it can virtually construct the thing in the empty air before our eyes. A monster takes shape from our fear and color from our confusion:

> Beware the Jabberwock, my son!
> The jaws that bite, the claws that catch!
> Beware the Jubjub bird, and shun
> The frumious Bandersnatch!

And you do: you become afraid of a Jabberwock who then begins to coalesce from your anxiety. When someone powerful — a teacher, a scholar — says that there are people out there who want to control people's thoughts and replace Shakespeare with Alice Walker, there are people for whom that begins to be true. And they are legion, all talking Jabberwocky.

Or you don't. Maybe at this point you're simply confused, tired, and bloodied. As Bandersnatches go, you are feeling less than frumious. What you want to do is run: across the border, into the trees, where Intellectual Integrity happily polishes the shoes of Justice, where the minuet breaks into a jazz riff, where the only route to Common Humanity follows the curious paths of Difference, where Shakespeare jitterbugs wildly with Alice Walker under a full, mad moon.

3. Crisis of Faith

In the best academic tradition, as I've said, we have failed to communicate to the non-academic public our own version of ourselves, our vision of the world beyond the border. At least we have failed to do so in terms that might stand a chance of being heard. The price of our failure has been to watch the term "politically correct" enter the popular lexicon with astonishing rapidity and completeness. If language tries for mimesis, this is a kind of fun-house-mirror word, stretching and distorting what it identifies. If, on the other hand, language constructs reality, then we are in even bigger trouble, for this term has constructed a Jabberwocky reality that is now larger than life and twice as hungry.

Initially, I was adamant about ignoring the term. Its sneering defensiveness was too obvious; its insubstantiality too patent. At this point, when I can no longer make it through a newspaper article or television show — or even one of my own classes — without hearing about political correctness or incorrectness, I have to acknowledge not only the success but the power of this notion. It's in the drinking water, like a cheap, lethal chemical weapon of the reactionary forces in and beyond academe. It has captured the sweeping backlash against the justice movements of the last generation, along with the eternal public suspicion of academe. The phrase is used now unselfconsciously and unsatirically, as if it described an objective reality objectively, so that, for instance, Penguin Classics can sponsor a teleconference called "Political Correctness: Free Speech on Campus." It has become virtually impossible to speak about efforts to crack hegemonic codes of knowledge and education without being sucked into the vortex of this notion so quickly that the issue is completely distorted by its frame before any intelligent or accurate discussion can take place. And so I find my mind has changed: we had better pay it attention, a great deal of attention. We had better sit it down, turn on the bright light, and interrogate it, this sneaky, corrupt little leech of a notion.

I am not the first to emphasize that "politically correct" is hardly a neutral term. It is used by, and takes meaning from, those who are opposed to what they believe it stands for. The term demands interrogation on two grounds. The first has to do with the notion of "correctness" it implies: it argues that the intellectual revolution has, in fact, succeeded and given way to the Reign of Terror, hardening into a new tyranny. To those who are working within this revolution, paying heavy prices in terms of tenure, salary, promotion, professional respect, peace and quiet, this assumption is a source of grim humor or incredulity. At the vast majority of colleges and universities in this country, the curricular changes have occurred in limited spaces (literature departments, largely) in very limited ways. Chaucer, Shakespeare, and Milton are very much with us, thanks, and likely to remain so. And since the corollary to the apocalyptic visions of curricular change is usually a vision of personnel change in which crowds of "minorities" are being hired (pretty much regardless of credentials) every day, it is worth saying that faculties remain overwhelmingly white and their leadership overwhelmingly male. It is infinitely easier to get a black woman into the curriculum than onto the faculty, believe me.

The second issue has to do with the term's implications about motives. This is the insult at the core of this language: someone who is called "P. C." is being accused of something — to wit, adhering to externally imposed standards and rules, toeing the party line, "being good," but hypocritically. The smirk at the heart of the term "politically correct" says that we all know better; our real sentiments are racist, or sexist, or heterosexist; at best the P. C. are just being polite, at worst caving in to cultural pressure or currying favor. They are motivated not by understanding and conviction, but by cowardice and conformity.

What fascinates and disturbs me is what people are willing to say about themselves, about our humanness, when they use this vocabulary. They imply that our societal and individual aspirations toward justice are either dishonest or naively admirable attempts to subdue the beast that we "naturally" are. For above all "P.C." signifies repression: certain deeply held essentialist notions of "uncivilized" human nature — Freud with strong dashes of Darwin and Rousseau — bubble under the surface of the term.

The assumptions coded in "P. C." spell a frightening despair, loss of faith. Ultimately, the designation "politically correct" severely limits our options by locking us into yet another grim dualism: either we are bigots, or we are hypocrites. We paint ourselves rhetorically into this corner where we sit, lonely, angry, frightened, disdaining our own best impulses and worthiest hungers.

It is finally the cynicism that troubles me most. Fearful and self-protective and simplistic, it is reflected in every facet of our culture. We are afraid of nothing so much as of getting taken, being seduced once more by belief or passion, vision or commitment. As the Who once put it, "we won't get fooled again." Cynicism comes easily enough to Generation X; as a teacher, I spend much of my time chipping away at it, working past the unyielding rock of this term down to the quick, the loam, where the need for meaning hides.

4. Reality Bites

But if "Politically Correct" means conformist, hypocritical, coward-ly, then what does its opposite mean? Even more unsettling than the ubiq-uity of the former is the way "Politically Incorrect" has taken on a kind of glory in the vernacular of popular culture. What does a new comedy show call itself to signify that it is daring? "Politically Incorrect." It has become a brag, a boast. Over the past year I have accumulated evidence, not as a lawyer would but as an anthropologist does, trying to understand the civilization in which I am crossing middle age. A few samples:

EXHIBIT A: a review of the recently edited and published letters of British poet Philip Larkin in the book review section of the Boston Globe.[6] In the first paragraph, Larkin is described as having been "about as politically incorrect as a white heterosexual male could be," regardless of which "readers on both sides of the Atlantic memorized his words, got a kick out of his opinions and held the poet himself . . . in affectionate regard. It was never any secret that the reclusive author was a reactionary and a xenophobe, a fussy bachelor, a blocked writer, misan-thropic, provincial, sour, profane, and full of base prejudices." The first dimension of political incorrectness worth scrutiny is that it seems to sub-sume and equalize characteristics as disparate as fussy bachelorism and base prejudices. In the course of the review, we are told that Larkin calls Italy "Wopland," ascribes the poor quality of one Indian writer's work to his "being an oriental," and urges someone to "Keep up the cracks about niggers and wogs." The reviewer himself, David Lehman, says of one of Larkin's poems that its "anti-Semitism stinks."

And yet Lehman finds need to defend Larkin against what he imagines as "politically correct critics." This is an important move: to label the opposition such that to object to Larkin's attitudes is to fall into an objectionable category oneself. If you find Larkin's fairly unambiguous racism hateful, it is you who are the problem: you're a party-pooper, spoiling the fun. Lehman's next move is to pull out an old lit-crit trick to salvage an "essential Larkin," innocent of his own statements: we "politically correct critics fail to discriminate between person and persona, and one feels one should temper one's disapproval with the knowledge that Larkin is at his lewdest and most unbecoming in correspondence with his closest, indeed lifelong friends." How did "racist and antisemitic" become "lewd and unbecoming," a matter of manners and behavior rather than character and spirit? And isn't it with our long-time, trusted friends that we are most honest, allowing our truest selves (whatever that might be) to speak? Furthermore, if Larkin cleaned up his act with less intimate associates so as not to seem racist and antisemitic, then isn't he the "politically correct" one?

Finally, the coup de grace: Larkin "is consciously posturing, delighting in being naughty — to the end of his life the Oxonian who missed his pals because now there was no one with whom he could utter forbidden words." By this end of this paragraph, Lehman has reduced a full-grown poet's racism and antisemitism to a schoolboy's delight in dirty words. Lehman does the same number when he quotes Larkin's reference to Emily Dickinson as "Emily Prick-in-son" as an example of "schoolboy crudeness" rather than some other category — "sexism," for instance. Words like "nigger" are not racist; they are only "naughty," "forbidden" — that is, by someone else, some resentable authority, who (like politically correct critics) spoils the fun. The language of racism and sexism is collapsed into the "bad words," usually scatological or sexual, prohibited in childhood. I think I've heard the moral of this story before: something like "boys will be boys"?

EXHIBIT B: An article from the *Detroit Free Press* on a computer game called "Man Enough."[7] Its first sentence begins, "You are a single male," so already I'm a little apprehensive, since I'm not. The game, billed as a "social adventure," offers "an unusual twist on adventure games, which usually require players to navigate a dangerous location using both wits and weapons. But here, your wits are your weapons." And guess who the dangerous location is?

. . . the player must first persuade each woman to give

him her phone number. In a subsequent call, he must
talk her into a date. On the date, the player must say all
the right things to achieve seduction. The action is
advanced by delivering one of three lines in response to
something the on-screen date says. Pick the right one,
and she responds favorably, often with a sleazy line of
her own. . . . every woman appears on-screen in some
form of undress. . . . it's supposed to look like a
Victoria's Secret catalog. There's no sex. Something happens to interrupt the action at the critical moment.

"Politically incorrect?" the article's author asks, and then answers happily:
"You bet."

But this time, no one defends against this label. On the contrary:
"We wanted to be politically incorrect," says the company president. "We
want to do products that are on the edge. . . . And maybe, just maybe,
there will be a few people who will play this game, and it may cause
them to think in a broader way." Now, let me see if I've got this straight:
political incorrectness broadens the mind; good old fashioned heterosexu-
ally predatory and objectifying porn, albeit on microchips, is "on the
edge"? Must be so: "Man Enough" (its title conveying its progressive
notion of masculine identity) sold 30,000 copies in its first month.

And yet these groundbreaking gender pioneers succumb to political correctness after all: they plan a feminine "corollary" version. Needless
to say, the corporate notion of feminine identity is equally cutting-edge:
women "tend to be more feeling, more emotional," so the company was
planning a game "that will appeal to women on an emotional level, for
Christmas 1994." Joy to the world.

EXHIBIT C: From the front page of the *Boston Globe*, a report on
Where the Boys Are '94 entitled: "Spring's PC Break."[8] The reporter stumbled on a wonderful geographic double-entendre: in the Florida panhan-
dle, "P.C. Beach" is Panama City Beach. The locals "would be hard-
pressed to concoct a more inaccurate nickname," he says. Apparently so:
his article opens with a balcony full of frat boys who have "downed a gal-
lon of whiskey and 14 cases of Old Milwaukee in only three days" aiming
a water rifle at a group of women below and threatening to open fire
unless the women drop their bikini tops, which they do (of their own
"free will," I'm certain).

From this scenario, the article proceeds to define a new allure —
or at least a reconstructed allure — for the old collegiate southern spring
migration. Places like P. C. Beach function as "seasonal demilitarized
zone[s] in the collegiate battle of the sexes, a refuge from campus political

correctness . . . . " As always, "P.C. Beach is all about escape" — but from a new enemy: "repressive attitudes about sex and dating sweeping college campuses." One college woman complains, "At school, everybody flips out over the littlest things. This is a totally different world. It's like the rules are off, and everyone can just relax." A male peer agrees: "Nobody cares if you're polite or politically correct. You don't have to worry whether a girl wants to have a relationship. You can just have fun." And they do, "carousing as wildly and mindlessly as they did before students were pressured to obtain step-by-step verbal consent for every sexual maneuver" — a paranoid overgeneralization of the Antioch College policy. Note that it is the predators, rather than the prey, who are now subject to "pressure." The article devotes one sentence to acknowledging that the "constant mingling of sex and alcohol can turn ugly," in the form of rape; nowhere does it deal with alcoholism itself or with the lethal incongruity of a sexual "free-for-all" (a male student's term) in the age of AIDS. For the author to consider, further, the effect on the women students' development of being at the business end of a water-rifle of sexual pressure would be, of course, asking too much. Free will, after all. Free speech. Free-for-all. It's a very, very free country.

5. The Wild Child

On cultural sites such as Philip Larkin's letters, Man Enough computer screens, and P.C. Beach, meaning has been made. The term "politically incorrect" has been constructed, insulated, decorated, and fully appointed. Entering its controlled climate, we see that it stands for an array of loosely but very crucially connected and deeply alluring notions that explain its ubiquity and potency. These fall into two important categories.

The first is a notion of *naturalness*. To be politically incorrect, in some cases, is to be relaxed, without tension — as one feels with one's "closest, indeed lifelong friends," for instance, or on a sunny Florida beach after 14 cases of Old Milwaukee. Or it is to be at peace, without conflict, especially without the conflicts of contemporary life, having returned, or regressed, to some kind of Edenic space — the sunny beach again. It is also to be honest, authentic in feeling and expression, resistant to polite hypocrisy. Ultimately, it is to be unrepressed — to have returned to a state of nature (the Edenic space again), eschewing the inhibitions and restraints of contemporary civilization.

The second important category of meanings collecting around "politically incorrect" is a notion of *rebelliousness, iconoclasm,* or *progressivism*. To be politically incorrect is to be outlaw, breaking rules and shattering codes; it is also to be risky, daring, "on the edge." The politically incorrect are those who think "in a broader way."

At first, these two branches of meaning might seem to be in conflict: the politically-incorrect-as-"natural," after all, suggests a return to an earlier world; the politically-incorrect-as-progressive implies forward motion. We can see one ready bridge in the notion of iconoclasm, the resistance to conformity, dear to the politically incorrect heart, that plays a leading role in American mythology. But the real link between the two, and the real lynch-pin in the construction of political incorrectness, is the image of the Child. The Wild Child, that is; the Romantic Child, who is at once Edenic and Rebellious, natural and daring, regressive and revolutionary.

And Male. Oh, yes; the child is male. If you watch closely where political incorrectness is being discussed or enacted, you will usually find that, sooner or later, as in the discussion of Larkin's letters, the issue becomes whether or not boys will be allowed to be boys. Complicated, serious adult verbal assaults will be, as Larkin's are, reformulated as naughtiness — sympathetic, daring, and masculine. "Man Enough" reduces adult heterosexuality to a high-tech boys' game. And P.C. beach is Animal House transplanted to Florida. It's the primal American myth: Huck Finn faces off against repressive old culture-reproducing Aunt Betsey the Politically Correct.

The profound danger of this linguistic trickery lies mostly in the notion of the natural and the repressed. A kind of K-Mart Freudianism is at work in the discourse of political in/correctness, clearly manifest in the P. C. Beach story. The campus environment, in which sexual behavior is regulated and interrogated with new and growing seriousness, is "politically correct," meaning that it is repressed and repressive. At the beach, sexuality seems totally unregulated, and therefore "free." Consciousness is not heavily monitored, and in fact unconsciousness (in the sexual and alcoholic senses) is encouraged (student get to carouse "mindlessly as they did before," remember) so the sexuality enacted must be "natural."

Of course the sexuality of Panama City Beach is neither: it is deeply constructed, anciently regulated, utterly in thrall to a strictly limited and limiting consciousness. The boys and girls of Florida are conforming to very traditional, "conservative," socioculturally determined sexual roles and behavior. If the boys on the balcony were sober enough merely to study the TV in their room, they would see the cultural scripts which their every move follows.

Neither is Philip Larkin's racism, sexism, and antisemitism innocent or childlike: since when do we take bigotry as inherent to childhood? Neither is "Man Enough" a cutting-edge, pioneering piece of technology: it is the tiredest of tired old misogynist stuff. But the selling of bigotry as rebellious, revolutionary, innovative: now that's something new. The real danger of this term "politically incorrect" is its reconstruction of cultural attitudes as "natural" and of adult preoccupations as "innocent."· To speak of racism as "bad words" and of pornography as "dirty pictures" allows us to escape serious analysis, responsibility, or consequences. It also perpetuates a view of actual male childhood development that, in fact, enables boys to continue being boys who grow up into bigoted men.

Implicit in the meanings of "politically incorrect," then, is an interesting escapism, a new romanticism. The term is charged with nostalgia for a lost Neverland. "I won't grow up!" sang Peter Pan. The term has caught the imagination of a society desperate to revert to childhood, to un-know what it has learned through the coming-of-age trials of Civil Rights and feminism, Stonewall and Los Angeles and many Marches on Washington. Such a term could gain currency only in a society whose dominant groups are yearning for freedom from the responsibility to be mindful. Yearning, that is, for mindlessness, like the children of P. C. Beach.

6. Why Ask Why?

And isn't it understandable that they should? Mindfulness, consciousness, are uncomfortable. As much as they expand and liberate, they constrict and limit. The most seemingly innocent of dearly and long-held assumptions about history, human nature, and interpersonal relations have been exploded. There seems to be no uncontested site, no conflict-free environment, no peace. The border wars rage inside our heads as well as our classrooms and departments. Small wonder that those among us likely to see more threat than promise in the outcome of these struggles should long for Neverland.

Our students, we're told, are confused by this new academic world, relativistic, pluralistic, deconstructive, multicultural. They need certainties; they need stability, a center. Quite true: so they do. But they do not need, or want, an education that ignores or fails to engage the complicated, conflicted reality around them. They need us, their teachers, and their classrooms to be the stable centers of the spinning world, people and places that can offer a vantage point, tools, language, attitudes and values with which to know what it is they see.

I think of a classroom again, this one quite unusual.

In April of 1992, the Simi Valley verdict in the Rodney King case came in, and a conversation began on the campus of Kalamazoo College. It started in the snack bar and a few dorm rooms, and it spread. It lasted all night and all the next day. It turned into a determination to seize one day from the normal academic week and give it over to what my generation called a "teach-in." It was organized entirely by a group of white students. I had to remind myself not only that these children had not lived through Kent State or Jackson State or Detroit or Watts, but that they were the video generation: reality came to them mediated through television. These students had seen a gang of white cops bludgeon a black man for over eighty seconds. They had seen it over and over and over again, ad nauseum. And yet the verdict was "not guilty." They needed to understand this. The memo soliciting faculty support was bewildered and beseeching, rather than belligerent. And it began with a disclaimer, phrased appropriately in media imagery: the students wished to dissociate themselves, they said, from the Generation X attitude of the Bud Dry ad that asks, "Why Ask Why?" They were tired of exhaustion, futility, cynicism; they wanted answers, complexities, meanings that would meet and shape their outrage and confusion, not anesthetize it.

During the committee meetings last year, I sometimes thought of that memo and the subsequent teach-in on the quad, which went on for over four hours on a cold, windy April afternoon. In the gaps and spaces left all around as we "debated P. C.," I could see the students' faces, hear their voices insisting that their tuition money buy them some strategies for comprehending the world into which they were born, the history they inherited. Even at the cost of our complacency or security, they said, make us mindful.

7. The Real Thing

The shift of cultural meanings makes for interesting study.

I used to have a maroon-colored button that read, in white letters, "Politically Incorrect." In the early eighties, I wore it happily. As a feminist, I thought I qualified. The phrase certainly captured how it felt to be me, on my campus, in the mesh of my daily encounters.

That's because I knew what Politically Correct meant. I knew what it looked like, and smelled like, and tasted like. I knew how it talked and walked and what color ties it preferred. I knew how it thought and wrote and where it got its Ph.D. For a long time I didn't realize that it was Political. But I sure knew it was Correct.

It had been invisible to me until I began to take shape myself. When I appeared, so did it: large and looming. I realized I hadn't seen it because I had been inside it, in its head most of my life. Once out (and, like Athena, armed), I began to understand its dimensions, its power. I understood the fealty I owed to it, and the revenge.

And I remember very well my grief upon first grasping the harm it had done, this genuine Political Correctness: in my discipline, the language I spoke, whole vast traditions of achievement and beauty were suppressed, silenced, erased. My students today, accustomed as they are to the presence and accessibility of women writers and writers of color, are a little embarrassed, I think, by the energy in my voice when I talk about these things. But to my mind it's all still very close: I see Alice Walker striding through the tall Florida weeds in search of a rise in the earth that might be Zora Neale Hurston's grave; I see Henry Louis Gates rescuing *Our Nig*, the first African American novel, from oblivion; I see *The Awakening* and "The Yellow Wallpaper" coming back into print after fifty years as a result of the work of women. I see myself asking questions of literature and of scholarship that I was taught not to ask — because it was Politically Incorrect to "politicize" literature. I see myself asking questions of history that Political Correctness taught me were unimportant and irrelevant. I see this Political Correctness as a giant Oz-like head whose first word is "SILENCE!" and whose first commandment is "Thou Shalt Not Know."

I think that we should remind each other and the rest of the world what Political Correctness really was and is, and why its suppressions generated a revolution. I think that we who have been continually hurt and undermined by this label should stop debating P. C. What we must do is to represent ourselves in our own terms, insisting on our own language, refusing to be reduced to straw men sitting on one end of a see-saw. We must repeatedly remind our genuinely bewildered colleagues and students and the non-academic public what this struggle is really about, where we have come from, and what we stand for.

There are many solid reasons to fight for curricular and cultural change that ends the dominance of white western male culture. Two of the most persuasive, as well as the most important, have to do with our clientele: our students will become increasingly diverse, and we are supposedly educating them to navigate in a multicultural world. But ultimately, I think we are fighting for change for the sake of Truth. Yes, you heard me: poor old beleaguered, deconstructed Truth. I think we should argue in terms of Truth more often. The truth is that the world is extremely diverse, that history reveals many cultures (and two genders) whose perspectives and achievements have shaped our world and are worthy of study. To ignore or deny this reality is to distort truth, to miseducate. The truth is that the United States of America has a particularly interesting multicultural history and identity, one that absolutely demands new intellectual approaches. The truth is that what we perceive and even cherish as absolute or universal often turns out, under a broader light, to be particular and relative.

This discovery can be devastating: it might be seen as the primal recurring experience of growing up. It has been my experience that fifty-year-old Ph.D.'s are not a great deal better at traversing this passage than their eighteen-year-old students. But it can also be as liberating, exhilarating, and revelatory for the fifty-year-olds as for the adolescents. It is usually the site of major intellectual leaps and paradigm shifts. And that is what the opening of the curriculum has meant, first and foremost: altered vision, a bigger world, greater possibilities. I think we should argue in these terms much more often, and more loudly, and for the purposes of these discussions, postmodern subtleties and cynicism be damned.

After all, which lies closer to the rigidity and narrowness embodied in the term "politically correct": an epistemology, or an orientation to life, that cultivates plurality, diversity, and multiplicity, or one that depends upon hierarchies of authority, exclusionary notions of significance and value, and theories of dominance? In the dualistic discourse I have railed against, the white light of truth is often claimed by the opponents of "P. C." and posited against the red light of passion, engagement, "politics." Don't believe it, and don't submit to argue in those terms. We are after the truth, the whole truth, the white light itself — which, as every objective, detached, apolitical physicist knows, is composed of a whole spectrum of colors.

12

Dear Katie
The Scarlet Letter

March, 1994

Dear Katie,

Surprise — here I am again. I've been thinking about your letter and especially about my response to it, and I realized I needed to send a fairly lengthy P.S.

I truly loved your letter. I have to admit that it's a shock to hear you posing these considered, probing questions about scholarship and academic life. In my mind, you are always about eleven, with your freckles, your heavy, dark hair brushing your chin, and your generous, graceful spirit always trying to bridge the gaps and heal the lacerations of our contorted family life. It's a jolt to realize that you're standing alongside the dozens of former students I'm in touch with, young women just out of college, full of intelligence, talent, and desire but not knowing where to take it all. Your questions were excellent, exactly the ones you should be asking. It was after I printed out my reply and put it in the mail to you that I saw a gap in my own response that was worth thinking about. Hence this second letter.

I think that our truest answers — mine, at least — are multiple. Or better yet: that the best evidence of our devotion to truth is our urge to revise. Spoken like an English teacher, I realize. I wonder if it is these philosophical positions that have formed my teaching strategies, or the other way around. Maybe it is years of discouraging singular answers and encouraging rewriting that have led me to this place.

I responded quickly and easily to all your questions but one. When you asked whether I felt respected in my place of work, I hesitated for a nanosecond. Something happened — a jarring, an old ache. I suppressed it almost as quickly as it came, and went on to answer you: Yes, I said, if you came to my place of work, you'd hear me described as a leader, something of a star, in fact, on that little campus. Of course, I went on, I have been a figure of controversy over the years, but that comes with the territory (the territory of feminism, though interestingly I never used that word anywhere in my letter to you). The sense of meaning and purpose comes from the struggle, I assured you grandly. And went on to the next question. When I finished answering them all, I printed out two copies and put them in the mail, one to you and one to my mother, your grandmother, who I knew would be pleased to see both your intelligent, mature questions and my confident, positive answers. Botta boom, botta bing.

And I meant it all. Didn't I? I'm sure I did. There is incontrovertible evidence. I chair a department and direct a Women's Studies program. Virtually every honor a little college has to give has come to me — for scholarship, teaching, involvement with students. My teaching evaluations help drag the divisional average way up. One or two of my courses have made it onto the Must Take list. I have a drawer full of testimony from students and colleagues as to the effect of my classes, my speeches and publications, my efforts in general. If that ain't respect, she said, you tell me what is.

So why is it that even as I typed my answer to your question into the computer, I was conscious of gulping something back, swallowing something down into silence? And why is it that for days after I posted the letter, your question stuck with me, re-presenting itself over and over again in the quiet of the back of my mind?

At some point in those days, I made a stunning realization: in my pages of single-spaced, small-font response to your letter, I don't believe I ever used the word "woman." You'd have to have lived alongside me for the past ten or fifteen years to know how remarkable that is. Given that you, a young woman and my niece, were asking me, a middle-aged woman and your aunt, about my professional existence, it's even more remarkable. And as I mulled this over, I saw suddenly what I had sublimated for the sake of a tight, smooth, cheerful response to your question.

What I gave you, Katie, was the version of my professional life that I tell not only others but even myself to try to keep myself in balance, to keep from toppling over into rage or despair. Not that it isn't true: I meant what I said at the top of this letter; I believe in multiple truths. It's pretty much impossible to live through our postmodern age (not to mention living it in academe) without acknowledging that. It's as true as true can be that I love my work (as distinct from my job), consider it meaningful and important, and am respected by my students and colleagues. But something else is true too, a darker, meaner truth. And as a young woman thinking about my profession, you need to hear it.

Maybe it's very simple: that the cost of that "loving-my-work" is

higher than I am sometimes willing to acknowledge, even to myself. Or
maybe it's very complicated: as old and complicated as the western male
notions of the Mind, of Knowledge, and of Woman. I'll try to find the
road between these two poles.

What I want to tell you about is sexism, specifically sexism in
academic settings. I want to tell you how it operates, but not in terms of
big splashy cases that make headlines: Eminent Researcher Quits Post,
Charges Years of Sexual Harassment; or Women's Studies Prof Denied
Tenure. Those cases speak for themselves — though it's pretty remarkable how they get interrupted in the process. What I want to talk about is
the dailiness of academic sexism, the way it functions as a part of your
work environment, like a particular chemical in the air or a pattern in the
carpet. I want to talk not about the foreground but about the background;
not the major collisions but the small frequent abrasions that leave you
sore and bruised and sometimes not really knowing why. I want to talk
about the slow, steady energy drain, the seeping away of your attention
and drive and focus, your imagination and strength and courage.

Where to start. Shall I start with sheer physical space? Never
mind the patronizing arms around shoulders, never mind the space-taking
positions and gestures that countless social scientists have written about.
There are other manifestations of what any anthropologist would identify
as dominance behavior. There are the men who come into your office
and, instead of sitting down, move in close to your chair, remaining
standing, forcing you to look up at them. When women colleagues come
to my office (whose door is always open unless I'm in a confidential conversation), they invariably knock softly on the open door, if I don't see
them; or if I do, they say, "Are you busy?" or "Can I talk to you for a
minute? Is this a good time?" I have a part-time female colleague who
always says, "When you have a free minute, can we talk?" Many of the
men have different patterns. Some of them simply charge in, regardless of
what I'm doing. I've had male colleagues walk in and start talking to me
when I was conferring with a student, without so much as an "Excuse
me" to me or the student. Once I was in a very serious, closed-door conference with one of the junior members of the department when a male
colleague knocked on my door and, when I opened it to tell him I was
busy (which the closed door should have signified), strolled right in and
started in on his agenda, regardless of the other person sitting there. One
remarkable little ritual has been a great source of interest among my
women colleagues: men — faculty and students — will stand in the
doorway, silent, waiting for me to realize they are there. Of course, the
effect is often startling; on occasion I've nearly jumped out of my chair
when I realized someone had been there, watching me, for who knows
how long. The effect can also be very invasive: I have peripherally

watched men stand there, five feet away, while I conduct a phone conversation. The power of that presence speaks volumes: "I'm here; it's
your job to notice me." If one's office is private, one's classroom is sacro-
sanct, yet a part-time female colleague of mine has twice had her class
interrupted by the entrance of senior male professors — one to announce
that someone's car was blocking his; another to pull her out of her own
class to confer with him about a student.

    And then there's the verbal arena, so important in an academic
setting. Again, never mind the well known, well documented male verbal
behavior: interruptions, the ignoring of women's comments in meetings,
contextually incongruous comments on appearance and clothing, monologue usurping dialogue (that is: men talking at you, regardless of where
you were going or what you might have on your mind, until you are
absolutely exhausted). There is the teasing, semi-sexual tone that men,
especially senior men, use toward women in meetings, which the other
women immediately notice and remark on. Sometimes it's used strategi-
cally, whether consciously so or not, to deflate the seriousness of a
woman's comment, her issue, her presence. Inappropriate humor can
work the same way. And there are outright diminishments: once a
provost — my "immediate superior" in hierarchical terms — actually
called me "little girl" when I expressed worry over something. On another
occasion, I was discussing a junior female colleague with the same man
when he said, "What are we going to do with that child?" Both of us, little
girl and child, were thirty-seven at the time.

    As a woman professor, you see the ancient double standard oper-
ating on a number of levels. Maybe you teach a particularly successful,
popular course; you hear a male colleague speaking of it in those ever-
so-slightly dismissive terms that suggest ever-so-clearly that it's probably a
gut — appealing, but not intellectually demanding or serious. In fact, its
appeal means it cannot be demanding or serious. He won't come right
out and say it, and if called on it he'll deny the implication, but you hear
it. You get excellent evaluations; they must indicate lower standards, or
pleasing personality, or personal attention — anything but effective teaching. Your personal life is much more a topic of conversation and concern
than that of your male colleagues. So is your appearance, your physical
being. Your collegial relationships are cast in a suspect light, too. (Not
that gossip isn't a part of any workplace; frankly, it can be one of the
redeeming features of an otherwise lousy day.) If you have no close relationship with a male colleague, you're a lesbian/separatist/man-hater; if
you do, you're obviously having an affair with him. And the likelihood is
that although you will hear about it regularly (from "concerned" friends
and other voyeurs), he will not.

    Maybe the most deadly operation of sexism has to do with work load. Workload inequities — women doing far more than their share, women cleaning up after man-made messes or finishing the jobs men start and abandon, women taking care of the human fallout from male-run systems — are so well known and obvious that they are a commonplace among women, and sometimes even acknowledged by men. A former colleague, male, liked to use the abusive overwork of what was then a handful of women on the faculty to argue that women really "ran the college" — a nod to that tired old notion of women's "influence" (the hand that rocks the cradle rules the world, etc.), which is nothing but insulting to women stretched very thin and seeing very few rewards, tangible or otherwise, for their commitment. You find yourself leaving a department meeting in which Dr. Full Professor has been extremely vocal about what needed to be done, but somehow the task has been assigned to your untenured self. It is true that some of the disproportionate female workload has to do with the way we often approach our work — holistically, inclusively, with a great deal of attention to process, to voice, and to human consequences. But instead of being used to set new standards of professional performance, so that the burden of a holistic approach to work might be more equitably distributed (i.e., that's a good and effective way to work, so let's all try it), we find ourselves used against ourselves, accused of creating the inequities that afflict us. We "take it on ourselves."

Maybe it's true. Once, when I left campus for my traditional winter off-campus research term, a senior colleague inherited my responsibility of a very important, time-consuming project. This was a guy notoriously allergic to hard work and details. When I returned in the spring, I discovered that a junior woman was doing it. Shall we blame her for it? Maybe she should have screamed bloody murder, called the provost's office, hired a lawyer. What I suspect is that she quickly realized that if she didn't pick up the slack, the job would be badly done or not done at all. For once, I choose not to ascribe the fault to her.

Once an administrator asked me if I would take on a major project. Not only was it part of the responsibility for which a senior male colleague was receiving a stipend, but it would have required me to stay on campus for at least part of my off-campus term (for which I am not paid — I am on a nine-month contract, though the checks are spread over twelve months). We both knew, the administrator suggested conspiratorially, that my colleague was probably not going to do a very presentable job. When I refused, the administrator, looking and sounding exasperated, told me that I was, in effect, asking for it: by refusing, I guaranteed that a bad job would be done. Do you see what happened there, my dear niece? Do you see that not only was the institution, represented by the administrator, quite willing to exploit me and to excuse my colleague's incompetence, but I was made responsible for his incompetence at the same time? Ah, but wasn't I shown respect, nonetheless, in the implica-tion that I would do the job well, better than he? Do you begin to see why this respect thing is the sharpest of double-edged knives?

Years earlier (years younger) I might actually have given in; the project meant a great deal, reflected on a whole group of people; and the administrator was quite right: my colleague would do — and did — a reprehensible job. He produced a document that not only was embarrass-ingly badly written but attacked the work of several others, including me. It was an even greater disaster than he or I predicted, so great that I con-sidered redoing it when I returned to campus. Finally we let it stand, sim-ply because nobody had time to take on a hasty revision.

My point is not so much that people suffered for his incompe-tence and self-indulgence as that he was never called to account for his product. He had had his say. Voice is an amazing drama at a college — who gets to speak, whose speech is validated, who gets heard, who is allowed to get angry, who gets forgiven for his "excesses" and eccentrici-ties, who gets deemed an Expert. As a woman you grow attuned to how easy it is for men in an organization to make noise, to get attention, to have their causes validated; and you watch women go silent, angry, and bitter. You are at first unwilling to believe that there is Gender Trouble at work when women's voices are devalued, contradicted, ridiculed, demo-nized, or otherwise diminished. But there is too much repetition to mean anything else.

The workload inequities come with an aftershock: after you've done the inordinate portion of the work, which often includes the undone or poorly done work of others, you find yourself criticized, sus-pected, or subverted for it. Your decisions, if you are in authority, are qui-etly eroded, questioned, destabilized behind your back. Alternately, men assume you are probably not doing your job. A few years ago, a woman professor found, in the personnel file of someone she supervised, a letter from a male colleague attributing the person's poor performance to lack of supervision. When she confronted him about it, he was abashed and apologetic (to his credit), and he confessed that he hadn't known any supervisory activities were taking place. But his ignorance hadn't stopped him from writing — that is, from using his considerable institutional voice at her expense. Who in the administration read that letter and drew con-clusions about her leadership?

The relationship of voice to expertise at a college is interesting. Colleges and universities are built on notions of expertise — faulty though they may be. According to the system, as it advertises itself, voice should depend on expertise: that is, you should be consulted, attended to, taken seriously, empowered because you know more than others about a subject. But those who by race or gender or some other force of fate or choice are marginal to a college (even if by talent, commitment, and tenure they are central) often find the relationship reversed: perceived expertise depends on voice. If you are someone without institutional voice, your expertise is regularly denied — in other, blunter words, if you're not one of us, you don't really know what you're talking about. If who you are and what you know leads you to question or contradict what the place habitually thinks about itself, you are likely to find yourself silenced. I don't mean that you will literally not be allowed to speak. We have the First Amendment, after all, and it's suddenly become tremendously popular at colleges these days. There are many ways to silence someone. To have your knowledge — your expertise — dismissed, constantly questioned, mistranslated, or otherwise rejected is to be denied voice. Faculty of color try to talk about institutional racism; instead of being acknowledged as experts, with insights no white person could possibly have, they are accused of making accusations and causing trouble; they are interrogated in the most suspicious or defensive tones; they are disparaged behind their backs and accused of the most heinous violations. I know women who have spent years on their campuses educating themselves and others about critical issues for women students — reading, networking, going to conferences, listening to and counseling students, doing workshops — and doing it on their own time and with little to no recognition; instead of being sought out as the obvious experts, they are likely to find themselves dismissed as "biased" or "not credible." Their judgment is still called into question with skeptical looks, trivializing comments, backbiting and gossip, reminders that there are two sides to every story. Expertise, coming from an unwelcome or threatening place, becomes "bias."

Bias: the problem that, as a feminist, you have tried to fight becomes the crime you're accused of. The surest way to damn yourself as biased or "not objective" is to evince loyalty to other women — your students, your colleagues, even the people who write the books you teach. You watch the men you work with. You see them bond at bars, on basketball courts, at strip clubs, and in faculty meetings; but your intimacy with woman colleagues is suspect, threatening — and of course a source of "bias." You note the way they validate each other's voices, grant each other implicit credibility; but when you choose to believe the voices of women — students describing harassment, black and Asian faculty describing racism, a colleague explaining why she feels unsafe in her department or her classroom — you are "biased." You watch the men you work with use their networks to hire their relatives, drinking buddies, and unemployed grad school cronies, not to mention new young Ph.D. clones of themselves; but when you lobby for a female candidate, you are accused of conspiracy, "going overboard," "trying to hire somebody just like you." (It takes a few days for the full insult to sink in.)

This is the disrespect that sometimes leaves you staggering, the heart-hurt that is worse than exhaustion. You work as bravely, as creatively as you can, and then you watch men around you describe what you have done in terms you do not recognize and ask you questions that say unambiguously that they don't believe or trust you. It is like "being called out of your name," as African Americans say. It feels like violation. It is.

I recently finished Patricia Williams' wonderful book about being a black woman law professor, *The Alchemy of Race and Rights*. One passage stopped my breath in recognition:

> There are moments in my life when I feel as though a part of me is missing. There are days when I feel so invisible that I can't remember what day of the week it is, when I feel so manipulated that I can't remember my own name, when I feel so lost and angry that I can't speak a civil word to the people who love me best. Those are the times when I catch sight of my reflection in store windows and am surprised to see a whole person looking back.[1]

That I have often felt this way, as a white woman from the same class, cultural, and educational background as most of the people I work with, gives me some hint of what life is like for a woman of color in my position.

This has been very hard to write, Katie. All the time there have been several editors in my head, leaning in over the computer screen, interrupting and advising and critiquing. One of them looks like ten or twelve men I work with. He has questioned every assertion I've made, reinterpreted every story I've told, and "wondered" at every point, "Is that really about gender, do you think?" He is full of anecdotes starring men of his acquaintance, even himself, who have suffered similar abuses. You will meet up with him a lot, and he's a subtle one: what better way to silence you than to make you doubt the validity of your own analysis of your own experience?

Another editor — gender indeterminate, sort of androgynous — has accused me of whining, of dumping, of dwelling on the negative. It's not so much the message, this voice insists; it's your tone. So I've gone back over this letter a lot, revising for tone, adding soupçons of humor, trying to make myself acceptable, trying not to lay too heavy a trip on you. I do this in my work all the time. Working with young people whom I don't want to terrify or alienate, I modulate myself. Working with men whose credence I need in order to function, I modulate myself.

Sometimes I modulate myself so successfully that when people ask, "How are you?" I have no idea.

A third editor has been the most dangerous. She's definitely female, and dressed very much for success — mauve suit, I believe, and neat, coifed hair; subtle make-up, perfect nails, and never a run in her pantyhose. Her agenda is this: I have been defining problems but offering no solutions. This is for your twenty-four-year-old niece, she says; you owe her advice, recommendations, strategies for surmounting these barriers. Teach her how to play the Games Mother Never Taught Her!

Katie, maybe I should. I know a whole lot of them. I could tell you ways to negotiate physical or verbal space with men who, intentionally or simply habitually, use it to dominate. I could recommend ways of keeping your workload under control. I could explore the pros and cons of workplace romances, modes of dress and grooming, teaching styles, and confrontation vs. transcendence as ways of dealing with sexist or racist statements. If you want me to, I will — in another letter, a nice letter on cream-colored college letterhead.

But this, Katie, is the Scarlet Letter. Here (I decided, finally, after the umpteenth interruption by the mauve suit) my goal is not to tell you how to navigate a sexist system. I recognize that you must do so, whatever system you enter. But if our sole response to sexism is to teach our daughters (and nieces) how to "get by" within it, haven't we also helped to stabilize the system? And if our focus is solely on how we can get by, haven't we shifted the responsibility for sexism to ourselves? Of course we are ultimately responsible for the lives we lead in this system. But part of our responsibility is to identify that system, blow its cover, name its parts. We cannot be outside of the system; no one can. But we must not be wholly swallowed by it either. I've worked with women who are, or who are trying to be, and it's not a pretty sight.

This returns me to my starting place, my fundamental ambivalence about my "job": I am Employee-of-the-Century, and I am also a Foreign Agent, stealing the blueprints so that the revolutionaries can blow up the factory. As a result, I work with a double consciousness that amounts, at times, almost to cognitive dissonance. I think the way I've been sustaining this dissonance all these years is by pretending to believe that the good redeems the bad. I think that's a true-sounding platitude we often use to rationalize our situations. But in fact, the good does not balance or compensate for the bad. They simply coexist, at odds with each other, creating a nearly constant contradiction that disturbs equilibrium and blurs focus. To hear that you're a goddess when you're being treated like a child or a witch or a drudge isn't redemptive; it's simply crazy-making.

I want you to know this, because you asked very direct questions and they deserve honest answers. I want you to know it, also, because I still believe the truth will set you free — or as close to free as a woman can get in this world. I want you to know that the crazy-making dissonance is there, and to know it has a name. I want you to know that you will meet with support, respect, and admiration from some of the men you work with, while others — or even the same ones later on the same day — will pull the rug out from under you. Same with the women: there are so many reasons for them to ally with men or with male hierarchies against you, and against their own best selves, and that may hurt most of all. I want you to know that you will sometimes feel you are doing two jobs, and here I'm not talking about workload: you will feel that on top of your job responsibilities you are also doing the additional psychic work of dealing with the ordinary, garden-variety sexism, subtle or not, that constantly erodes your edges, making you at the very least tired and cranky, at the most half-mad and physically ill. No degree of talent, accomplishment, or privilege will protect you, ultimately; being white, middle-class, heterosexual, educated, and physically near the cultural ideal affords certain buffers, but they are not absolute. And if your head is in the right place, these buffers function as reminders that for others, lacking such protections, the burden is much heavier.

And finally, I want you to know all this so that when it gets you, however it gets you, you might know you are not crazy and not alone. When you speak up about what you see happening, a chorus of voices, male and female, will contradict you; they will tell you that it's better than before, or that it's not about gender, or that it's not intentional, or that it's not even happening. But over in the corner you'll see another woman, or two, or three, who are nodding their heads.

One of them will look familiar. That will be me,

Your devoted Scarlet Aunt,

Gail

13

The Space Between
Maternal Pedagogy and the Position of the Woman Teacher [1]

*Was there ever a life more riddled with self-doubt
than that of a female professor?* [2]

Since being invited to speak on this topic, I have been very nervous. We are in treacherous waters, talking about teaching and motherhood in the same breath. The opportunities for shipwreck seem ubiquitous. There is, first and perhaps foremost, the fact that I have no children and therefore might well be accused of ignorance, if not arrogance. There are the Scylla and Charybdis of heterosexism on the one hand and essentialism on the other. There is the dreadful iceberg of sentimentalism toward which all discussions of motherhood in post-industrial western societies seem to be inescapable drawn. I think I am doomed unless I make two claims, or disclaimers if you like, from the beginning. The first is that I do not see mothering as biological or even as necessarily deriving from a biological role. I see it as women's propagation and nourishment of life. While I don't see it as universal among women, essential to women, or exclusive to women, I do see it as a historically developed female expertise in the nourishment of life, including the raising of the young. And second, I don't see anything sentimental about it. I don't see it as primarily a matter of feeling, but as a matter of skill, an exercise of strength and intelligence. When I say that we are called upon, as female teachers, to mother our students, then, I don't mean what my male colleagues usually think I mean or usually mean themselves: that we are to be emotional sponges, soaking up and then cleaning up. I mean that the academic world, *for better and for worse,* is familial. The "worse" part is that in so many ways it replicates the heterosexual nuclear family, with all of its abuses and inequities. But it is familiar in another, quite separate sense in that it is devoted (supposedly) to the development of children into adulthood. I wholeheartedly agree with the African proverb that says it takes a village to raise a child, and from eighteen to twenty-two that village is often an "academical" one, as Mr. Jefferson used to call it in Virginia. Faculty members, for better and for worse, are in loco parentis, and thus we are in the place of mothers. But not merely by accident of gender; we can make a political, historically informed choice to situate ourselves as mothers in explicit contradistinction to the paternal tradition that has shaped academe as we know it. I mean that taking ourselves seriously as maternal pedagogues can give us revolutionary energy. End of claims and disclaimers.

I find that my thinking on many issues is shaped by my most recent academic encounters — with students, colleagues, and texts — and so I want to begin at the place where I ended this past academic term at Kalamazoo College (which was in September): a remarkable poem from the latest book by our new poet laureate, Rita Dove. The book is *Grace Notes* and the poem is called "Arrow."

> The eminent scholar "took the bull by the horns,"
> substituting urban black speech for the voice
> of an illiterate cop in Aristophanes' *Thesmophoriazusae.*
> And we sat there.
> Dana's purple eyes deepened. Becky
> twitched to her hairtips
> and Janice in her red shoes
> scribbled *he's an arschloch; do you want*
> *to leave? He's a model product of his*
> *education,* I scribbled back; *we can learn from this.*
>
> So we sat through the applause
> and my chest flashed hot, a void
> sucking at my guts until I was all
> flamed surface. I would have to speak up.
> Then the scholar progressed
> to his prize-winning translations of
> the Italian Nobel Laureate. He explained the poet
> to us: immense difficulty
> with human relationships; sensitive;
> women were a scrim through which he could see
> heaven.
> We sat through it. Quite lovely, those poems.
> We could learn from them although they were saying
> *you women are nothing, nothing at all.*

When the moment came I raised my hand,
phrased my question as I had to: sardonic,
eminently civil my condemnation
phrased in the language of fathers —
felt the room freeze behind me.
And the answer came as it had to:
humanity—celebrate our differences—
the virility of ethnicity. My students
sat there already devising

their different ways of coping:
Dana knowing it best to have
the migraine at once, get the poison out quickly
Becky holding it back for five hours   and Janice
making it to the evening reading and
party afterwards
in black pants and tunic with silver mirrors
her shoes pointed and studded, wicked witch shoes:
Janice who will wear red for three days or
yellow brighter
than her hair so she can't be
seen   at all

I suspect that in any room full of female academics, this poem is going to ring wild bells. What pleasantly surprised me in late August was the similar response from most of the twenty women in my twenty-three-student Contemporary American Women Poets course. A highly charged discussion ensued, charged with what felt like accumulated frustration and a common stock of memories. Apparently this poem captures a primary experience of women in the academic world: the experience of sitting through the self-serving, racist, sexist monologue of an eminent arschloch. (By the way, though I had some contextual notion of the meaning of this word, I don't speak German, so I asked the class. At Kalamazoo, 80% of the students study overseas, many of them at the three German universities where we maintain programs. So when I asked, there came a wonderful chorus from about a third of the class: "ASS-HOLE!" Thankfully, the class also included numerous theater majors who could tell me how to pronounce Thesmophoriazusae, not to mention enlightening the science majors about what a scrim is.)

Usually I ask the class to choose poems from the day's reading to discuss, but this time I said I had dibs. I thought I chose this one because it would appeal to them, being about student responses to academic life; but in the course of our wonderful discussion, as the students focused almost completely on Dana, Becky and Janice, I realized I had my own motives. I wanted to talk about that speaker.

When one of my students said that at first she hadn't realized the speaker was a teacher, I was surprised. Glancing at the poem, I saw that there was good reason for her ignorance: that point, to me glaringly obvious, is in fact not revealed until the end of the second-to-last stanza of the poem. Before that, the reader does not "officially" know about the speaker, or for that matter about the identified trio in relation to her. Why was it so obvious to me that the speaker was their female teacher? Perhaps only because I know that Rita Dove teaches in the English Department of the University of Virginia, where I did hard time as a graduate student. But perhaps not. Perhaps I recognized her, like my own face in a mirror, from other data. I want to chart those data carefully, for I realize they define, for me, a consistent relationship with students and with the academic world that I call maternal pedagogy — or pedagogical maternity, if you prefer. I want to use Dove's text as a defined space in which to search out the corners of that difficult, controversial notion, the maternal metaphor of teaching, that we are here today to think about.

The first stanza of the poem establishes a genuine conspiracy, in the original sense of the term. First it defines an opposition: there is "The eminent scholar," up there taking bulls by horns; and then there is "we," who "sat there." Dana, Becky, Janice, and "I." Then a secondary opposition emerges, this one discursive: the speaker's dominant, monological voice, doing its awful verbal blackface, versus the dialogical, subversive, scrawled messages between Janice and the speaker. Talk about your oppositional discourse! Janice uses the strategy common to kids in the presence of adults, students subjected to teachers: she 'writes notes,' as they used to say when they sent me to the principal's office for doing it. I always saw writing, as opposed to speech, as secret, subversive, and immensely powerful, whether I was writing to a friend in class or writing poetry in my notebook instead of watching the film or taking notes. Girls write notes. It is one of the ways their little subversive voices stay alive. The relationship between Janice and the speaker is immediately established as one of "girlfriend" intimacy, implied not only by the note-writing, but by Janice's language — she uses the word "asshole" to her professor, about another professor — and by her very question: she asks her professor if she wants to blow this popstand, as if she were asking a peer. In fact, that blurriness in their relationship is part of what probably confused my student, just as, conversely, it helped me identify the speaker as a teacher like me, a woman who has never found established categories of teacher/student or professor/student relationships to be adequate, useful, or reliable.

But while Janice and the speaker are conspiratorial, they are also in opposition. Janice's tendency is to jump ship; she has minimal ambiguity. The speaker's response to her question is what, for me, instantly identified her as a teacher, their teacher. *"He's a model product of his education,"* she begins, and those who know her as intimately as I do know this is not an attempt to rationalize or justify his offenses. What she is doing is asking her student to see this *arschloch* as a *product,* a symbol, a sign, a text, an artifact — an object, that is, in response to which she encourages the students to become knowing subjects, reversing the established order of such situations, where he, the "expert," is the knower and they the silent recipients — or receptacles — of his knowledge.

And then she continues: *"we can learn from this."* Here I clearly hear the sound of my own voice. What I hear is all my best and worst teacherly instincts, all my ambivalent relationship with the academic world. She asks Janice — who by the subtle strokes of poetry has already been established as the ringleader — to stay, but she does not say outright, "No, stay." She asks Janice to regard the speaker as more than simply an *arschloch,* but she neither quarrels with Janice's definition of him nor reprimands her for the insouciance of her dismissal. What she offers is another option: staying at the lecture, but not as powerless subordinates, duped by the expert's minstrel show; rather, as anthropologists, studying him culturally, as *"a model product of his education,"* and as sophisticated researchers, who can learn, not from *him,* but from *"this."* In two sentences, this speaker — this obviously female teacher — has transformed her students (and here I will call upon the categorical terms from *Women's Ways of Knowing)* from "silent" receptacles to constructed knowers[3] superior to the expert himself. And, last but definitely not least, she has also positioned the four of them as peers, allies in the construction of knowledge: *"we can learn from this."*

But I said I could hear my ambiguity in her voice, too. Do you hear it? Her resistance to the radicalism of Janice's suggestion? Her loyalty to the proceedings, despite her implicit concurrence in Janice's judgment? Some whiff of rationalization in her response to Janice, something wishful, as if she needed to find a reason to stay in the room, or felt an obligation to make her students stay? The ambivalence of girlfriend/teacher in her exchange with Janice? It is precisely in this ambivalence that I locate myself as a woman/teacher. I used to see it as something to resolve, an indication of my lack of professional development or deficient ego structure or something. Since it hasn't gone away in the past twenty years, I've decided to make it normal. In fact, I've come to see it as a normal response of women to our academic situation, our particular *marginality,* not so much in the sense of our being excluded, but in the sense of our occupying *spaces between,* spaces on the edge. In this poem, both the speaker's ambiguity and her potency come from her between-ness: She occupies a space between peer and superior, the two choices offered us by male academic tradition. She is also situated between the students and the eminent scholar, for she is a professor, an academic, a scholar/intellectual like him; but she is also in opposition to him, allied by many factors with her students. And, of course, she is in-between in her attitude toward the lecture, wanting to stay but only in a resistant, critical mode. This marginal zone, while it can be confusing, confining, a site of intense ambivalence, is also potentially freeing, mobilizing, and creative. It is what I call the out-law zone. I have been helped in coming to this satisfying recognition of the potential of academic marginality, in my use of the term, by Madeleine Grumet's discussion of the classroom as "a real space in the middle" rather than a "conveyance, designed to transport children from the private to the public world. . . ."4 Here at this very point in the poem, in fact, the speaker creates a "space between" the two options that have presented themselves so far: subordinating themselves to the "eminent scholar," or leaving, abandoning the proceedings entirely. She verbally concocts a third option: staying as critical observers, subversive analysts, spies in the halls of the fathers, as it were.

So the foursome sits through the applause and into that most dangerous ground in any such academic occasion, the dreaded question/answer period. But somewhere in this process of sitting through it, the speaker formulates, viscerally rather than rationally, a decision: she will have to speak up. Why? And what was is about this sequence — obliquely convincing her charges to stay the course, and then experiencing those vividly described symptoms of sickness and rage — that leads to the decision? Or is it a decision? *"I would have to speak up."* It is expressed as more of a recognition, a dawning awareness, not that she wanted to speak up, or that she simply "would" speak up, but that she "would have to" do so. Why?

There are two possibilities. The one my students recognized is the overt one: that the speaker, despite her modulating influence on Janice, has had to acknowledge her own fury and upset and thus cannot keep silent. Quite true, I think. But then there's the other, obscured motive. She "would have to speak up," suggesting a sense of responsibility, obligation. To whom? Of course, to Janice and Dana and Becky. And this is the next clue that identifies the speaker as a teacher. How often have I, how often have you realized — sometimes with a sickening feeling — that *we will have to speak up* in such a situation, specifically for the sake of, or on behalf of, the students in the room, and particularly the women? He's an *arschloch* and we want to cut and run, or at least sit in safe, disgusted silence; but the room is full of students to whom this guy has been presented as an authority. We have what our students don't have in such situations — similar authority to his; maybe greater articulateness than they; perhaps a clearer understanding of the issues and of what is really going down. So it is incumbent upon us to speak, to use our power to counter his, to provide a counter to the eminent scholar's dominant narrative, to model intellectual dissent for the students watching us.

Full of this obligation wrought by her own anger in league with her commitment to her students, the speaker moves us to what the poet has established as the pivotal moment in the poem by placing it in the very middle of the middle stanza: the moment that the eminent scholar's racism is capped by his sexism. Again, "We sat through it." Notice the recurrence of this phrase: "And we sat there"; "So we sat through"; "We sat through it." The repetition emphasizes the "we," the unit comprised by the speaker, Janice, Becky, and Dana; it also underscores the enforced passivity of being audience to such a performance — the endurance required, the frustration. Now the speaker's tone gets very complicated:

> Quite lovely, those poems.
> We could learn from them although they were saying
> *you women are nothing, nothing at all.*

Has her voice changed since the last time she asserted the possibility of benefiting from that which demeans you? Is it sharpened with irony? Is she regretting her earlier advice to Janice, critiquing her own collusion with the proceedings? She has encouraged her students to stay in order to hear that they are nothing, nothing at all — not a new message, surely, but always a harmful one. The "we" that is all-important in this poem is specifically gendered here, so that the opposition between eminent scholar and foursome deepens considerably.

The penultimate stanza pits speaker directly against eminent scholar. The moment comes. This might be the moment when the poem resolves, too; the moment we are led, I think, to hope for, when the maternal teacher triumphs on behalf of her pedagogical daughters, raising her lone voice against the perpetrator. But this is not what happens. In fact, this tensely awaited moment is anticlimactic, a fraudulent verbal interaction on both sides, as my students were quick to note. The speaker phrases her question as she had to; the scholar's response comes as it had to; both seem chained to inauthentic language. Hers is false because it is "sardonic" and "eminently civil," instead of angry and direct, and because it is "phrased in the language of fathers" (which *is* usually sardonic and

eminently civil). When I asked my class why she had to speak this language, they answered that, of course, that's the only language in which
she could be heard. You have to speak the *lingua franca,* they said, with
all the pragmatism, or is it cynicism, of twenty years old. Invisible to them
was the bitterness of such a compromise, such a translation of the self
into alien terms as I knew the speaker felt because I know I feel it —
daily. And then there is the question of whether, in fact, she is heard.
She feels "the room freeze" behind her; clearly the audience recognizes
her dissent. Perhaps that's enough, though I might suggest that when
rooms freeze like that, it's because people read *through* the eminently
civil and sardonic tone to the rage beneath. But what about the eminent
scholar? Does he hear her? He responds in what my students deemed
"politically correct language." That horrible phrase comes so readily to
their lips; I wondered if they could read through the fragments to the text
of his actual response, as Rita Dove sketches it for us: he defended his
imitation of black speech on grounds of *"celebrating our differences"* —
that is, a minstrel show was rationalized in the discursive terms of multiculturalism. He spoke of ethnicity as *"virile,"* meaning of course strong,
rich, vivid. His mockery of black speech is defended as a tribute to its
masculinity. And *"humanity"?* We can all imagine the uses to which he
put this word.

It is as this stanza closes — in fact, as the poem moves into its
next, final movement — that we finally get clear evidence of the relationship between the speaker and Janice, Becky, and Dana. That this crucial
information is disclosed just as this climactic and anticlimactic exchange
has taken place and the eminent scholar has perpetrated his final insult
seems significant. The revelation sheds retrospective light on everything
before it, most especially the internal struggles of the speaker, so sparely
implied throughout the poem. The object, the cause for which she struggles and speaks becomes clear: Janice, Becky, Dana. But what has she
been able to do for them, after enticing them to stay? She vanishes as a
character in the poem; what remains is her account of the various coping
mechanisms engaged by her three students. This was where our class discussion really took off — not surprisingly, given my students' natural
attention to images of themselves, but also given the extreme ambiguity
of the final stanza.

Dana, it is suggested by the deepening of her purple eyes, takes
things to heart, internalizes, feels strongly and immediately; so of course
she has "the migraine" right away. Becky tries to avoid it — she of the
electric hair that twitches, perhaps suggesting a tendency to repress, to try
to control her responses. Their teacher speaks of them exactly as mothers
speak of children, with that detailed bodily knowledge that reads the
heart. It is Janice's response to the lecture that blows the poem wide

open, as it did my class. My own original position was that Janice's response is valorized: she "takes the bull by the horns," as the eminent scholar did; throws herself into the fray, acts out, projects all the vitality, energy, and in-your-face fearlessness we recognize from her only statement in the poem. Becky and Dana, I argued, turn into victims, suffering "the" migraine, the same headache, taking the event into themselves like their Victorian predecessors, while Janice refuses to be cowed by it, responding aggressively, subversively, even humorously. But my students weren't so sure. Emily reminded me that Dana "get[s] the poison out quickly," and Becky only a little less so. Perhaps they are the ones dealing efficiently with it. Does that mean the poison is still in Janice? Is her evening performance a kind of tarantella, then, a way of dancing the poison out? Her tunic is covered in small mirrors: what does it mean that she becomes a walking reflector of her surroundings? That when people look at her, they see fragments of themselves? And what about those twice-mentioned wicked-witch shoes? The witch image is surely a powerful, positive one. The shoes, we were told earlier, are red, which is also the color her teacher imagines Janice wearing "for three days" after the lecture — the color of rage, of blood. But the red or, alternatively, the "yellow brighter / than her hair" will make Janice, paradoxically, invisible. So do the mirrors, for that matter. Janice becomes less than a scrim through which some man can glimpse his notion of heaven; "she can't be / seen   at all". Or am I missing the point? Has Janice the witch devised the perfect armor, the magic garment that renders the victim invisible to her tormentors? Isn't making yourself invisible preferable to being turned into a scrim by somebody else? I asked my students if they had ever seen a young women so dolled up, so visible, that she became invisible, and a universal knowing nod went around the room. The outfit, the make-up, the extroversion become a mask behind which the hurt girl-woman can hide from the legions of eminent scholars ready to tell her, *"you women are nothing, nothing at all."*

In hiding, though, is that what Janice becomes, especially with the care-ful repetition of those last two words? What about Becky and Dana? And what about our speaker, who vanishes after her obligatory challenge to the scholar? I reiterate my earlier question: what has she been able to do for her girls? Is the ambivalence I hear throughout the poem the echo of her own reflections on her options? Should she have agreed with Janice to begin with, and left? Did she rightly urge the students to stay, or did she thus perpetuate their subjection to further insult and injury? She said they could all learn from this experience; what did they learn? Anything they can use? If I am correct that her compunction to speak originates in part in a maternal obligation to them, what does her challenge to the scholar accomplish? And in the end, is Janice foregrounded because she exemplifies her teacher's lesson by staying engaged in the proceedings, not cutting loose? If so, how does her teacher feel about seeing her at the party, imagining her days later, brightly armed and invis- ible?

I have no answers to these questions. Or rather, I have partial and changing answers. I said I saw myself clearly in this poem, along with many of the women I've taught with over the years; what I meant was that I see our dilemma, our sense of obligation, our ambivalence. I don't see any obvious solution — which is probably why the poem nags at me. I see what I think is our essential between-ness, our marginality, throughout this poem, in the speaker's situation, her words, her feelings. As she stands between her female students and the *arschloch* scholar, I believe that we women who teach stand between our students and patri- archy itself, in the form of the culture they inherit, the society they enter, the history that has produced them and their situation, not to mention the actual institutions in which we work with them. But what does "standing between" mean? Do we stand there as the voice through which their cul- tural heritage is translated to them? Do we stand there to shield the young from the saturnine Father who might devour them? Or do we stand there as guide, as medium through which the child enters the Father's world? As Grumet has written, this is the traditional position of the mother, a position of awful power, similarly awful powerlessness, precious little clarity, and monstrous self-doubt. Jo Anne Pagano identifies this as pre- cisely the position of the female teacher: for every young woman, she argues, "entry into the fathers' order is predicated on her own absence."[5] Thus, "as women teachers bearing the word of patriarchal culture, we . . . seduce our female students with the same stories that seduced us, the sto- ries of our cultural heritage." [6] As academic Demeters, we collaborate with the rape of Persephone, delivering her to Hades: "In teaching women, we lead them into exile, giving them up to the forms and lan- guage of the fathers." [7]

For me, this is the drama beneath the text of Rita Dove's poem. The question Dove leaves us with — and the question I'm afraid I'm going to leave you with — is the one I am left with every time I leave a classroom or finish a conference with a young woman with purple eyes, electric hair, or pointy red shoes: what is it that, as maternal teachers, we aim to do to/with/for our students, in particular those women students who often look to us with a more or less conscious hunger? We cannot keep the patriarchal poison from them; that's impossible. Do we teach them to get rid of the poison as quickly as possible with a good, honest, miserable migraine? Or to dance through the party in witchy shoes? Do we enjoin them to stick around, learning what they can? Or do we lead the way out of the room, leaving the *arschloch* behind? Do we instruct them in phrasing their subversive questions in the language of fathers, or in unearthing the mother tongue, obscured as it is by the debris of history?

Does the text of the poem give us any hints? Perhaps one, just one, and it's as trivial *and* as important as typography. It took me about five readings before I realized that the final stanza of the poem differs typographically from the four preceding it. In the first place, with the exception of two colons, all punctuation drops away. In the second place, there are those spaces, those interesting gaps, at two points: just before we hear about Janice's coping mechanism, and again just before the two final, weighty words. There are always many ways to read the lack of punctuation and the presence of space in poems, but for me what this sudden change means is that the poem opens up, in two provocative ways. First of all, it lacks closure, especially at the very end. The absence of final punctuation typographically suggests ambivalence and possibility, just like Janice's striking outfits. And second, spaces emerge where there were none before, silences full of meaning because they are wider than the usual gaps between words. Both typographical strategies, occurring late in the poem as they do, suggest transformation and point forward, beyond the poem. The speaker, as a character, has exited her own story, leaving the stage to her three charges. Perhaps the only finality this poem offers is the fact that they go on, the Beckys and Danas and Janices, and whatever we may do to mediate and facilitate their passage, they will find, and I quote the first line of the stanza, "their different ways of coping." These modes, as my class discussion revealed, have their deficiencies and their strengths, just as do the teacher's strategies. The maternal/pedagogical worry about these strategies is palpable. But finally, she has done what she can do, so the next thing she does is let go, let them go — Becky and Dana to their respective headaches, Janice to her marvelous masquerade, and the poem itself to whatever might happen next.

What kind of conclusion is this, you ask? None, none at all, and that is the precise point, I think. What this poem does, for me, is to sketch brilliantly the situation of the maternal teacher, including her limited control over her situation and that of her students. That the poem is markedly open-ended suggests this lack of control, this letting go. And it also suggests potentiality, the power of the future. The empty spaces at the ends of sentences or between groups of words are also the marginal spaces of women — the terra incognita we find or make in the carefully mapped patriarchal world. The white spaces are not so much blanks as silences, in which we wait to hear what has not been heard before, or to speak what has not been spoken.

Ultimately, I think that what we do to or for our women students is indeed *what we can*. As people and situations vary, we do what we can, adaptable and resourceful and ultimately conflicted as mothers can be. And that is what the speaker in this poem does. When she urges Janice to stay and analyze the *arschloch,* she places herself "in-between" by acting as guide, giving the younger women a way of being in the patriarchal world *insubordinately,* navigating academic patriarchy as critical, constructive subjects. This is motherwork, I believe. But when it is time to confront patriarchy head-on, she knows it and does it, and that is motherwork too. Sometimes we do so "in the language of fathers"; sometimes we choose another, mother tongue. And sometimes we must stand "in-between" as shield and defense. At such times, as academic mothers we must raise bloody hell, I think — for instance, when a professor at the University of Massachusetts (formerly at the University of Virginia, my alma mater and Rita Dove's current employer) states that as part of his professorial role he relieves students of what he diagnoses as "unnaturally prolonged . . . virginity," which is "presented" to him, rather than to a peer of the student, "as something that [he], not quite another man, half an authority figure, can handle . . . ."[8] In such a situation, we maternal pedagogues should yell. Loudly. This academic father is Saturn devouring his children. We should not collaborate in an incestual family situation, as many women have done for many reasons. We should stand up and call it by its true name. That too is motherwork. And then sometimes — ultimately *always,* as all mothers know — our work is to let go, releasing the children into the cruel, beautiful world, to suffer their own migraines and to dance in their witchy red shoes.

Toward the end of the class period, as our discussion was winding down, a student suddenly asked, "Why is it called 'Arrow'?" Now, I had dreaded this question, because I had no clue. The title seemed cryptic, inaccessible, unconnected to the poem in any way. We all puzzled silently. Suddenly Emily spoke up again: Maybe Janice is the teacher's arrow. Everything got still in the room and I felt my eyes widen. I heard one "Ooh!" and a "Wow." Maybe all three of them are her arrows, Emily continued.[9] And maybe they are, flying out in front of her, beyond her. As we all know, when you shoot an arrow into the air, it falls to earth you know not where. Maybe she fledges her arrows as best she can and then pulls back and releases them into the air, beyond the visit of the eminent scholar, beyond graduation, beyond her own experience and language, beyond this poem into the future that is theirs.

14

Dirty Pictures
or
Who's the Fairest One of All?

December 6

My friend Marigene has a name for days like these. When I see her looking particularly driven and haggard and I ask after her, she says, "It's the Day That Will Not Die." Sometimes it's a day that simply goes on forever, a non-stop string of contiguous classes, meetings, and appointments from early morning through a dinner on campus and an evening meeting or event, getting you home after ten with classes to prepare for the next day. Sometimes it's not the degree or level of activity but the gruesome cast of the whole day, everything difficult, painful, or screwed up.

I should have known when I walked into Humphrey House that it was going to be One of Those. I brought in with me the incorrigible illness I had dragged around (or vice versa) for about a month now. Its primary symptoms were few and simple, a sore throat varying from slight to throbbing according to time of day, and a constant aching weariness. But it was the end of the quarter — exam week, in fact — and what you do at that point is keep on truckin' until you can get a few hours to see a doctor, a few days to lie low and try to kick it.

Tuesday of exam week, actually, and I had promised the students I would be in the office from 9:00 on. The final portfolios from the freshman seminar were due at 4 p.m., those from the other class in two more days, so I expected visitors. I felt both classes had gone well, and I was looking forward to closure, to the quieting and emptying of the campus as the students disappeared, to turning in my grades and having ten days or so to call my own before Christmas.

All quiet upstairs. I switched on the lights and the public radio station, got coffee, turned on the computer. I had worked on various projects for about an hour when Donna brought in the morning mail.

I think I knew it when I saw it, before I even read the address. Something about it — the thickness, the distinctly masculine handwriting, the name and return address that told me it was local but from no one I knew. It was the only first-class mail in the stack, so I went for it first. It was addressed as follows:

Ms. Gail Griffin
Professor of English and Director of the Feminist Agenda
Kalamazoo College
Kalamazoo, MI 49006

Whoa.

The first two pages were heavily annotated xeroxes of an article in the local paper the week before, in which I and others had been interviewed about the direction and accomplishments of the women's movement. The first thing I saw was the really terrible photo of me that headed the article. I was sitting exactly where I was at that moment, with a weird, twisted grin that came from responding to the photographer's insistence that I smile while I tried to keep my crooked front teeth covered. Beside the photo the author of the letter had written, "Is there a Ten 'Least Wanted' List?"

In the margins of the article, he wrote that everything I had said was garbage; that I was clearly interested not in education but in furthering the feminist agenda; that it was no wonder our kids were being dumbed down at college nowadays; and that, as an alum, he would now not send his dogs to multicultural, politically correct Kalamazoo College. The rest of the pages included a copy of an article about the local (woman) director of Right to Life, approvingly annotated, and an extremely unimaginative riddle about Clinton (describing him as a baby-killer and a thief, among other things), below which was a note to me, warning me that Hillary (whom I had spoken of in the article as the most obvious example of antifeminist backlash) was "a very dangerous 'lady.'"

Finally, I went back to the two small pieces of notepaper clipped to the front of the packet. Another riddle:

Q: What's the difference between a dead dog and a dead radical feminist in the middle of the road?
A: There are skid marks in front of the dog.

And, crammed onto the bottom edge of the second piece, a PS: "You do have that self-righteous feminist smirk."

Well. And good morning to you, sir. Nice to see that the alums are taking an interest in the College. Can we count on a generous contribution this year?

I went through it all several times, until the airless feeling in my head went away and my breathing returned to normal. Obviously a garden-variety crank. Still, there is something about hate mail from a stranger, even when signed. Is it the hate, or the stranger? Is it the sense of invasion, similar to what comes with an obscene phone call?

And still, when I came back to the riddle (a serviceable all-purpose bash which I had first heard as a lawyer joke), I was unable to dismiss the small, chill finger of fear numbering my vertebrae.

———

By 5 p.m, the throat having gone into high throb mode, it was definitely time to go home. Dark had come down, snow and freezing rain predicted. That initial communiqué from the heartland had lent a steely-grey cast to the day. Nothing extraordinary happened subsequently; pretty much the usual department-chair fare. A guy I work with came to see me with a serious student complaint about a member of my department. Another came by to whine, yet once more, about having to teach too many introductory courses and too many students. I spent two hours in a committee meeting listening to very senior male faculty and administrators worry about protecting themselves at the expense of junior, untenured people. Students came and went, agonizing, asking questions, showing me drafts, dropping off portfolios — a category comprising everything from pristine, colorful, illustrated, bound volumes with title pages, acknowledgments and dedication, to ratty manila folders full of wrinkled paper, much of it bearing my comments and corrections from the first time I looked at it eight weeks ago.

I am just gathering my energies to pack up my tent and move out when Lisa appears in the doorway. Since she was here not twenty minutes before to drop off a portfolio, I'm surprised. "Hello again," I smile.

"Um, hi." Although I know from the first visit that she is seriously sleep-deprived, she looks worse now than before: scattered, pale, eyes darting off sideways.

"What's up?"

She mumbles, halts, laughs, finally says, "Listen, if you get a package? In the mail? That looks like it might be photos? Just throw it away, OK? Just burn it or something, OK?"

"Lisa, come in." She does. "Sit down." She does. "Now: I promise I will throw it away if you will tell me what you're talking about."

A smile flickers at the edges of her mouth. Lisa is eighteen, a first-year student from the far west. I have seen her a lot this quarter; she loves to write and likes my class. She is extremely bright and supremely talented. Throughout the past term I have sensed that she and I will see more of each other in the next three years. I have also sensed, from what she writes but more from the way she occupies her skin, that this girl was sexualized too early.

Slowly she tells me the story: a former boyfriend (twenty-five to her fifteen and physically abusive) was a photographer. He has "these pictures" of her. She hasn't seen him for two years, and suddenly this afternoon he calls her room. "I don't know how he found out where I was," she says, shaking her head. He wants to see her. She resists, and he reminds her of the pictures. "He said he was going to send them to my parents, and to my grandparents, and to my professors," she whispers. "He said everybody would know what I was really like. I told him he couldn't send anything to you because you were leaving town for the winter, and he said, 'I found you, didn't I?'"

Deja vu: I am ten years back, with another student telling me the same story, only it's videotape, not photos. There is another striking similarity: that earlier camera-toting perpetrator destroyed the girl's school-books; this one wants to destroy her in her professors' eyes. Both see (correctly) the girl's academic self — her *mind* — as their adversary. What terrible astuteness, trying to violate that mind, inscribe it with a wholly sexual, objectified self-image. Literally trying to fuck with her head. If twice in one decade I deal with women students being terrorized by pornographic images of themselves, imagine how many more there are, here at this little college. Everywhere else. A peculiarly contemporary mode of sexual assault and battery.

A curious paradox flashes through my mind as I listen to her: in order to prevent my seeing those pictures, she has had to come tell me about them. I am the person she most wants to keep them from, and I am also the person she most needs to tell about them.

"OK," I say, when she has fallen silent. "I want you to listen to me. He's bluffing. First of all, if he sends those pictures through the mail, he's breaking several laws."

"He is?"

"Yes. Obscene material through the mails, not to mention child pornography. You were a minor, remember? Second, he can't find me or any of your other profs. Think about it: where could he possibly find out who your instructors are? The College won't give out that information. Or where I'm going after Christmas — how could he find that out?"

She smiles a little, but her eyes don't track.

"Lisa, he's bluffing. He wants you to believe he would do this, but he won't. It's a way to control you, to make you afraid. Do you know that?"

She nods almost imperceptibly.

"What he's counting on, Lisa, listen to me, what he's counting on is that you will believe in the image of you in those pictures. As long as you believe it, he's in control. You have to try not to believe it. I know that part of you does right now, but you won't always."

Silence on both sides for a long moment.

"Lisa: do you know that if I saw those pictures, I would think no less of you?"

She looks directly into my eyes.

"It's true. I would think you were a kid who was victimized, and I'd be very sorry about that, but I would not think less of *you*."

A long silence. Her eyes, wandering around my office, suddenly stop at the framed poster over the fireplace. "Who's that?"

"Virginia Woolf," I explain. "She was molested by her half-brothers."

Lisa smiles wearily, and I wonder whether Woolf has ever been introduced to a student in quite those terms before.

An hour-and-a-quarter later, when I hug her goodbye for the second time today, we have at least reached agreement on one strategy: before she leaves campus, she will request unlisted room and phone numbers and arrange for the College to give out no information about her. She is moving to another dorm next quarter. If he attempts to contact her again, he will find a dry trail. But beyond this practical maneuver, I get nowhere. Like Angela, ten years before, she is lost in someone else's images of her, in frightening fantasies of what he might do, resourceless to fight back, drowning in her own impotent silence. Like my own floundering self ten years ago, I am lost in her silence too, looking away down the years it will take before she can even begin to dismantle those images. Why can't the truth be passed on whole, at once? Why can't I just tell her what is true about what's happened to her, as I would explain subject-verb agreement, and have her know it as the truth?

When I walk out the front door of the building to my car, it is very dark, very cold.

———

Those who see the body, in part, as metaphor for the mind and spirit sometimes interpret a sore throat as an indicator of something that can't be swallowed. When suddenly, after dinner that night, I walked into the bathroom and vomited, I suspected that the turkey I'd eaten had perhaps not expired in a state of grace, but it also crossed my mind that there was something here that I could not stomach.

For the rest of that week, an old seventies song ran over and over in my brain, the one where the guy keeps telling the girl to "Smile for the camera." I have always despised being told to smile, especially by male photographers. I remember one, here in Kalamazoo, who kept teas-

ing me (then aged thirty-eight) about my putative "boyfriend" to get me
to laugh. When the session was over I left his studio hurriedly, feeling
angry, demeaned, and also, oddly, embarrassed. And I'd had all my
clothes on.

"Images of women" — that old saw from Early Women's Studies.
We used it to talk about stereotypes, to overview our cultural landscape,
to name our alienation from ourselves. As the beginning and end of my
Very Bad Day came slowly, inexorably together in my mind, like ends of
a snake curling into a circle to swallow its tail, the urgent power of
images came back to me renewed, expanded, and deadly personal: our
images are taken from us and given back to us, sold or sent or otherwise
inflicted, to frighten us into line. Lisa and I, first-year student and associate professor, a generation apart, both threatened with images of ourselves coming through the mail. How very personal these images are,
geared to our worst fears: hers that she's not an apprentice writer with a
future but a sexy pubescent body mired in the past; mine that I'm not an
educator but an exploiter. And how archetypal, too: I was portrayed as
the patriarchal nightmare — shrew, witch, corrupter of children, unlovable ("least wanted"; no skid marks). She was the patriarchal (wet) dream
— the mindless slut, the baby vamp. The dream and the nightmare collapse, conflate; they are inseparable. Yet they are different, too; hers is
harder, more complicated, for her as for most of us, because it is adver-
tised and inculcated as desirable, as adorable, as beautiful, even while it
is also despised and viciously punished. And hers is harder because she is
eighteen. I understand the imagery of women like me that proliferates in
my culture (in fact, it was the imaging of feminists as witches that I was
discussing in the newspaper interview), and while that imagery hurts and
frightens me, I have contexts and strategies for dealing with it. At this
point Lisa is virtually defenseless against these razor-edged reflections of
her own "beauty." How could she recognize a true image of herself if she
saw it?

Virginia Woolf, whose lovely image — age eighteen — domi-
nates my office, whose similarly vacant, faraway eyes caught Lisa's: as a
little girl, she climbed up to look into a mirror in the hallway of the
Stephen home and was terrified to see a demonic animal looking back.
Before she was tall enough to see the mirror Virginia Stephen had learned
how vile she was, how corrupt her flesh, her femaleness.

"Mirror, mirror, on the wall, who's the fairest one of all?" An
indelible image from childhood: Disney's beautiful, haughty, wicked
queen interrogating her mirror, asking the central question of womanhood, the one we girls learned by heart. And what image looked back at
her? A long, drawn, deathly male mask, giving her the answer she
doesn't want to hear.

What if, instead, Snow White herself appeared in the mirror? Not as an answer to her stepmother's damning question, but as its antidote? Imagine: the older and younger woman looking through the dark glass at each other, in reunion and recognition.

Lisa, I can see you so clearly, though I know you cannot see yourself yet. Try to look past the demons swimming in the glass. Look deeper. Look in my eyes, Lisa. Look in my eyes.

Part Three

The Giant Waking
On Memory, Myth, and Transformation

Yes, that fear is there, but I will try to be at the edge
between my fear and outside, on the edge at my skin,
listening, asking what new thing will I hear, will I see,
will I let myself feel, beyond the fear. . . . How do we begin
to change, and then keep going, and act on this in the world?
How do we *want* to be different from what we have been?. . .
I began when I jumped from my edge and outside myself,
into radical change, for love: simply love:
for myself and for other women.

—Minnie Bruce Pratt

Tell us what it is to be a woman so that we may know
what it is to be a man. What moves at the margin.
What it is to have no home in this place.
To be set adrift from the one you knew.
What it is to live at the edge of towns
that cannot bear your company.

—Toni Morrison

15

In Salem

In the fall of 1993, I moved from Michigan to western Massachusetts for a year. One day soon after my arrival, I took a walk in vicinity of the lake cottage I was renting. Noticing a faint path from the road up a rise through an opening in the trees, I followed it and found myself suddenly in a clearing totally invisible from the road, among gravestones. Some were crumbled and time-scoured to nothing; others were illegible; but the readable ones, given some time, told a wonderful family saga of the Civil War. I spent a hallowed hour, walking among the dead, listening to their whispers.

I came to associate this experience with one of the things that charmed me about Massachusetts: the presence of the dead. No, really. They're everywhere — in monuments and inscriptions and museums, in place names and in the ubiquity of cemeteries. Town and countryside alike, you turn a corner and come upon a tiny, fenced or walled cemetery full of stones that years and weather have worn smooth and nearly silent.

So I guess I shouldn't have been surprised by what they did with Halloween. In western Massachusetts, they take Halloween seriously. Every porch is laden with pumpkins — not two, but eight or ten, carved or not. In Michigan, these would be in pieces on the sidewalk in a matter of hours. People decorate their houses too, as exhaustively as they do for Christmas, for comparable periods of time and in similarly varying degrees of taste. You see black and orange crepe paper webbed across porches, garage doors covered in cardboard witches and black cats and pumpkins, ghosts made of sheets perched in bushes or hanging from eaves.

And then there are the corpses. The first time I came speeding around a curve on a country road and saw a man swinging by the neck from a tree, I nearly drove off the pavement. I had to get quite close before I realized he was a product of old clothes and stuffing. It was early October and I thought it was a clever, if kind of ghoulish, anomaly. But as the month progressed, I saw them everywhere. I mean *everywhere:*

bodies slouched in lawn chairs, sprawled high in trees, sitting on swing seats. I saw one with a hatchet in his back. And not only the victims, but the perpetrators: one night, driving home late, I saw a figure leaning out toward the road with a huge scythe in his hand. My heart skipped only once; I was growing acculturated. Further on up the road a whole nuclear family of ghouls with purple faces stood by the driveway like emissaries from some kind of netherworld Welcome Wagon.

I admire adults who take Halloween seriously. I've always had a particular affection for it. All Hallows Eve, the night before the Day of Saints, seems to me like an interesting kind of window of opportunity between "this" world and the "other," the realm of darkness, however we think of it. On Halloween, all that we repress, deny, outlaw, ridicule, or otherwise exile from our rational daylight concerns walks abroad, revels, shouts, shows up at the door demanding its due. In this, Halloween functions a lot like Mardi Gras or other pre-Easter carnivals around the Christian world. These are residual outcroppings of a pre-Christian spirit that is chaotic, greedy, comical, sexy, and, of course, scary.

But why Massachusetts? I thought, passing a headless woman lying in a garden. And the answer came to me immediately: Salem. This is the Bay Colony, where Puritanism met up with its own dark side. Of course Halloween would be a kind of unofficial state holiday here (in this state that to a newcomer seems to have official state holidays every other week). They have always had corpses in the garden here.

Shortly after Halloween, when some, though by no means all, of the stuffed figures had disappeared, I went over to Bedford for a small reunion with two college roommates, one of whom I hadn't seen since graduation twenty years before. After Friday night, spent in "Remember that guy you were dating?" and "Have you heard from?" and "What ever happened to?", Saturday morning left us ready to contemplate an outing. After some fruitless discussion, Salem suddenly emerged as an option interesting to all three of us. For Rachel, a museum curator, the Peabody-Essex museum was the draw. For Beth, it was historical curiosity. For me, it was nothing less than a feminist pilgrimage.

A couple years earlier I had had occasion to do a little research on the witch persecutions of the seventeenth century in England. The deeper I went, the deeper I wanted to go into this colossal psycho-social trauma that consumed western Europe in the centuries we call the Renaissance. The numbers amazed me, ranging from low figures in the tens of thousand upward into the millions, overwhelmingly female.[1] The spectrum of explanations fascinated me too, all of them potent and plausible. The "burning years," as they're sometimes called, were the final effort of the patriarchal Christian Church to wipe out the Old Religion, where women and womanpower were sacred. The rise of capitalism and the resulting agricultural and economic upheavals pitted families against each other. The women who were likely to be accused as witches were distinguished by some combination of a range of characteristics that rendered them dangerous: they stood to inherit property in a time when private property and thus male inheritance attained new importance; they were midwives and healers at a time when medicine was being professionalized and masculinized; they were intellectually, theologically, or sexually unorthodox under a repressive, doctrinaire church that said their minds were Satan's snares and their bodies Satan's doorway; they were old or single or lesbian, no safer then than now. They were terrorized, tortured, and killed in huge numbers. And in 1692, the fire sweeping Europe burst out in Massachusetts Bay Colony, briefly and violently, taking with it twenty-two people, twenty of them female, devastating the communities of Salem Village and Salem Town, and leaving a permanent scar on the national psyche, a recurrent bad national dream, a cultural reference point for playwrights and politicians alike.

As we drove into Salem, I was thinking about the sexual politics of witch persecutions. I hoped the Witch Museum we were trying to find would address that somehow. We found it, housed in a likely looking Gothic church near the water. But what we found inside was something else. First of all, they get you coming and going: there's no way to enter or exit except through the gift shop. It struck me as suffering from a certain schizophrenia: it offered an array of scholarly books and videos, plus shelves of neat-looking sweatshirts, alongside display cases full of skeleton earrings and Tarot cards and candy in the shape of devils. When showtime finally arrives, you're ushered into what was the sanctuary of the church, in total darkness except for a bright red glass circle on the floor, a wheel full of names and symbols, lit from below. Phantom-of-the-Opera-type organ music plays in the background. You gather around the glass wheel and an artificially deep male voice begins the Salem Story.

The show consists of dioramas, in cubicles up above your head, around the sanctuary space. In each, the actors of Salem, reproduced in wax and cloth, appear as the story is told. The figures are grotesquely unnatural looking, as if the wax were melting. The Voice tells an interesting version of the story, in which the women are pawns or demons and, as the three of us noted, John Proctor (of *Crucible* fame) turns out to be the hero. It did remind me that the first person accused at Salem was black: Tituba, a Carib slave whose subsequent confession, beaten out of her, bought her freedom. The horror at Salem was born in the turning of an adolescent white girl against the black woman who cared for her. At the end of the show, the Voice intones that what happened in 1692 was the result of intolerance and superstition. The lights go back on and you file out into the gift shop again.

Disappointed, we took pictures of each other in front of the building and headed for the Peabody-Essex. Lo and behold, one of the exhibits is devoted to the events of 1692. While Rachel explored upstairs, Beth and I edged into a tour-in-progress, where an extremely informed, articulate docent told another version of what happened, surrounded by documents and artifacts from the period. This story was significantly different: a story of land disputes, family rivalries, slavery, Puritan paranoia, and adolescent girlhood. We hung around for questions and then went through the display carefully. There is a draft of the recantation of Ann Putnam, Jr., one of the possessed girls who accused her neighbors. Years later, as an adult, she stood in the Salem meetinghouse and apologized to the community for her part in the tragedy. She didn't do it out of malice, she said repeatedly. Why she did do it, she never said.

Before we knew it, the early November dark had fallen outside. We were hungry and tired. We decided to walk to a waterfront restaurant so that we could find the Witch Memorial we'd been hearing about all day.

We were upon it almost before we knew it. Strangely wedged between an old churchyard cemetery and a high-rise apartment building, it consists of a plot of grass, with a few trees, surrounded on three sides by a low wall of granite. At stages around these walls, shelves obtrude, polished and engraved with the name of one of the victims and the date and mode of death. In place of the fourth wall, the ground is laid with stones on which are carved statements from the trials. "God knows I am innocent," reads one. They taper off into the walls, interrupted, unfinished, like snatches of voices on the wind.

It is a quirky, disturbing construction, stuck there in the middle of downtown Salem, like an empty lot in which someone has happened to place stones. It feels like a mental space as well, a pause in the middle of contemporary Massachusetts, filled by a strange and terrible memory. The names and words fill the space like ghosts. Over the walls, old gravestones keep watch like guardians.

Driving out of Salem that night, I felt I somehow hadn't got what I came for. My pilgrimage had brought me to three different shrines, all bearing a different account of the story I'd come to hear. At the first I got the Shock Theater version, in cartoon red-and-black, spooky and spine-chilling, with a moral tacked on about tolerance. At the second, 1692 was a complex, interesting historical event in which various forces in the culture of Massachusetts Bay Colony came together. And at the third, what occurred at Salem was a human tragedy, a community debacle whose truth whispers in the wind over the stones. We never made it to the Witch Dungeon or the Salem Wax Museum to get those angles on the story.

Maybe all three versions have their truth. Maybe Salem was just that composite: a horror show, a layered historical phenomenon, and a collective drama about what people do to one another. But above all three, Salem is a myth, one in which all the forces at work in European witch hysteria somehow became distinctively American. In a way, the schizophrenia of the Witch Museum Gift Shop speaks of a larger confusion: Salem itself can't decide how to tell its own story.

And neither can this country. The traditional versions have been irredeemably subverted. The myths are in revision. And if any kind of truth is to come, we will have to move like tourists through our own horror shows, our museums, our memorial sites, the places where our collective memory rests with its sorrows. It is Massachusetts where we began this process. Massachusetts, where they know there are bodies in the garden, killers on the lawn, spirits in the trees.

16

A Fable

*And the woman saw that the tree was good for food,
and that it was a delight to the eyes, and that it was
to be desired to make one wise; and she took of the
fruit and ate. And she gave of the fruit to her
husband, and he ate. . . .*

. . . And all at once a great wind swept through the garden, all the way to
the East Gate, whose doors flew open.

The man began to shriek. "SHE DID IT! SHE DID IT!"

The Voice came. "Time to go."

"I didn't even swallow!" cried the man. But the two of them were
picked up by a gust and carried through the East Gate, which shut firmly
behind them. They were set gently but unceremoniously on the ground.

The woman picked herself up and began to speak. "Look," she
said, "this isn't fair. You tell us not to eat from this one particular tree,
because if we do, we'll be like you. What kind of deterrant do you call
that?"

"Not much of one," the Voice replied. "I'd say it's quite a tempta-
tion."

"Damn straight it is," the woman continued. "Any reasonable person would eat the stupid apple."

"Probably, yes."

"So what's the point?"

"To teach you a lesson."

"How patronizing!"

"No, just parental. There's something you needed to learn, and
there was no other way."

"Such as?"

And the Voice answered, "Choice. You needed to learn about
choice."

"So how does the snake fit in?" the woman asked, more quietly.

"Oh, that was me. I thought you'd figure that out on your own. In order for the choice to be a real one, the other side needed representation."

"You went through all that just to confuse us?"

"Of course not. What do you take me for? I did it so that you could choose, as I said."

"So we failed your little test."

"Not a test," the Voice interrupted. "A lesson. There's a difference."

"OK, lesson. We failed to learn your little lesson."

"Who said you failed?"

"You did!"

"But I didn't."

The woman furrowed her brow. "You didn't?"

"Never."

"So, um, did we? Or what?"

"Did you what?"

"Fail."

"Certainly not. In fact, I think you did quite well. YOU did. HIM I'm not so sure about."

The man looked up from where he sat on the ground, throwing stones at chipmunks. "Huh?"

The woman became angry again. "Then if we didn't fail, why are you punishing us?"

"Who's punishing you?"

"YOU are!"

"And how is it that I'm punishing you?"

"You're kicking us out! "

"No: I'm letting you go. There's a difference."

The woman thought about this for a minute. "But it's a wilderness out here! Where will we go?"

"That's my point: you'll have to choose."

She looked around her. "What if something comes after us? I doubt the snakes out here are all that sociable. Are we allowed to kill things?"

"You're not listening: you'll have to *choose*."

"What are we not allowed to eat this time?"

"Are you hearing me at all?"

The woman sighed deeply. "This isn't going to be much fun."

The Voice softened. "You would have said that about the garden in a few months."

"OK, listen," said the woman, moving a few yards away from the man, who was whimpering and peering into the dark trees. "I think this is kind of sudden, and I don't like your methods. But OK, I see your point. Here's my question: do I stay with him, or find someone a little more like myself?"

In the short silence, a bird called. Then the Voice responded, "I'm sorry, but you'll have to . . . "

"Yeah, yeah, I know," said the woman, turning back. She looked around her, in every direction, shrugged, motioned to the man, and started walking due east. After a few yards she stopped and turned.

"One more thing — what you said about bringing forth children in sorrow: do I have to go through with it?"

But all she heard was the wind.

*—for the Kalamazoo Chapter,
National Organization for Women,
to commemorate the twentieth
anniversary of Roe v. Wade*

17

Imagining Whiteness
A Meditation

*I state that 'whiteness' is the unrecognized
and unspoken racial category
and that we must end this silence. . . .*

—*Hazel Carby*[1]

1. Beginning

The black woman urges me to "interrogate whiteness."[2] To cease the hungry white (female, feminist) attention to people of color and to reel my gaze back in to myself. At once I understand the charge: whiteness must be interrogated . . .

— to specify, to peculiarize it. When white is left generalized and universalized, as dominance has rendered it, it remains dominant. It is permitted to see itself as unraced. But while it fails to see its particularity, it also fails to see its dominance. I think of my own exasperation when men will not or really cannot see the gendered character of their thinking, their behavior, their institutions and practices — when they talk about that elusive creature, the Generic Human. Whiteness, for whites, is Everything—and therefore Nothing in particular. As nothing in particular, it is therefore Everything in general.

— to make it accountable. If it is constantly subject, never object, it is always asking the questions, framing the definitions, writing the stories.

— to make it self-knowing. Otherwise it can't see itself; it goes on arrogantly and ignorantly observing the "Other" colors, irritated when its gaze is returned.

— to make it remember. It says it does not remember: it is blank. And as long as it fails to remember itself, it erases everyone else.

Yet I cannot understand, at first, how to proceed. Interrogating whiteness feels like being locked in a big empty room, or being wrapped in cotton. I am childlike, inarticulate, and slow, as we feel in a new language. I am on the edge of a profoundly snowbound landscape I am supposed to survey and chart. Interrogated, whiteness does not answer my questions. Whiteness (ironically) behaves like the Tar Baby, panicking me by its refusal to respond — or to let me go. Whiteness is sticky business.

"Whiteness, alone," says Toni Morrison, "is mute, meaningless, unfathomable, pointless, frozen, veiled, curtained, dreaded, senseless, implacable. Or so our [white] writers seem to say."[3]

What is it we imagine waiting at the heart of Whiteness? "The horror! The horror!"

Begin instead with what is known, visible: the face, the everyday images of whiteness.

2. In the White Museum

Gallery A: Perfect Innocence

White Christmas. White wedding. White light. White knight. White tie and tails. Free, white, and twenty-one. White is ultimate, perfect, epitomized, absolute. *Dare you see a soul at the White Heat?*

White lace, white lies, Snow White, lily-white, another White Wedding. White is virginal, pure, innocent, unstained, honorable. "That's mighty white of you."

Gallery B: Mysteries of Nonbeing

White Rabbit. White Stallion. Great White Shark, known to his friends simply as Great White. His great-granddad, Melville's White Whale. Whiteness is mysterious, unknown, unknowable, unnamable, terrifying, beyond definition: the white screen against which fantasies and terrors are projected. "You're white as a ghost!" "Well, you're white as a sheet!"

White bread, white milk, white rice, white noise. Whiteness is without character, void and formless, bleached out, wishy-washy, indistinct, mediocre, homogenized. The White Album is the one where the Beatles dis-integrate before our very ears; the album with no coherent identity, not even a real title.

Crayola made one of its 64-pack resemble us and called it "flesh." But in *Beloved,* when Sethe's ghostly daughter recalls the Middle Passage, she designates the white men as "men without skin." And in *The Woman Warrior,* the Chinese immigrant community sees white people as "ghosts."

Gallery C: Shades of White

Stills from TV ads: the White Knight who is Stronger Than Dirt. The White Tornado. The detergent that gets your clothes Whiter Than White.

An ad for Clorox: the kid's shirt gets progressively "dingier," and the comically guilty mother concocts new euphemisms to describe its color: "Uhhh, TAUPE! It's taupe!" "If you're not using Clorox," the ad ends ominously, "it's not white."

In the deep-structure of laundry detergent marketing, as in American racial psychology, white is a kind of archetype. What we *might* identify as white is suspect: is it *really* white? Nothing is ever white enough. Somewhere, in some bottle or box or level of feminine exhaustion, there is Absolute White.

Whiteness is cleanness, sterility, purity, then — and also a standard against which all pretenders must be measured and found wanting. (I suddenly think of discussions I've been in on where white academics are evaluating people of color and their work.)

———

In our images of whiteness are embedded our racial confusions, contradictions, paradoxes: whiteness is everything, whiteness is nothing; whiteness is complete presence, whiteness is utter absence. The paradox contains the arrogance of whiteness, and also its sometimes deep sense of deprivation, its yearning for Being.

Remember in elementary school, arguing about whether white was all colors combined, or no color at all?

3. The blank page

The blank page: for a writer, whiteness at its most terrifying. But why, I have asked myself, watching students struggle to write papers. Is it because this whiteness demands to be filled, or is it the opposite: that it resists its own inscription? Is there something in the writer, as strong as the urge to inscribe that whiteness, that wants to preserve it, that fears to mark it? I hear students (women in particular?) speak of the as-yet-nonexistent paper as terrifying precisely because it won't be, in print, what it is in the head. Another raid on the (big, white) inarticulate, to amplify T. S. Eliot. Whatever is inscribed is partial, real, a particular color split off by the prism of the pen from the Ultimate Unspeakable Whiteness, the Ideal Paper. While the sheet of paper is pristine white, the essay might be anything, anything at all. It is All Possible Essays, says the student. It is also absolutely Nothing, the teacher reminds her.

To write is to specify. To write is to defile the pure, to chip away at the absolute. Toni Morrison finds in the writing of white Americans recurring images of "an impenetrable, an inarticulate whiteness."[4] To write is to penetrate the whiteness and make it speak. But in inscribing the white page, writing destroys whiteness, deconstructs it, if you will, with its Other, the non-white, the dark ink. What does it mean, then, to write whiteness?

To write is always to "make history," to inscribe memory. Morrison writes of the lure of the "New World" for white Europeans: "One could be released from a useless, binding, repulsive past into a kind of historylessness, *a blank page waiting to be inscribed*"[5] (emphasis mine). Onto the continent before them, they wrote their sense of themselves, their whiteness, which included their innocence, their newbornness, their indeterminacy, all tenacious white American myths. They who would become a nation of inventors began by reinventing themselves — as Adam, given the whole garden to name and classify.

The denial of history included the history of the new place itself. From the notion of "discovery" on down, they inflicted a form of "whiteout": nothing was here until "we" made it. A "new nation, carved out of the wilderness," like a sculpture from formless stone. The story that appears on the white page was conceived, written, and repeatedly revised in denial, in erasure.

Forgetfulness becomes a habit of whiteness. Especially self-forgetfulness, an unconsciousness that settles into the mind. In an effort to render her status as a white person visible to herself, Peggy McIntosh began to make mental lists of privileges accruing to her simply because of skin color. "I repeatedly forgot each of the realizations on this list," she says, "until I wrote it down. For me, white privilege has turned out to be an elusive and fugitive subject."[6] Like a ghost, disappearing through the wall.

Again, past conversations come back: white people, my students, my colleagues, exasperated with black people's insistence upon remembering. The impatience of white America with memory; the tendency to speak, to analyze, to judge in "clean-slate" terms, as if there were no past. The fascination with abstraction, which has no memory.

Onto the continent we wrote our whiteness, our pastlessness. The overinscribed European page had been thrown into the revolutionary fire; we landed on the margins of a new one, blank and white and clean.

The virgin land.

4. White/Woman

If whiteness is, in Morrison's term, "impenetrable," what happens to it when it is penetrated?

In *A Room of One's Own* Virginia Woolf links chastity and anonymity, both historically assigned to women. The unpenetrated and the unnamed. The pure and the blank, both white. The woman who is unknown to any literary public equals the woman who is unknown to man, terra incognita.

The pure women is a blank page: she waits to be inscribed. She too is without history: in conventional male plots, she cannot be the "hero" because she has no story. It used to be said of a woman, to denote impurity, that she "had a past" — so she who has a story is also disqualified from heroism, or from heroinism at least. The traditional proof of virginity: blood stains on white sheets, the red ink telling the story of whiteness permeated.

Whiteness as purity: thus it is that racial politics in this country were, and often still are, centered on female sexuality. The image of white women "violated" by black men, the ultimate horror of blackness vitiating the blank white page: this story was the pornographic fuel for white male violence. The white woman and the black man were both crucial figures in the white man's version of his own story, both projections of himself — he who had been raping black women as a matter of privilege and as a functional prop to the slave economy since the first African woman was dragged onto this page of her history.

And she—that African woman: in the psychic economy of American patriarchy, she became the requisite counterpart to the white virgin: the black whore, wholly inscribed, utterly determined, totally materialized. So the white woman learned a kind of survival, a kind of definition, dependent upon her blankness, her silence — and her alterity to this dark Other.

5. Over and Against Darkness

Another paradox: whiteness is absolute, universal, "uncolored," and yet it knows itself only in opposition, in contrast. "'White' is used only to distinguish from black and other nonwhites. The absence of 'white' thus signals that 'everyone' is white," as Patricia Williams puts it.[7] "As a mindset," Adrienne Rich sees whiteness "bent only on distinguishing concrete bands of color from itself. That is its obsession — to distinguish, discriminate, categorize, exclude on the basis of clearly defined color. What else is the function of being white?"[8]

Is this a reason why white people so often resist specifying themselves or being specified racially? An African American colleague has said that white men are so accustomed to playing Adam, doing the naming, that when they in turn are named, they react to the identification as an attack.[9] Introduce the phrase "white men" into a conversation with white men and you will be accused of "blaming" (if not of reverse something-or-other). This is the resistance of the dominant to seeing themselves as limited, as defined in any way. But is it also their forcefully repressed knowledge that in this country, to be white means to be white-as-opposed-to-black (or another color, but especially black)? The testiness of the white person identified as white bespeaks the anxiety of being implicitly *in opposition to*. History has suddenly entered the room and claimed us as its children.

For this reason (again in Rich's words), "there is no study of race — only of racism. . . . Race itself is a meaningless category. But people have defined themselves as white over and against darkness, with disastrous results for human community."[10] And when we are "called" on our whiteness, we suddenly belong to the history of — not race, but racism. We no longer have the luxury of "universality" to hide in; we are present and accountable, and not safe.

James Baldwin, writing in 1963:

> . . . a vast amount of the energy that goes into what we call the Negro problem is produced by the white man's profound desire not to be judged by those who are not white, not to be seen as he is, and at the same time a vast amount of the white anguish is rooted in the white man's equally profound need to be seen as he is, to be released from the tyranny of his mirror.[11]

6. The Unbearable Whiteness of Being

Not safe.
And not innocent.
And not pure.
And no longer virgins.

If we are inscribed by history, we lose our claim to innocence. If we take our eyes from the mirror, we will have to meet the dark eyes of the one who watches us, knows us. What white people fear in the process of racial specifying is that we will be *found guilty*.

In listening to white women talk about race, Ruth Frankenburg noted a crucial point: "the status of the white subject was at stake . . . as much as, if not more than, that of the subject of color." Liberal white women took great pains to construct "a white self innocent of racism."[12] Racism, then, becomes not primarily a matter of harm to people of color, or of institutional systems, but a matter of the state of white souls. This distinction almost replicates the old theological argument about grace versus good works, spiritual versus active and material virtue, that undergirded the foundation of this country: which will get us to nonracist heaven faster, the internal purity of white people, or the demise of practices and institutions that harm people of color? Racism, Frankenburg continues, seems to represent to white people not institutions and behaviors but "a static condition of being, possibly even an 'original sin' that the white individual could never undo." [13]

Her metaphor is precise: racism is the "original sin" that entered the garden of the New World, damning white Europeans' attempts to escape history and live in eternity. But to see racism primarily in these terms also makes it once again an issue of white people's goodness or badness. It is this monumental egocentricity that exasperates people of color in interracial conversations where instead of talking about how racism functions, white people are bent on either exonerating themselves or being exonerated: getting a clean bill of spiritual health, a verdict of Innocent.

"[I]t is not permissible that the authors of devastation should be innocent," wrote James Baldwin to his young nephew. "It is the innocence which constitutes the crime."[14] To interrogate whiteness is indeed to forfeit our claim to innocence — the innocence that means "not guilty," but more importantly the other, literal innocence that means "not knowing." To accept and begin to understand oneself as white is to forfeit unknowing, another version of blankness and virginity. Another tactic employed by white people in discussions of racism is the ignorance defense: "But I didn't know all that!" or "How am I supposed to know that?" This defense is a desperate clinging to innocence in the face of history. It is innocence well lost.

First, we need to remember: to "have a past." Then, we need to confess, in the old sense of the word that meant simply "to acknowledge — or *admit knowledge* — together." What a relief it will be. And then, stripped of the shroud of our innocence, we can breathe and move; our silence broken, we can make whiteness articulate. In doing so, we compromise whiteness; we problematize and subvert white absolutism. White becomes a color, a heavily weighted color, rather than a blank ground against which all things are projected. And we become people with skin, participating in history, writing our story, rather than baleful, evasive ghosts, dragging the chains of history behind us, vanishing through the walls.

18

The Giant Waking
Memory and Survival

*What can I possess
But the history that possesses me?*

—Alicia Ostriker[1]

1. Flashbacks

I go to a reading by the author of an autobiographical book on surviving ritual cult abuse. I enter the room with terrific trepidation. I have been dreading this all week. Yet I know I must be here, and not only because the author is an acquaintance. I must be here because I have been avoiding this topic for years now. How many years? Since the McMartin Preschool case. Since Elizabeth, my student ten years ago, whose physical and psychological symptoms bespoke a horrific past to which her lover referred considerately in generalities that let us know the shape of what had been done to Elizabeth, but not its lineaments. I never asked; Elizabeth's eyes were too scary: hunted, haunted, suspicious, terrified, yet somehow vacant, as if her mind were almost cut loose from its moorings. *Like the eyes of an abused animal,* I used to think, looking at her. My avoidance was not denial: I believed what had happened to her before knowing it. My avoidance was more like an invisible electric fence around me, keeping me in, safe from the subject. I knew ritual abuse existed; I didn't want to know more.

I still don't, of course. And yet I'm here — because my cowardice has finally caught up with me. I think of Toni Morrison's saying that she was finally able to write *Beloved,* years after learning the events on which it is based, when she said to herself, "If they could live this, I can write it." If she can live this, and live to write about it, I can hear it, I can know it. So I hang on tight for the descent into hell.

And if it's not hell, it's close enough. The author is a thoroughly credible and remarkably astute witness to the evil coiled around her girlhood. She is eloquently undramatic, but unsparing, uncensored. Her recovery of these memories is relatively recent; they surfaced, as they often do, when she lifted the alcoholic numbness that had kept them submerged. Yet she has sufficient distance to examine the processes of memory with an almost dispassionate, scientific eye. She says the most difficult time in the remembering process was the span during which she sustained two entirely distinct versions of her childhood. One was the narrative of upper-middle-class familial normalcy. The other was the hallucinatory narrative of rape, torture, murder, cannibalism, terror. The second version is horrific enough. But what her memory would not give her for a long time, she says, is any bridge between them, any memory of a connection between these two lives. It was the dissonance, she says, that was maddening.

Is it this dissonance I've been holding at bay? I think of the day in the office when Carl, my beautiful, brilliant student, started to tell me he'd been unable to sleep, kept wakeful by dreams, or waking visions, of a circle of people in black robes, pointing at him. I hastened to assure him that it was entirely possible he'd internalized this imagery from other people, from the media. Even as I spoke I knew I wasn't simply consoling Carl; I was protecting myself. If I acknowledge the reality of such visions, they become, on some level, my own.

My only autobiographical angle into such experience is an attempted rape in graduate school. Afterward, what obsessed me, incommunicable to anyone, was a similar dissonance: between the world I had known and in fact saw around me, full of sun, trees, people living their lives, and its underside, a nightworld of fear and violation. *Now I will know this* I said to myself. *I will remember this always, and this other world will always be visible to me. How will those two worlds ever come together? How will I live if they don't?*

On this level I begin to understand the phenomenon of denial, individual and collective, personal and historical. In the discussion after the author's reading, the question of denial arises and someone says, angrily, that it is a simple issue of power: people deny others' testimony in order to preserve the institutions that perpetrate these horrors. But what of those who are not invested in those institutions? For them, the answer is not so pure. I think we deny others' monstrous truths for the same reason we can deny our own for years, decades: because to know would shatter us. We lack paradigms and tools to integrate such knowledge; it is too much to be borne. The self is constructed of memory, and there are some memories so heavy the construct can't support them. The walls come tumbling down.

I think of a conversation with my mother years ago about "the War": did she and her friends know about the camps? "We heard rumors, whispers," she said. "But we just couldn't believe such things were happening." I wonder: did she mean that they figured it for war propaganda, or did she mean perhaps that they had no context for understanding, no way yet to digest this information and go on living their lives?

So then, I think, as I leave the hall, what explains memory's return? Individually and collectively, when we come to revise our narratives, reconstruct our selves, what is going on? What is it that makes a formerly unbearable memory — one so profoundly threatening to the psychic or social body that it had to be repressed — suddenly so critical to that body's survival that it will endure the trauma of recovery, the dissonance and despair of memory's waking?

2. Mimir

The children of the West — the children of privilege and plenty — are waking and reporting bad dreams. The very baddest. The testimony about childhood abuse, often recollected years later, has reached proportions such that we struggle to comprehend it. Cartoons, cynicism, and labels such as False Memory Syndrome are only evidence of our struggle. The memories of abused children — pre-schoolers, altar boys, stepdaughters — are deeply threatening to the collective consciousness not only because they jar horribly with persistent notions of childhood, but because they undermine some of the institutional pillars of our society and culture: school, church, family. Even the wholly incredulous can and should concede the symbolic significance of the nightmares of these now-grown children. They carry in their subconscious minds — the realm of dream, hallucination, and repressed memory — the "bad dreams" of western culture, its dark side, its demonic potential.

On our current embattled cultural ground, memory is precisely the issue. The question is what version or versions of memory will prevail as "truth," especially when truth itself is a suspect category. New, submerged narratives surface — the formerly obscured or denied histories and literatures of marginalized peoples — and are met by the forces of denial, from accusations of "political correctness" to assaults on "revisionist historians." This latter category, unfortunately and very ironically, lumps together those struggling to make the submerged narratives heard again — historians of women or African Americans, for instance — with Holocaust deniers. Some revisions unearth truth; some attempt to bury it. I believe that the defining battle of our time pits the forces of remembrance against those of forgetfulness and denial.

But how to affirm the validity of memory, its potential for truth, when as post-Freudians and post-moderns we know too much to the contrary? If the self is constructed primarily of and by memory, its instability is a given: it is grounded in quicksand. What an irony that at this cultural moment autobiography should come forcefully into its own as a literary genre attracting tremendous critical and pedagogical attention. And yet maybe not. Maybe it's quite logical that our need for autobiography should increase as our faith in an enduring rememorable self erodes. Autobiography might be seen not as the presentation or representation of a self, or even as an account of the construction of a self, but instead as the very enactment of self-construction through the conscious, fallible, selective exertion of memory. In other words, autobiography demonstrates the process of self-revision. It is the Operator's Manual for a fluid, dynamic self, a self-in-time.

The ultimate post-modern autobiography will have multiple narrators. One of the basic rules of literary study is that when the narrator changes, so does the story; but the reverse is also true: when the narrative changes, behold, the narrator becomes different. The narrative is likely to change when a rival narrative erupts — from without or from within, a voice from the very margins of the story we thought we "owned." This process is disruptive and fearful. Our collective self, like our individual selves, is shaken to its roots. The competing narratives feel like chaos, like madness. This is the periodic "revolutionary" reconstruction of our selfhood.

The excavation of lost memory has been critical to the project of Women's Studies and to the individual projects of women within it. "Women's Studies itself," write the editors of a collection on women and memory, "may be viewed as the construction of a 'counter-memory,' to use Michel Foucault's term. This act of re-membering does not sentimentalize or sacralize what has been lost or suppressed, although it may always contain . . . an element of nostalgia. More important, however, the practice of re-membering, as the emblem of the Women's Studies enterprise, marks the desire to bring to consciousness all that the symbolic system represses in order to maintain and perpetuate itself: a return of the repressed, as Julia Kristeva has pointed out, that has the power to disturb, subvert, and transform the existing patriarchal order."[2]

The authors make a common feminist lexicographic move in hyphenating "remember," making it yield the secondary meaning of "putting the parts back together." In fact, "remember" and "member" are etymological strangers. "Remember," like "memory," comes from the Latin *memor,* meaning "mindful." It means, literally, to become or remain mindful. In the discourse of psychoanalytic feminism, then, to remember is to recall the repressed Feminine, the exiled Mother, to mindfulness. But the hyphenated version brings a provocative adopted child into this word family: to "re-member" is to reunify the members of the body, to make whole. Its opposite is not "to forget" but "to dismember": to destroy by taking apart, to render unwhole, unholy, without integrity.

Memor has a northern European cousin: Mimir, of Norse mythology, a giant who guarded the well of wisdom. Those who would drink had
to confront the colossus of memory. What if the re-repressed, being
recalled to life once again, is not the exiled Mother but something huge
and dreadful, constructed of incongruent dismembered parts? What if the
re-membered jerks to life, opens its yellow eyes, and rises before us like
the gigantic shape of our worst fears, our ugliest shame?

3. Re-membering the Monster

Frankenstein was begun in 1816, by an eighteen-year-old who, in
mining her imagination, somehow struck the gold of a most resonant
myth. Coming in the midst of the Industrial Revolution, it was probably
the first fictional treatment of the modern horror of human scientific
power turning on its owners — technology run amok. The moment of its
publication, like the moment Victor Frankenstein's creation jerks to life,
marks a watershed, beyond which modernity looks backward, nostalgic
for a lost, innocent natural world. In this sense and on the many other
levels on which its myth operates, the novel is a study in the curse of
memory and responsibility, the doom of living with what we have done
and what has been done in our name.

Mary Shelley gives us precious few details of the watershed
moment itself. We know Victor procures spare parts from "charnel houses," the "dissecting room and the slaughter-house" (ch. 3); but we do not
watch him splice them together into his eight-foot nightmare, or infuse it
with life. This most famous literary act of re-membering covers a mere
two or three pages in most texts, and more attention is given to Victor's
state of mind than to his physical operations.

What Victor chooses to remember in more detail is his childhood.
If we see *Frankenstein* as a novel in many ways about memory, this
emphasis is interesting, for it foregrounds the angelic mother whom the
rest of Victor's career will repress. Victor's memory paints an idyllic,
indeed Edenic, period that closes with the death of his mother — "that
most irreparable evil" (ch. 2). Her dying wish is Victor's union with her
foster-daughter and surrogate, Elizabeth Lavenza. Victor's departure for
the University of Ingolstadt — clearly a fall into the symbolic order, the
Fathers' world — ensues immediately. By the end of the same chapter he
is completely committed to his scientific career, which has been defined
by his mentor, Professor Waldman, in his description of contemporary
natural philosophers: "They penetrate into the recesses of nature and
show how she works in her hiding places" (ch. 3).

Other readers, including Anne Mellor [3], have amply examined the
connection between Victor's motherlessness and his scientific mission of

probing Mother Nature's womb, seeking her deepest secret, the reproduction of life. The trope is brilliantly triple-faceted, for Victor wants to crawl back into the womb, to rape it, and to usurp it, replacing the mother himself. But this search for the dead/mother can be read as a mnemonic search as well. Victor searches for the repressed/lost maternal, the angelic queen of that supremely happy, prelapsarian childhood before the fall into the logocentric charnel-house of modern western science that he finds closing in on him at college.

The problem, of course, is that he uses the tools and philosophies of the latter in order to recover the former. He uses technology to recover Paradise. He employs the scientific rape of Nature's womb to remember mama. That is, he denies and re-represses Mother in the course of unearthing her. His remembering becomes monstrous.

I teach *Frankenstein* frequently. To my students, the most astonishing moment in the novel occurs just after the Creature comes to life: "He might have spoken," says Victor, "but I did not hear; one hand was stretched out, seemingly to detain me, but I escaped, and rushed down stairs. I took refuge in the court-yard belonging to the house which I inhabited; where I remained during the rest of the night . . . " (ch. 4). The next day, he runs into his happy, healthy, androgynous friend Henry Clerval and returns to his rooms, terrified, but they are empty. His ensuing delirium turns into real fever, from which Clerval nurses him to health, taking him then on a walking tour in the country, where, in Victor's words, "I became the same happy creature who, a few years ago, loving and beloved by all, had no sorrow or care" (ch. 5). In other words: a clean slate, through the kind offices of a male nurse and Mother Nature herself. Victor's consciousness begins to split because he is caught between double narratives, two sets of memories and corresponding self-images, one represented by his old friend Clerval and associated with Victor's beatified youth, the other by the yellow-eyed, speechless giant he left behind in his rooms.

More incredible than the actual construction of the Creature, to my students, is this denial. You create a monster, but it runs away, so you decide to forget about it and get on with your life? Not only is it incredible at this point in the novel, but it will become exactly the heart of the matter: Victor's continuing denial of the Creature, in one way or another, drives them to their mutual doom. The compelling, layered relationship between Creator and Creature lends itself to a wide array of readings. But it works splendidly as a near-allegory of memory and denial. And with each denial, the Creature grows more monstrous.

The identification between Victor and the Creature — the *doppelgänger* effect — deepens the effect of the novel as a narrative of memory. Just as the Creature is at once Victor's abandoned, abused child and his tormentor, Victor is both perpetrator and victim vis-a-vis his creature. To remember the monster is, for him, to feel the complex coupling of guilt and victimization, sorrow and anger. But unless the Creature accuses him, Victor almost completely represses the guilt; otherwise, what he remembers is his own victimization, his own pain. When he feels guilt, it is not for what he has done to the Creature, but what he has done *through* the Creature, his instrument or surrogate. In one way or another, the Creature hounds Victor with the specter of moral responsibility for what he pieced together and then ran out on, slamming the door behind him.

What the Creature wants from Victor is very simple: a figure of disturbing memory, he wants to be acknowledged (an archaic meaning of "remembered"). To be *owned,* in all the senses of that word: possessed, admitted to, taken responsibility for. His long narrative, the centerpiece of the novel, recounts his own passage from a blank slate to a being of cultural memory, derived through his surrogate family, the DeLaceys, and their books. Now, armed with a past of his own, he confronts his maker with *his* past. His request for a mate is doubly horrifying to Victor. First, the mate is explicitly a surrogate for the maker who won't acknowledge him. Second, the request comes in the wake of Victor's betrothal to Elizabeth, implying a monstrous parody of Victor's own sexuality. In other words, to acknowledge the Creature would be, for Victor, to touch his own sexual humanity, to *own* himself as a sexual being, child of his mother's sexual body.

He comes close — and does so in another act of re-membering, this one even closer to the lost mother, for he re-members a female. The metaphorical implications of Victor Frankenstein — white, male, privileged, intellectual, scientist, eldest son — remembering Woman are enormous, and frightening; so this repression must be considerably more violent:

> I thought with a sensation of madness on my promise of
> creating another like to him, and, trembling with passion,
> tore to pieces the thing on which I was engaged.

He closes the laboratory door on his destruction, just as he did on his creation, and wanders for some hours. Determining to leave the island, he decides to pack his instruments, which necessitates re-entering the locked room:

> The remains of the half-finished creature, whom
> I had destroyed, lay scattered on the floor, and I almost
> felt as if I had mangled the living flesh of a human being.
> . . . I reflected that I ought not to leave the relics of my

work to excite the horror and suspicion of the peasants,
and I accordingly put them into a basket, with a great
quantity of stones . . . .

He loads his skiff and sails out under the moon, suddenly covered by
cloud:

> I took advantage of the moment of darkness, and cast my
> basket into the sea; I listened to the gurgling sound as it
> sunk, and then sailed away from the spot. (v. III, ch. 3)

Total submergence of the dis-membered female. Victor drifts ashore he
knows not where and is immediately taken into custody — for murder.

For me, the dis-integration of the female creature — including
that grisly after-image of discarded body parts on the floor of the locked
room — is by far the most frightening image in *Frankenstein*. I have been
surprised by how many of my students believe Victor is quite right to do
as he does, renege on his compact with the Creature. They reasonably
cite his very arguments: Who knows if the Monster's truthful? Who
knows if the female would turn out to be even worse? But to my eyes
Victor's sudden turnabout and the violence it precipitates so clearly constitute a fatal error, a step backward rather than a turn in the right direction — a denial. The female, literal and figurative, has been sunk to the
bottom of the psyche. This dis-memberment, which goes on before our
very eyes, requires another, as the Creature says: "*I will be with you on
your wedding-night.*"

The corresponding death of Elizabeth resonates on many levels
of this allegory. She is Victor's mother, dead for the second time (or the
third, if one counts Justine Moritz, another of Caroline Frankenstein's sur-
rogates and likewise murdered indirectly by Victor, through his refusal to
deal with the Creature). Her death also signifies the personal consequences of denial: what is repressed often surfaces in sexual and relational dysfunction; Elizabeth was Victor's last chance for connection with
his kind and, implicitly, for "natural" reproductive creativity. Her death
leaves him alone — or rather, alone with his terrible un-natural offspring,
which amounts to the same thing.

The rest of Victor's life is an ironic reversal of what has gone
before: pursued to this terrible end by his own personal Mimir, giant of
memory, he now turns pursuer, though in fact the Creature is still in
charge, luring Victor after him into the region of ice, where the last
remaining "female" force in this novel, Nature herself, seems all but dead.
Victor's own longed-for death, most appropriately, cannot come until he
makes his "confession," as autobiographies were originally termed, to

Walton. That is, he re-members his own monstrous life.

The embedded multiple narration in Frankenstein serves to structure the novel's concern with memory. The memories of Safie and the
DeLaceys (not to mention the cultural memories of his Great Books curriculum) are internalized by the Creature; the Creature's memories
become Victor's; Victor's story becomes part of Walton's. But ultimately
memory is sustained through the female: Margaret Walton Saville, the
silent repository of her brother's letters. More specifically, the horrific
memory of male violation finally rests with a woman.

This invisible, silent woman, as her initials suggest, is a surrogate
for the author,[4] Mary Wollstonecraft Godwin, who at her marriage
dropped her father's surname and kept her mother's, writing as Mary
Wollstonecraft Shelley. Her 1831 Preface introduces the novel by remembering its inception, the "waking dream" produced by her "imagination,
unbidden," in the long-ago summer of 1816 on the shores of Lake
Geneva, one late night when "even the witching hour had gone by."[5]
This much-analyzed Preface is, among other things, a condensed account
of Mary Shelley's own wrestle with the giant of memory, for she has written it, she says, in response to a perennial question: how did a young
girl, as she was then, come to write such a horrific story? She attributes
her notorious, unfeminine creation to various external agencies — her
illustrious parents, her husband, Lord Byron, her "unbidden" imagination.
But then she captures the memory itself, coming as a dream vision:
"When I placed my head on my pillow . . . I saw the pale student of
unhallowed arts kneeling beside the thing he had put together."
Immediately, the pale student imitates the author, lying down to sleep
and waking to the monstrous: "He sleeps, but he is awakened; he opens
his eyes; behold the horrid thing stands at his bedside, opening his curtains, and looking on him with yellow, watery, but speculative eyes."[6] In
full identification with her "protagonist," Shelley writes, "I could not so
easily get rid of my hideous phantom; still it haunted me."[7]

Mary Shelley's life/story is replete with metaphors for the operations of memory. Surrounded in childhood by powerful intellectual men,
she wrote a fictional world in which the female principle is silenced by
powerful male intellects. Like Victor, she was haunted by the ghost of a
fabulous mother for whose death she felt crushing guilt. In her romantic
(and Romantic) elopement with Percy Shelley, she both embraced and
violated her heritage, behaving like her mother and alienating her father.
In writing her most famous work, she too had to exhume the buried: her
own dead mother, her own dead child.

But her response to her "hideous phantom" is exactly opposite to
Victor's. In closing her preface, she acknowledges the novel as her own,
her "hideous progeny" this time, and rather than denying or dis-member-

ing it, she bids it "go forth and prosper." And so it did. Part of its enduring power is its multivalence: like all plots that achieve the level of myth,
it speaks in many voices and tells many stories to different readers in different times. To our own time, it has spoken of the rape of the environment, the dangers of technology, the anxieties of motherhood, female creativity, patriarchal science, the nature and politics of narrative, western
imperialist constructions of the Other. But at its very heart is a mythos
equally pertinent to our times: the terror and guilt of re-membering, the
flight from memory, and memory's relentless pursuit.

4. Ashes and Bones

> . . . the entire history of the brief 'millenial Reich'
> can be reread as a war against memory. . . .
> [Hitler's] collapse was not only a salvation for mankind,
> but also a demonstration of the price to be paid
> when one dismembers the truth.
>
> —Primo Levi[8]

All around us are people walking the desolate boundary between
two worlds, memories running on separate tracks. At any moment, the
nightmare may surge up through the surface of "normal" life, demanding
its due, just as the Creature intrudes ever more insistently and violently
into Victor's domestic life. Like Victor, those in the full thrall of these conflicting worlds often find themselves caught and tangled in the slippery
distinctions between perpetrator and victim, self and other, victim and
survivor, past and present.

Those who have taken the nightmare memories into their psyches for good have crossed a dark, wide water. From the other side they
watch us watching them, or trying not to see them. For them, survival
depends on memory, on the very monstrousness of the memory itself.
Denial and repression belong to the rest of us; for them, the horror must
be kept alive, acknowledged, made present always.

Eva Kor stands at the front of a large room at Kalamazoo College,
packed to the rafters with students and faculty. She and her twin sister
survived Mengele's experiments at Birkenau. With her she has brought
photo albums — pages of pictures of her family before the war, and then
a few images from Auschwitz. She can point herself and her sister out in
a crowd shot, as well as in a photo of a group of twin adolescent girls,
naked and skeletal, bearing no signs of the changes that should have
been altering their bodies.

Alongside the albums is a clear plastic bag full of grey ash flecked with chips of white bone. She retrieved them in a recent return to Auschwitz. She speaks with disconcerting (but characteristic of survivors) ease and nonchalance, telling us we can examine and touch whatever we want. I reach for the bag, feeling bound to touch it, but my hand starts to shake and I draw it back.

Does she bring this relic simply to educate? To thwart unbelievers? Or does she keep it with her for other reasons, as an amulet of gruesome power that paradoxically keeps her safe by keeping her whole, literally in touch with the past, intact?

A similar literalness and practicality mark Kor's attitude toward Mengele, whom she believes to be alive — I take the liberty of believing she hopes he is alive. She is asked by a student whether she would like to get revenge or to see him brought to justice. No, she says; she has never thought in terms of revenge (there is none possible, after all), and she gave up long ago on the possibility of justice. From this far-bank of a land beyond nightmare, she says that what she wants now is simply the truth. Mengele, she says, could confirm what occurred and could identify what was injected into her ten-year-old body that nearly killed her. Perhaps he could explain why it was done. Eva Kor will settle for the truth.

Her particular Monster — the memorably beautiful man standing above her infirmary cot — is probably dead. If he weren't, it is doubtful that he could or would give Eva Kor the truth she seeks. In any case, there may not be truth enough finally to satisfy that hunger. But surely the plastic bag is a totem of the most fundamental, indissoluble truth: the reduction of human bodies to irreducible components, the terrible common denominator of bone and ash. The truth of this massive destruction is the truth that sustains Eva Kor, on a daily basis. The damning memory becomes the saving re-membering of a people. Adrienne Rich writes: "What is represented as intolerable — as crushing — becomes the figure of its own transformation."9 It occurs to me that this is the secret of the paradox of tragic art as well.

The psychic damage of such extreme victimization is *shattering:* the self dis-integrates. Victims remember leaving their bodies while things are being done to them, watching from the ceiling. Some dissociate from their bodies for good. One common effect of severe sexual abuse is multiple personality disorder.

To remember can mean to begin to re-integrate, but the various pieces of the self come into communication with each other with their own pain. This is the survivor's slow crawl toward integrity, which often carries both its meanings: wholeness, and moral health. To be whole, they who have felt morally polluted need to see themselves as good people — not innocent, for innocence is impossible; but agents for good, beings worthy of light and love. How people manage to reach this end is worthy of the most careful study. These are the people — Evil's elect — who can teach us what to do with an unmanageable past. Their confrontations with the monster of memory can be seen, not as pathological exceptions, but as more dramatic versions of our own, we whose traumas are of the range deemed "normal," the thousand natural shocks that flesh is heir to. They are the sages of a society sadly incompetent to deal with its memories. We are their disciples.

5. American Dreams

> The question for a North American poet
> is how to bear witness to a reality from which
> the public — and maybe part of the poet —
> wants, or is persuaded it wants, to turn away.
>
> —Adrienne Rich[10]

The Holocaust is a very particular horror. But it was not the first of our collective nightmares, and it will not be the last.

It seems that the United States was founded in forgetfulness, that denial was incorporated from the very first into the national consciousness. Racism: the supreme repressed memory of white America. Is it coincidence that the structures of racism were themselves so often grounded in enforced forgetfulness? Africans of diverse ethnicities mixed so that their various languages were useless and soon forgotten; Native children sent to government schools far from home, where their languages were forbidden. Among enslaved Africans, literacy banned outright. Cultural practices and gatherings proscribed. Parents and children separated. So many tools of communication, heritage, and memory shattered.

The price of these stolen memories is the loss of our own. Racism becomes the nightmare that must be smothered. So history is whitewashed; racial discourse becomes unbearable, either terrifying and enraging; racism's victims become white people's victimizers, *deserving* their poverty, their addiction, their despair. Ours has been a "social compact built on fantasy and collective secrets," says Adrienne Rich[11] — exactly like a family where something unspeakable is happening.

As a result, "episodes of collective, civil loss, shame, betrayal dwell in the national psyche unacknowledged, embedded like shrapnel, leaving a deep, recurrent ache in the body politic . . . . "[12] Our scapegoats and sacrifices enact these effects of repression for us: the Viet Nam vet regularly blasted by explosive nightmares or permanently isolated by paranoia; the survivor of extreme abuse who enters the office of a therapist with a body literally deformed, contorted by tangled recollections that can be neither fully remembered or suppressed. For the luckier of us, there is the option of anesthesia. In Rich's words: "we hibernate; we numb ourselves with chemicals; we migrate internally into fictions of past and future; we thirst for guns; but *as a people* we have rarely, if ever, known what it is to tremble with fear, to lament, to rage, to praise, to solemnize, to say *We have done this, to our sorrow* . . . ."[13] On the road to becoming "memory" and "remember," *memor* took a significant detour in Old English to become *murnan,* to mourn. We miss the communal exorcism, I think, precisely because we fail to see that the acts of praise and solemnization are inextricable from the acknowledgment of fear, of grief, of rage, and especially of memory: *We have done this.*

So we live in a "destabilizing national fantasy from which all our work has suffered . . . ."[14] As a writer I feel it, the strain of writing clearly from a consciousness that includes these collective memories. As a teacher I feel it probably even more piercingly, the tension of trying to raise these memories to consciousness in classrooms where, in addition to all the other forces of denial working in the minds of eighteen-year-old, privileged, white students, there is now a readily available antidote to memory: such consciousness can be dismissed as "P. C."

As we slouch toward millennium, more sophisticated resistance comes in a variety of forms. One says we're becoming a Culture of Victims, "disempowering" ourselves by identifying what has been done to us. But there are no survivors who have not first acknowledged victimization. If there seems to be a victim bandwagon, growing very crowded, perhaps it should be heralded as a compelling sign of a profound sociocultural dis-ease, not as an indictment of victims as weaklings or masochists.

Another form of resistance says we impose contemporary values on the past in, for instance, our analyses of historical racism or sexism. This argument often assumes a monolithic view of past attitudes that is itself quite ahistorical: e.g., everybody thought Indians were savages; everybody thought women were inferior; everybody hated homosexuals. (Notice that "everybody" in the past seems always to have been white, straight, and male.) This is a form of denial in another sense, too: it suggests that the past is inaccessible to contemporary moral or political consciousness, as if we could not condemn slavery because many people supported it in the eighteenth century.

Minimization is a form of denial too: unpleasant aspects of the past are reduced to footnotes or details. So is the "blank-slate" thinking beloved of Americans, which weighs contemporary issues in pastless terms, as if we were all starting afresh. Thus we can speak of "reverse racism" and "reverse sexism," wiping out a complicated, oppressive past with a sweep of the tongue. Much as this tendency annoys me, I understand it; it's a wish, more than anything else. When we say, "I don't see you as black at all," or "Let's not talk about gender, let's talk about humanity," what we're really saying is *Couldn't we just pretend this ugly past doesn't stretch between us? Couldn't we forget? Couldn't we leave the Old World behind and invent a new one?* Surely this is the real American dream.

I remember the sixties and seventies as a time of remembrance — the waking of the giant. Civil Rights brought slavery into present-time white consciousness. The lies and erasures surrounding our terrible engagement in Southeast Asia were repeatedly stripped away. My memories of Watergate are energetic and positive: the uncovering of a cover-up, the unseating of a crook, the System my generation learned to regard with cynicism actually functioning in service of the truth. And women began excavating their past.

Then came the eighties, embodied in a president whose own memory was obviously impaired. It was morning in America, we were told, and we could wake from the bad dreams of the past two decades to colorized reruns of Father Knows Best — better technology. The decade ended (regardless of calendars) with a quick, "clean" techno-war brought to us as a video game — a war without body bags, disturbing photos — without memories.

Here we are. Millennium approaches. Girls come to school expecting to learn their history; African American children celebrate Kwanzaa; the AIDS quilt will soon cover the country with names of the unforgotten; Holocaust museums are open; celebrations of the twenty-fifth anniversary of Stonewall are beginning as I write. The children are waking from their terrible dreams. "Could we still," Rich asks, "in the name of transforming ourselves as a people, make some national recognition of our past, of the lies we have told and have told our children — could we then, as a people, break through despair?"[15]

The question hangs in the air.

6. Ancestral Help

> It's gonna hurt now," said Amy.
> Anything coming back to life hurts.
>
> —Toni Morrison[16]

It used to be said that women functioned as the bearers of culture. Men were the official chroniclers, but women carried within them the unwritten stories, rules, values. In a radical sense, perhaps what we carry is the counter-narratives, the collective memories repressed from the official story. This might explain in part both the volume and the tremendous vitality of the literature coming from women of color in the past quarter century: they know the untold stories, tales of horror and beauty full of damning and saving power. And often these accounts are edged in this very ambivalence.

"This is not a story to pass on," Toni Morrison writes at the end of *Beloved.* A tremendous irony, since the story has just been passed on. "The story" belongs to a group of people who have crossed the water — literally, the Ohio River, separating slavery from freedom; figuratively, the water of the Middle Passage, the water of the River Styx, the water of consciousness that separates those who know the worst from the rest of us, the water of unconsciousness, where memory and dream sleep. Each of their stories is sufficient to break a heart. But "the story" is also the collective saga of African America. This is true of all of Morrison's novels, but especially of *Beloved* because it treats the experience of slavery, the core shaping experience of African America, the crucible in which a racial consciousness was forged.

And yet in truth, *Beloved* is not so much about slavery as about the *memory* of slavery, or more accurately the *remembering* of slavery — the effect of slavery on the memory and the self constructed from memory. Its complex, shifting narratives are shaped so as to foreground the operations of memory. The eye of the hurricane, the horrific central action of the novel — the entry of the slavecatchers into Baby Suggs' yard and Sethe's murder of her baby daughter to preserve her from their hands — literalizes memory's "return" to rob the survivors. So does the murdered child, Beloved: memory returns as a force field that gradually achieves human form and takes over the house, devouring its inhabitants' lives. Beloved carries in her hungry form not only the memory of what was done to her, but the collective memory of the Middle Passage, where the nightmare began.

The memory at the center of the story belongs to her mother, Sethe. Much of Sethe's story recounts her struggle with the double-edged power of memory — her need to remember, her need to refuse to remember, the very unclear margin between the remembering that is salutary and the remembering that is deadly. For a time — for years — it seems her survival depends upon "the serious work of beating back the past."[17] But this amounts to beating back the ocean. Sethe wonders wearily at the hungry capacity of her mind to remember: "Why was there nothing it refused? No misery, no regret, no hateful picture too rotten to accept?" Why, she demands, is there no limit at which the brain says, "No thank you. I don't want to know or have to remember that."[18]

To save this woman from drowning in memory's dark water requires a collaboration of forces. It takes Paul D' s persistent love, which tells her at the lip of the bottomless hole of memory, "Go as far inside as you need to, I'll hold your ankles. Make sure you come back out."[19] It demands daughter Denver's courage in seeking help to evacuate memory's devouring ghost, an act which in turn stimulates the black community to embrace Sethe once more. Perhaps above all it depends upon Sethe's own life force, nearly exhausted but ultimately capable of entertaining the possibility that Paul D. is right: that she is, indeed, her own "best thing," despite her store of defiling memories.

The memories defile doubly: Sethe has been a victim (of the violations of slavery), and she has been a perpetrator (of her daughter's death). Sethe stands at the crux of these two versions of herself, the crossroads of innocence and guilt, action and passion salvation and damnation. Her sacrifice of her unnamed child testifies clearly to the enormity of slavery: the baby's death is preferable to her re-enslavement. But this act also shatters Sethe's consciousness to its foundations.

The giant of memory is perhaps most fearsome when it wears this double face. If "innocent bystanders" are rare, so are "pure" victims; often oppression comes with a sense of having collaborated on some level, if only passively. Our significant engagements with collective memory must include this complexity.

It is exactly this conundrum that opens Maxine Hong Kingston's *The Woman Warrior: Memoirs of a Girlhood Among Ghosts*.[20] Kingston's book ranges through memory's tricks and minefields in the process of exploring how individual and communal memories interpenetrate, how the past seeps into the present. The first chapter, "No Name Woman," is also not a story to pass on; it begins, like *Beloved,* with an injunction to silence: "'You must not tell anyone,' my mother said, 'what I am about to tell you." But it then proceeds, along with Kingston's mother, to tell the forbidden story. This act of remembrance is thus swaddled in ambivalence from the outset.

The forbidden story is that of Maxine's father's sister, in China, who became pregnant by someone other than her husband and in so doing brought down the wrath of the village on the family. Beyond her shame and her infanticide/suicide, she has incurred the worst of fates: namelessness. She has "never been born," in Chinese parlance. She is a blank, an absence — a forgetting.

Yet she is not forgotten. She rises from her watery grave, with the help of Maxine's mother — but only to serve as a warning to the young Maxine against untrammeled female sexuality and social deviance. A second level of ambivalence: both necessary and prohibited, No-Name Aunt

is gift and curse at once — like most powerful memories. But her message is at first obscure. Given only the stark, violent skeleton of the story
by her mother, Maxine proceeds to reconstruct the story repeatedly, one
version replacing another as she tries to find the meaning hidden in her
Aunt's buried life: was she an adulteress? a rape victim? a romantic indi-
vidualist in a collectivist culture? Who would the man have been? In
other words, the "memory" becomes Kingston's fiction; she constructs an
aunt she can comprehend: "Unless I see her life branching into mine, she
gives me no ancestral help."

At the close of this first chapter of her own "biomythography,"
Kingston faces the moral conundrum: now it is she who passes the story
on. On the one hand, she fears the wrath of the dead, the woman whose
shame she is baring to strangers, not to mention the live woman who has
said, "Don't let your father know that I told you." But on the other, to
keep silence is to collaborate in her aunt's erasure, in the misogyny that
killed her in the first place, and in the silence that threatens to swallow
the lives, the desires, the names of women today.

Kingston's resolution of this conundrum is obvious: she tells. She
re-members the dead body. So must we. We contact our ghosts at our
peril, but contact them we must. They may rise angry, demanding attention and reparation that we are unprepared to give. They may, as
Kingston fears, drag us down after them. But if we do not remember, we
forfeit what we need desperately at this juncture of history: ancestral
help. If we forget, we expand the silence, which then turns to swallow
us, drown us, deprive us of our names.

Pass it on.

19

Season of the Witch

October 30, 1992
Stetson Chapel, Kalamazoo College

> *I have been invisible,*
> *weird and supernatural.*
> *I want my black dress.*
> *I want my hair*
> *curling wild around me.*
> *I want my broomstick*
> *from the closet where I hid it.*
> *Tonight I meet my sisters*
> *in the graveyard.*
> *Around midnight*
> *if you stop at a red traffic light*
> *in the wet city traffic,*
> *watch for us against the moon.*
> *We are screaming,*
> *we are flying,*
> *laughing, and won't stop.*
>
> *—Jean Tepperman*[1]

1.

Tomorrow night, we celebrate a remarkable holiday. It survives as a vestige of lost ritual, marginalized as a children's holiday, robbed of its ancient spiritual significance — except for certain fundamentalist Christian groups out to ban it. All Hallows Eve: a sad case, devolving down the centuries to its present status as an opportunity for orgiastic marketing of paper objects by Hallmark in Kalamazoo College colors.[2] But originally, as the night before the celebration of saints, Halloween was a fleeting dark gap through which the things of the other world could slip into this one. It was the one night when everything denied, exiled, repressed by the very concept of "saints" and by the Church itself rose up from its shallow grave and walked, and howled, and demanded to be fed. And we toss it some Mars Miniatures and make it go away.

Sometime tomorrow night, if you are a pumpkin-carving candy-giver like myself, you will open the door to a group of kids. An older boy will be a rock star, the younger one a ghost. But the little sister will be wearing green face paint, a long, hooked nose with a black wart, and a tall, pointed hat. Look at this little girl. Study her carefully. Who is she?

There's in my mind a woman
of innocence, unadorned but

fair-featured, and smelling of
apples or grass. She wears

a utopian smock or shift, her hair
is light brown and smooth, and she

is kind and very clean without
ostentation—
                         but she has
no imagination.

                         And there's a
turbulent, moon-ridden girl

or old woman, or both,
dressed in opals and rags, feathers

and torn taffeta,
who knows strange songs—

but she is not kind.

—*Denise Levertov*[3]

2.

Dictionaries are such wonderfully succinct, honest repositories of cultural history. Look up "witch" in the *American Heritage* and you will find these three definitions:

1. a woman who practices sorcery or is believed to have
                         dealings with the devil.
2. an ugly, vicious old woman.
3. a bewitching young woman or girl.

How can we account for such a contradiction as two and three? And even in number one, it is unclear whether, to qualify as a witch, you have actually to do something, or merely to be *believed* to do something — a rather dangerous ambiguity. A deconstructionist's dream, it would seem: a word that contradicts itself. But the deconstructionist's conclusion would be that there is no ultimate, stable meaning here. My conclusion is different. There is definite, clear, irrefutable meaning here, known to every woman who has been called a witch. They know that the ugly, vicious old woman is the flipside of the bewitching young woman or girl. They know that both are projections of a fantasy, a need, a terror that is not female at all. And they know that the old woman and the young girl are equally likely to burn at the stake.

The word *witch* derives from *wicca,* an Anglo-Saxon word probably coming from a Latin root meaning "to bend, to wind, to make" — the same root as *wicker* and *wicket,* not to mention *wicked.* The witch was a maker, a shaper, a bender of reality. Her power derived from the ultimate power of the Goddess, the Great Mother, worshipped in the forms of the natural world, with its distinctly female cycles and seasons, its comprehension of the yin and yang of production and destruction, birth and death. As the Christian church spread its ritual across Europe, its most formidable opponent was the ancient, deeply rooted Goddess, the so-called "Old Religion." The rituals and celebrations of the various communicants of this religion were gradually supplanted by new feasts and festivals, having at their center a new god. The fertility fest of spring became Easter; the feast of light in winter, celebrating the return of the sun, became Christmas; the Mother Goddess became the Mother of God. And in the course of this conquest, wicca began to shrivel, to turn green and ugly and malevolent. A worshipper of life, she became a devourer of children. A celebrant of the female principle, she became the devil's bride. And thus demonized, she had to burn.

In numbers too big to ignore, as Helen Reddy once sang. The estimates of the number of woman executed as witches from the beginning of the persecutions in Europe in the fifteenth century to the last flicker in places like Salem, Massachusetts, two centuries later have ranged into the millions, though the most recent scholarly study puts the number at one hundred thousand. The percentage of executed witches who were female stayed remarkably steady, throughout western Europe, between eighty and eighty-five percent.[4] Clearly there was something very powerful here which had to be obliterated.

Contemporary scholars usually set the "witch" persecutions in the context of the numerous and profound social, economic, intellectual, and religious upheavals of the late Middle Ages: the Protestant Reformation and rise of Puritanism; the movement from feudal toward national political organization; the rise of capitalism; the so-called Scientific Revolution; and, of course, the "Age of Exploration." An interesting historical moment: is it coincidental that the European culture that stumbled upon the people of the Americas and proceeded to misname them, enslave them, exploit them, and ultimately decimate them is the same culture that so energetically transformed wicca into the Devil's Handmaid? Can it be coincidence that in 1486, just six years before Columbus set sail, Jakob Sprenger and Heinrich Kramer published *Malleus Maleficarum (The Hammer of Witches)*, which theorized for the first time the connection between witchcraft and womanhood, not to mention offering detailed, helpful instructions for the detection and persecution of witches? Kramer and Sprenger's rationale for the gender connection was forthright:

> There are more women than men found infected with the heresy of witchcraft. . . . And blessed be the Highest who has so far preserved the male sex from so great a crime: for since He was willing to be born and to suffer for us, therefore He has granted to men this privilege.

It included the standard depiction of female intellect:

> There are more superstitious woman found than men . . . They are more credulous: and since the chief aim of the Devil is to corrupt faith, therefore he rather attacks them. . . . As regards intellect, or the understanding of spiritual things, they seem to be of a different nature from men, a fact which is vouched for by the logic of the authorities, backed by various examples from the Scriptures. Women are intellectually like children.

of female sexuality:

> All witchcraft comes from carnal lust, which is in women insatiable . . . . Wherefore for the sake of fulfilling their lust they consort even with devils.

and of the danger women pose to men:

> Witches can with the help of the Devil bring harm upon men and their affairs . . . their reputation, their body, their reason, and their life.

They also included an interesting twist on the mother-daughter bond:

Daughters of witches are always suspected of similar
practices as imitators of their mothers' crimes. . . . Their
reason for this . . is that according to their pact with the
Devil, they always have to leave behind them and carefully instruct a survivor, so that they may fulfill their vow
to do all they can to increase the number of witches.

And most importantly, Kramer and Sprenger saw in women, a population
without significant actual power in the world, a fabulously subversive
power:

if we inquire, we find that nearly all the kingdoms of the
world have been overthrown by women . . . . Therefore
it is no wonder if the world now suffers through the malice of women.

This year — this very month — we commemorate the initial contact between the world of Kramer and Sprenger and the world which
became its designated Other. But exactly two hundred years *after*
Columbus, three hundred years ago exactly, another definitive American
event took place, at Salem, Massachusetts. The so-called "witch trials" of
1692 gave to our national parlance a metaphor for our persistent tendency
to define and demonize an Enemy "out there" to avoid confrontation with
demons within. In the context of the flames across Europe, Salem was a
brief, intense conflagration, taking only twenty people. Afterward, the
persecution of women as witches slowed and died out. Or did it?

Before we can know that, we need to know who these women
were, these vast populations of women. Before their inquisitors sought
telltale marks on their bodies, what were the telltale marks on their lives,
identifying them as dangerous? Contemporary scholarship has, again,
given us a splendid group portrait:

Many of them were women who had inherited or stood to inherit
money or property. Carol Karlsen has argued that this was the most significant common denominator at Salem;[5] it was also true of the first
woman executed as a witch in Ireland, Alice Kytelar, a survivor of four
husbands who, contrary to common patterns, inherited a bundle.

Many were old woman, at a time when life expectancy was about
forty and a woman's value was defined by her reproductive capacity. Old
women defied both expectations.

Many were midwives and herbalists, at a time when the traditionally female practice of medicine was slowly, surely being "professionalized" — that is, masculinized. That women should collaborate with
women to bring life was formidable; that women should know secrets to

sustain, prevent, or terminate pregnancy was, in patriarchy, diabolical.

Sometimes they were deviant women — unmarried, educated, lesbian, presuming to teach, differing in some way from established patriarchal orthodoxy. Such were the two most famous American witches. One was Anne Hutchinson, who narrowly escaped a witchcraft charge in 1637 after daring to hold religious discussions in her home, where she openly espoused doctrine differing from the Puritan line. She was exiled. The other was Tituba, a slave, African and Carib Indian by heritage, the first woman accused at Salem, presumably for having taught secrets of her native Barbados — "black magic," as it was so tellingly called — to a group of young girls. She escaped the gallows by confessing and naming others, was sold to pay for her jail costs, and disappeared from history.

And the persecutors? Who were they? You know who they were: they were men in power, in the Church, in the economy, in the home, in the government. They were aided by women aligned with them for safety or advancement. But did they consciously target women who posed a threat to established order? Or were they driven by subconscious demons of their own? Were the witches real, powerful women, or were they male hallucinations? But there's the rub, you see; there's the heart of the matter: the external and internal witches are mirror images. The persecutors' external worldly power and their internal terror are inseparable. Together this power and terror ignite a fire that demands to be fed. It positively requires a witch or two. Or a hundred thousand.

> *in salem*
>
> *weird sister*
> *the black witches know that*
> *the terror is not in the moon*
> *choreographing the dance of wereladies*
> *and the terror is not in the broom*
> *swinging around to the hum of cat music*
> *nor the wild clock face grinning from the wall,*
> *the terror is in the plain pink*
> *at the window*
> *and the hedges moral as fire*
> *and the plain face of the white woman watching us*
> *as she beats her ordinary bread.*
>
> *—Lucille Clifton*[6]

3.

How appropriate that those who began the terror in Salem were girls — pubescent and prepubescent girls. The road to adult womanhood

takes us through a deep woods, populated by witches. Grownups tell us
that they are the danger lurking within the candy house of our dreams.
They will eat us alive.

In many fairy tales the witch is conflated with the evil and/or
ugly stepmother. There is good, solid historical reason for this. Take again
the case of Alice Kytelar: all that money inherited from her four dead
husbands would normally have gone to his children, if he had them. How
do you suppose they might have felt about Alice? But there is a psychic
reason for this coupling of witch and stepmother, too. The witch is the
Bad Mommy, the dark side of the maternal moon, the shape of our fear
that we will not be nurtured and cherished, the silhouette of our anger at
the woman who somehow does not meet what we think are our needs.
In "Snow White," the wicked stepmother, sexually jealous of the superior
beauty of her husband's simpering daughter, actually turns into the witch
who offers the girl the poisoned apple. At least one contemporary inter-
pretation unravels this tangled gender drama for us: the witch-queen provides the apple of forbidden insight and knowledge to the virginal daughter as a signal to abandon her snow-whiteness and get a life, apart from
the seven little men she's cooking and cleaning for.[7] In such a reading,
Snow White's ensuing coma is not female passivity or unconsciousness,
but rather the symbolic death of the traditionally feminine, victimized
daughter-self. Whether the Prince's restorative kiss wakens a new, regen-
erate womanhood or revives that tired old princess, I will leave to others
to ponder.

The fairy-tale witch tends to be all the dimensions of female identity that get marginalized and estranged from the woman who is trying to
pursue a career as a princess. Isn't it interesting that Sleeping Beauty gets
into trouble precisely because her father neglected to invite a particular
"bad fairy" to his child's christening? Dorothy Parker, known otherwise for
cynical, world-weary satire, wrote a version of this story, a poem called
"Godmother":

> The day that I was christened—
>   It's a hundred years, and more!
> A hag came and listened
>   At the white church door,
> A-hearing her that bore me
>   And all my kith and kin
> Considerately, for me,
>   renouncing sin.
> While some gave me corals,
>   And some gave me gold,
> And porringers, with morals

Agreeably scrolled,
The hag stood, buckled
In a dim gray cloak;
Stood there and chuckled,
Spat, and spoke:
"There's few enough in life'll
Be needing my help,
But I've got a trifle
For your fine young whelp.
I give her sadness
And the gift of pain,
The new-moon madness,
And the love of rain."
And little good to lave me
In their holy silver bowl
After what she gave me—
Rest her soul! [8]

"Sleeping Beauty" becomes a warning: don't forget the witch. Her complex, unpretty gifts make the difference between princesses and real women. She won't be shut out.

If you grew up with television, you saw what happens when the dominant popular culture tries to deal with the witch in yet another way, by domesticating her: she turns into Samantha Stevens, whose wiccan powers reduce to nose-twitching and the secret competence of the American housewife, hidden from her half-witted husband, Darren, like a guilty secret. All the nasty stuff, then, gets funneled into Endora, the witch-as-mother-in-law-joke.

But we weren't fooled, we little girls preparing for Halloween. We knew what a real witch looked like, didn't we? And we knew what she sounded like, too. She looked and sounded like Margaret Hamilton, hurling fireballs from the roof and screeching, "HOW ABOUT A LITTLE FIRE, SCARECROW?" in a voice that was half squeaky door, half nails on a blackboard. Hamilton gave us the definitive witch for at least the last two-third of this century, and probably for as long as the film holds out: a lean, green, mean archetype. For me, she was and is far and away the most compelling thing about Dorothy's cinematic sojourn in Oz, from the moment she explodes into the dismal kindergarten of Munchkin Land in a cloud of black smoke, bewailing the demise of her sister under Dorothy's house, to the moment she melts away, her "byoooooootiful wickedness" drowned out by an adolescent girl. "What a world, what a world!"

What a world, indeed, this place where you, Dorothy the Small and Meek, are hailed as none other than a witch, a personage of untold, mysterious power. You seek the mythical Wizard, but you keep getting deflected back to the Witch. You call out for soft, grey old Auntie Em, your lost Mother, and she vanishes in the glass, replaced by the leering green face, mimicking and mocking your cries. Here you are, seemingly, unmothered; here you must rely on your own brain, heart, courage — and on the broomstick and the shoes: traveling gear, legacies from that Bad Mother you couldn't bear to look at, the angry one, infuriated by the death of her sister.

> *I have gone out, a possessed witch,*
> *haunting the black air, braver at night;*
> *dreaming evil, I have done my hitch*
> *over the plain houses, light by light;*
> *lonely thing, twelve-fingered, out of mind.*
> *A woman like that is not a woman, quite.*
> *I have been her kind.*

—*Anne Sexton*[9]

4.

In her play *Vinegar Tom,* British playwright Caryl Churchill explores the witch persecutions of seventeenth-century England. But her real subject is how women get turned into witches, then and now. Toward the end comes a song called "Lament for the Witches." The lyrics lose some power apart from music, but here is an excerpt that asks some questions that stayed with me:

> *Where have the witches gone?*
> *Where are the witches now?*
> *Here we are . . .*
> *Look in the mirror tonight.*
> *Would they have hanged you then?*
> *Ask how they're stopping you now.*
> *Where have the witches gone?*
> *Who are the witches now?*
> *Ask how they're stopping you now.*
> *Here we are . . . .*[10]

Who are the witches now?

In Lucille Clifton's poem, the white women have decided that the black women are the witches, but as the black sisters watch the white woman beating that bread behind those moral-as-fire hedges and those terrible pink curtains, they know different. The evil is in our back yards. Our neat, pretty back yards — or departments, or colleges, or classes, or businesses, or nations. When those we call Other speak up, when they tell us about ourselves, when they let us know, as Sojourner Truth said, "what time of night it is," we call them witches; we burn them at the stake of our privilege, in the flames of our outrage.

Who are the witches now?

Pat Buchanan takes the stage at the Republican convention to accuse Hillary Clinton of "radical feminism" — by which, apparently, he means her years of groundbreaking work on the legal position of abused children. Sooner or later, Hillary Clinton is reduced to offering her chocolate-chip cookie recipe as evidence of her innocence. [11]

Who are the witches now?

When opponents want to embarrass Ross Perot, they organize a campaign to depict his daughter as the worst thing they (or he) can think of — a lesbian. Meanwhile, the states of Oregon and Colorado vote on proposals not only to abolish civil rights for homosexuals, but to mandate that schools teach that homosexuality is unnatural and immoral.

Who are the witches now?

An Equal Rights Amendment referendum in Iowa is narrowly defeated after Pat Robertson says it would encourage women to "leave their husbands, kill their children, [and] practice witchcraft."[12]

Who are the witches now? The same women they have always been. Women who have or threaten to get power. Women who claim knowledge of and control over their reproduction. Women who teach the young what the fathers don't want them to know. Women of color who pass on their heritage. Women who claim authority. Women whose primary loyalty is to each other.

Ask how they're stopping you now. Is it a word, a terrible word, that haunts you? Is it *lesbian?* Is it *man-hater?* Is it the f-word itself? It is intellectual standards that say your experience is not valid or important? Is it eyes and hands and laws that take your body away from you? Is it the violence that stalks you everywhere, especially at home? Or is it words, just words, casually tossed at you on the street, or written on a wall, or speaking from your telephone late at night?

Never fear, little sister — you in the pointed hat, with the green make-up. There are a lot more of us than you know. And remember, we "always have to leave behind [us] and carefully instruct a survivor, so that [we] may fulfill [our] vow to do all [we] can to increase the number." Listen: we are everywhere. And tomorrow is our night. We are flying, laughing. And won't stop.

Sources for Epigraphs

Introduction

A. S. Byatt, *Possession: A Romance* (New York: Random House, 1990), pp. 168 and 467.

Part One

Maxine Hong Kingston, quoted in Paula Rabinowitz, "Eccentric Memories: A Conversation with Maxine Hong Kingston," *Michigan Quarterly Review: Women and Memory*, v. XXVI, no. 1, winter 1987, p. 179.

A. S. Byatt, *Possession*, pp. 367-368.

Patricia J. Williams, *The Alchemy of Race and Rights* (Cambridge: Harvard University Press, 1992), p. 204.

Part Two

Paul Tillich, *Religious Realization (Reliöse Verwirklichung* [Berlin: Furch, 1929]).

Madeleine R. Grumet, *Bitter Milk: Women & Teaching* (Amherst: University of Massachusetts Press, 1988), p. 20.

Part Three

Minnie Bruce Pratt, "Identity: Skin Blood Heart," *Yours in Struggle: Three Feminist Perspectives on Anti-Semitism and Racism* (New York: Long Haul Press, 1984), pp. 18-19.

Toni Morrison, *Nobel Lecture in Literature* (New York: Alfred Knopf, 1994), pp. 28-29.

Notes

Introduction: Marginalia

1. "Young Mothers V," *Satan Says* (Pittsburgh: University of Pittsburgh, 1980), p. 43.
2. *Yearning: race, gender, and cultural politics* (Boston: South End Press, 1990), p. 153.
3. *Yearning*, p. 149.
4. Interview in *Poets and Writers*, January/February 1993, p. 42. ·
5. Quoted in a profile in *Ms*, January/February 1994, p. 71.
6. "The Art of Fiction," *Paris Review*, fall 1993, pp. 119-120.
7. *What is Found There: Notebooks on Poetry and Politics* (New York: W. W. Norton: 1993), p. 242.
8. *Refuge: An Unnatural History of Family and Place* (New York: Vintage, 1992), p. 24.
9. *The Alchemy of Race and Rights* (Cambridge: Harvard University Press, 1992), p. 130.
10. *On the Boundary: An Autobiographical Sketch* (New York: Scribner's, 1966), p. 13.
11. *What Is Found There*, 25.
12. *What Is Found There*, 85.
13. Williams, pp. 129-130.
14. *Yearning*, 153.

Chapter 2: Snapshots from an Uncolored Girlhood

1. *What is Found There: Notebooks on Poetry and Politics* (New York: W. W. Norton, 1993), p. 181.
2. "Unspeakable Things Unspoken: The Afro-American Presence in American Literature," *Michigan Quarterly Review*, winter 1989, p. 11.
3. Ruth Frankenberg, *White Women, Race Matters: The Social Construction of Whiteness* (Minneapolis: U. of Minnesota Press, 1993), p. 55.

4. This is not her real name.
5. Frankenberg, pp. 49-50.
6. *Rolling Stone*, April 19, 1990; quoted in Gillian G. Gaar, *She's A Rebel: The History of Women in Rock & Roll* (Seattle: Seal Press, 1992), p. 1
7. Quoted in Steve Turner, *A Hard Day's Write: The Stories Behind Every Beatles' Song* (New York: Harper, 1994), p. 35.
8. "Sweet Honey: a distinctly female voice of African America." *Boston Globe*, Sunday, November 14, 1993, p. B7.
9. "after Kent State," *Good Woman: Poems and a Memoir* 1969-1980 (Brockport, N. Y.: BOA Editions, 1987, p. 57.
10. The title of her book on white U.S.writers' use of African or African American characters in fiction.
11. Gaar, 86-87.

Chapter 4: A Good Little Girl Like You

1. *Yearning: race, gender, and cultural politics* (Boston: South End Press, 1990), p. 148.
2. "Out of Kansas," *The New Yorker*, May 11, 1992, p. 93. A longer version was published as *The Wizard of Oz* in the British Film Institute's Film Classics series in the same year.
3. Terry McMillan, "The Wizard of Oz," *The Movie that Changed My Life*, ed. David Rosenberg (New York: Viking, 1991), p. 254..
4. McMillan, 260.
5. Rushdie, 93-103.
6. *Archetypal Patterns in Women's Fiction* (Bloomington: Indiana University Press, 1981), p. 14. Pratt's second chapter deals in depth with this concept.
7. Thanks to Diane Seuss-Brakeman, my alter-ego in thinking about "Oz," for putting this together for me.
8. Rushdie, 100.
9. Rushdie, 100.
10. The trio calls up other cultural archetypes too: the proverbial straw man; T. S. Eliot's modernist symbol, the Hollow Man; and the legendary warrior Lionheart.
11. Rushdie, 100.
12. McMillan, 255-56.
13. McMillan, 255.
14. Rushdie, 95
15. I'm grateful to Denise Mumm, my fellow colonist at the Virginia Center for the Creative Arts in March of 1992, for bringing the nature of the shoes to my attention.

16. It is likewise a witch, Circe, who sends Odysseus into the Land of the Dead.
17. Linda Hamel reminds me that the death of the first witch was also a consequence, if indirect, of Dorothy's action, if we see the cyclone as emanating from her own fury.
18. Rushdie, 93.
19. Rushdie, 90.
20. Rushdie, 96.
21. Rushdie, 96.
22. Rushdie, 103.
23. Rushdie, 103

Chapter 5: Letting It Be

1. From Linda Burrowes to Richard Freeman, in Freeman's *The Beatles: A Private View* (New York: Barnes & Noble, 1990), p. 21.
2. "Help! The Day the Mania Came to Washington," *The Washington Post,* February 7, 1994, sec. C, p. 4
3. "The Revolution: They Changed the World," *The Washington Post,* February 7, 1994, sec. C, p. 3.
4. The phrase is Adrienne Rich's, from an eponymous essay included in *On Lies, Secrets, and Silence: Selected Prose, 1966 - 1978* (New York: W. W. Norton, 1979).
5. When he is asked "How did you find America?" by a British reporter in *A Hard Day's Night,* John's deadpan answer is "Turn left at Greenland."
6. Quoted by Bill Harry in *The Ultimate Beatles Encyclopedia* (New York: Hyperion, 1992), p. 308.
7. The name the teenaged John and Paul used for a short-lived duo act.
8. "Laughing it Off" (review of revival of Joe Orton's *What the Butler Saw*), *The New Yorker,* February 21, 1994, p. 107.

Chapter 6: Girlfriend

1. Toni Morrison, *Sula* (NY: Penguin, 1973), p. 147.
2. Morrison, 66.
3. Morrison, 53.
4. *A Room of One's Own* (New York: Harcourt Brace Jovanovich, 1929), p. 86.
5. "To My Excellent Lucasia, on Our Friendship."
6. The phrase is Walter Pater's.

7. Morrison, 58-9.
8. Morrison, 168.
9. Morrison, 169.
10. Morrison, 146.
11. Andrea Dworkin, *Mercy* (Village Station, N.Y.: Four Walls Eight Windows, 1991), p. 339.
12. Morrison, 95.
13. Morrison, 174.

Chapter 7: We All Shine On

1. *What is Found There: Notebooks on Poetry and Politics* (New York: W. W. Norton, 1993), pp. 105-06.
2. in the film *Imagine: John Lennon.*
3. ibid.
4. ibid.

Chapter 8: On Not Knowing What We're Doing

1. Florence J. Lucasse, an alumna of Kalamazoo College and a teacher, left a million-dollar bequest to establish annual awards to faculty members for teaching and for research. The recipients are asked to give a lecture.
2. Four Quartets, "East Coker," V, ll. 7-9.
3. Quoted in *Black Women Writers at Work*, ed. Claudia Tate (Harpenden, Hertfordshire: Oldcastle Press, 1985), pp. 114-115.
4. Mary Field Belenky et. al., *Women's Ways of Knowing* (New York: Basic Books, 1986).
5. from an interview in the PBS television series "Joseph Campbell and the Power of Myth: with Bill Moyers."

Chapter 9: Who's "We," White Man?

1. So far as I know, our then-brand-new president, Lawrence W. Bryan, being a man of great humor and small ego, didn't.
2. by Laurence Barrett, Professor Emeritus of English.
3. *Three Guineas* (New York: Harcourt, Brace, & World, 1938), p. 63.

Chapter 10: The Bluest Eyes

1. An abridged version of this essay was delivered at the Great Lakes Colleges Association Women's Studies Program conference

University, April 8-10, 1994, I'm grateful to the conference plan-
ners and to the session participants for the chance to explore
these ideas initially.

2. Patricia J. Williams, *The Alchemy of Race and Rights* (Cambridge:
   Harvard University Press, 1991), p. 129.

3. bell hooks, *Yearning: race, gender, and cultural politics* (Boston: South
   End Press, 1990), pp. 151-52.

4. "White Feminists Who Study Black Writers, *The Chronicle of Higher
   Education*, October 12, 1994, p. A48.

5. Williams, 49-50.

6. Toni Morrison, *The Bluest Eye*, reprinted in *The Norton Anthology of
   Literature By Women*, ed. Sandra M. Gilbert and Susan Gubar
   (New York: Norton, 1985). Subsequent page citations will refer to
   this edition.

7. Ruth Frankenburg, *White Women, Race Matters: The Social
   Construction of Whiteness* (Minneapolis: U. of Minnesota Press,
   1993), pp. 228-29.

8. Frankenburg, 228.

9. Frankenburg, 192.

10. Frankenburg, 204.. Frankenburg, 198.

12. Frankenburg, 6.

13. Frankenburg, 198.

14. Frankenburg, 173.

15. Frankenburg, 197-98.

16. Frankenburg, 231.

17. Frankenburg, 202.

18. Beverly Daniel Tatum, "Teaching White Students about Racism: The
    Search for White Allies and the Restoration of Hope," *Teachers
    College Record*, Summer, 1994.

19. See her essay "City Limits, Village Values: Concepts of the
    Neighborhood in Black Fiction." Literature and the Urban
    Experience, ed. Michael C. Jaye and Ann C. Watt (New
    Brunswick, N.J.: Rutgers University Press, 1981), pp.39 ff.

20. In "City Limits, Village Values: Concepts of the Neighborhood in Black
    Fiction."

21. The statement comes from a television interview with Charlie Rose,
    May 7, 1993.

22. "Identity: Skin Blood Heart," *Yours in Struggle: Three Feminist
    Perspectives on Anti-Semitism and Racism* (New York: Long Haul
    Press, 1984), pp. 41-42.

23. bell hooks explores the concept of marginality in these terms in her
    essay "On Claiming the Margins" in *Yearning: race, gender, and
    cultural politics*.

24. The maternal figure in *Tar Baby*.
25. A concept of community Morrison discusses in "City Limits, Village Values."
26. A reference to the myth of the Flying African that informs *Song of Solomon*.
27. The disruptive male protagonist of *Tar Baby*.
28. A paraphrase of Claudia's statement near the beginning of *The Bluest Eye*.
29. Frankenburg, 171.
30. Frankenburg, 238.
31. "Down at the Cross: Letter from a Region in My Mind," *The Fire Next Time* (New York: Dial Press, 1963), p. 95.

Chapter 11: Beware the Jabberwock

1. *Nobel Lecture in Literature* (New York: Knopf, 1994), p. 19.
2. *Bitter Milk: Women & Teaching* (Amherst: University of Massachusetts Press, 1988), p. xiii.
3. Michael J. Gillman, letter to *The Michigan Alumnus*, March/April 1994, p. 5.
4. April 8, 1994.
5. Paul Berman, Ed., *Debating P.C.: The Controversy Over Political Correctness on College Campuses* (NY: Laurel, 1992).
6. David Lehman, "Larkin: Bellicose lettres," *The Boston Sunday Globe*, December 12, 1993, pp. B34 & B37.
7. Dwight Silverman, "Computer game has hot dates," *Detroit Free Press*, December 27, 1993, pp. 1E & 4E.
8. Michael Grunwald, "Spring's PC break: The beach has changed, but hedonism is the same in cease-fire between sexes," *The Boston Sunday Globe*, March 27, 1994, pp. 1 & 18.

Chapter 12: Dear Katie

1. Patricia J. Williams, *The Alchemy of Race and Rights* (Cambridge: Harvard University Press, 1991), p. 228.

Chapter 13: The Space Between

1. A version of this essay was delivered in a symposium on maternal metaphors in teaching hosted by the women's studies program at Loyola University in Chicago in October, 1993. I'm grateful to my

hosts and to the audience for the chance to explore the ideas in this essay in such an encouraging context.

2. May Sarton, *The Small Room* (N.Y.: Norton, 1961), p. 29.
3. Mary Field Belenky, et. al, *Women's Ways of Knowing: The Development of Self, Voice, and Mind* (New York: Basic Books, 1986).
4. Madeleine Grumet, *Bitter Milk: Women and Teaching* (Amherst: U. of Massachusetts Press, 1988), p. 20.
5. Jo Anne Pagano, *Exiles and Communities: Teaching in the Patriarchal Wilderness* (Albany: SUNY Press, 1990), p. 5.
6. Pagano, 9-10.
7. Pagano, 128.
8. William Kerrigan, quoted in "The New Rules About Sex On Campus," *Harper's,* September 1993, p. 36.
9. Emily is Emily Galloway, Kalamazoo College class of 1994. Rita Dove, in response to a draft of this essay, wrote me a gracious letter in which she called Emily's reading of the title "simply dazzling."

Chapter 15: In Salem

1. In *Witchcraze* (San Francisco: Pandora [Harper Collins], 1994), the most recent scholarly work with which I am familiar, Anne Llewelyn Barstow argues persuasively for a figure of 100,000.

Chapter 17: Imagining Whiteness

1. "The Canon: Civil War and Reconstruction," *Michigan Quarterly Review*, vol. XXVIII, no. 1, winter 1989, p. 39.
2. The question came, not to me but to a roomful of people, from bell hooks in her Gloria Watkins incarnation, in a lecture at Kalamazoo College. I am grateful to her for all the rich thinking her charge provoked.
3. *Playing in the Dark* (Cambridge: Harvard University Press, 1992), p. 59.
4. Morrison, 58.
5. Morrison, 35.
6. "White Privilege and Male Privilege: A Personal Account of Coming to See Correspondences Through Work in Women's Studies." Paper #189, Wellesley College Center for Research on Women (1988), p. 10.
7. Patricia J. Williams, *The Alchemy of Race and Rights* (Cambridge: Harvard University Press, 1991), p. 88.
8. Adrienne Rich, *What is Found There: Notebooks on Poetry and Politics* (N.Y.: Norton, 1993), p. 203.

9. Jeanne Baraka-Love, Director of Multicultural Affairs, in a talk in Stetson Chapel, Kalamazoo College, July 10, 1992.
10. Rich, p. 204.
11. "Down at the Cross: Letter from a Region in My Mind," *The Fire Next Time* (New York: Dial Press, 1963), p. 109.
12. Frankenburg, p. 188.
13. Frankenburg, p. 173..
14. "My Dungeon Shook: Letter to My Nephew on the One Hundredth Anniversary of the Emancipation," *The Fire Next Time* (New York: Dial Press, 1963), pp. 19-20.

Chapter 18: The Giant Waking

1. "A Meditation in Seven Days," *Michigan Quarterly Review: Women & Memory*, v. XXVI, no. 1, Winter 1987, p. 194.
2. Margaret A. Lourie, Domna Stanton, Martha Vicinus, "Introduction," *Michigan Quarterly Review*, p. 3.
3. Anne K. Mellor, *Mary Shelley: Her Life, Her Fiction, Her Monsters* (N.Y.: Methuen, 1988), ch. 5, "A Feminist Critique of Science."
4. Mellor first drew this parallel to my attention.
5. Mary W. Shelley, *Frankenstein, or The Modern Prometheus* (London: Oxford University Press, 1969), p. 9.
6. Shelley, 9
7. Shelley, 10.
8. *The Drowned and the Saved* (New York: Simon & Shuster, 1988), pp. 31-32.
9. Rich, 249.
10. *What is Found There: Notebooks on Poetry and Politics* (New York: W. W. Norton, 1993), p. 115.
11. Rich, 122.
12. Rich, 106.
13. Rich, 20.
14. Rich, 122.
15. Rich, 17-18.
16. *Beloved* (New York: New American Library, 1987), p. 35.
17. ibid., 73.
18. ibid., 30
19. ibid., 46.
20. New York: Knopf, 1976.

Chapter 19: Season of the Witch

1. From "Witch," originally published in *Women: A Journal of Liberation* (1969); reprinted in *No More Masks! An Anthology of Poems by Women,* ed. Florence Howe and Ellen Bass (Garden City, New York: Anchor/Doubleday, 1973), p. 333.
2. Princeton, too. That's where we got them.
3. "In Mind," *The Freeing of the Dust* (N. Y.: New Directions, 1975).
4. Anne Llewellyn Barstow, *Witchcraze: A New History of the European Witch Hunts* (San Francisco: Pandora, 1994). The first chapter analyzes the numbers, which are rigorously presented in an appendix.
5. *The Devil in the Shape of a Woman: Witchcraft in Colonial New England* (New York: W. W. Norton, 1987).
6. *Good Woman: Poems and a Memoir 1969-1980* (Brockport, N.Y.: BOA Editions, 1987), p. 111.
7. For this insight I am grateful to Jennifer Babcock, whose Senior Individualized Project on revisionist readings of fairy tales I had the pleasure of directing in 1991.
8. I am grateful to the late Xarifa Greenquist, a witch if ever there was one, for first sending me this poem via campus mail. "Rest her soul" indeed.
9. "Her Kind," *To Bedlam and Part Way Back* (N. Y.: Houghton Mifflin, 1960).
10. "Lament for the Witches," *Vinegar Tom* (New York: Samuel French, 1982), pp. 59-60.
11. And subsequently, like a good witch, she has been burned, though only in effigy.
12. Quoted in *Ms.,* January/February 1993, p. 24.